Educating the Evolved Mind

Conceptual Foundations for an Evolutionary Educational Psychology

a volume in
**Psychological Perspectives
on Contemporary Educational Issues**

Series Editors:
Jerry S. Carlson, University of California, Riverside
Joel R. Levin, University of Arizona

Psychological Perspectives on Contemporary Educational Issues

Jerry S. Carlson and Joel R. Levin, Series Editors

The No Child Left Behind Legislation:
Educational Research and Federal Funding (2006)
edited by Jerry S. Carlson and Joel R. Levin

Educating the Evolved Mind

Conceptual Foundations for an Evolutionary Educational Psychology

edited by

Jerry S. Carlson
University of California, Riverside

and

Joel R. Levin
University of Arizona

Information Age Publishing, Inc.
Charlotte, North Carolina • www.infoagepub.com

Library of Congress Cataloging-in-Publication Data

Educating the evolved mind : conceptual foundations for an evolutionary
educational psychology / edited by Jerry S. Carlson and Joel R. Levin.
    p. cm. — (Psychological perspectives on contemporary educational
issues)
  Includes bibliographical references.
  ISBN 978-1-59311-611-8 (pbk.) — ISBN 978-1-59311-612-5 (hardcover)
1. Educational psychology. 2. Evolutionary psychology. I. Carlson, Jerry
S. II. Levin, Joel R.
  LB1051.E217 2007
  370.15--dc22

                                                    2007003670

ISBN 13: 978-1-59311-611-8 (pbk.)
ISBN 13: 978-1-59311-612-5 (hardcover)
ISBN 10:   1-59311-611-X (pbk.)
ISBN 10:   1-59311-612-8 (hardcover)

Printed in the United States of America

CONTENTS

INTRODUCTION

Jerry S. Carlson and Joel R. Levin

Several challenging issues confront education today. Perhaps the most discussed among these is the academic achievement of American youth. Some critics point to international comparisons, where performance levels of American students lag behind those of their counterparts in other countries. Other critics focus on the "achievement gap" in the United States between students of different ethnic, cultural, and social backgrounds and traditions. Still others point to the inadequate and disproportionate allocation of educational resources. A common theme among the critics is that educational standards are not high enough and academic achievement, which is generally assessed by means of standardized testing, is insufficient. Included in the critiques are issues related to school reform, curriculum and instructional approaches, and the multitude of social, cultural, and political issues that affect schools and educational achievement.

The first volume in this book series, *Psychological Perspectives on Contemporary Educational Issues*, was published in 2005 and focused on the No Child Left Behind and the Education Sciences Reform acts. Valerie Reyna, author of the target essay ("The No Child Left Behind Act and Scientific Research: A View From Washington, DC"), provided a wide-ranging perspective on the legislation, its implementation and implications

*Educating the Evolved Mind: Conceptual Foundations for an
Evolutionary Educational Psychology*, pp. vii–xii
Copyright © 2007 by Information Age Publishing

for educational practice and research. The title of the volume is *The No Child Left Behind Legislation: Educational Research and Federal Funding*. Consistent with the format of the series, several commentaries, representing a variety of perspectives, followed the Reyna essay. These were prepared by Patricia Alexander and Michelle M. Risconscente ("A Matter of Proof: Why Academic Achievement Learning"), Richard L. Allington ("Federal Intrusion in Research and Teaching and the Medical Myth Model"), Robert Calfee ("Educational Research and the NCLB: A View From the Past"), Earl Hunt ("The Education Acts: Political Practice Meets Practical Problems, Scientific Processes, Process Control, and Parkinson's Law"), G. Reid Lyon ("Why Converging Scientific Evidence Must Guide Educational Policies and Practices"), Douglas E. Mitchell ("Response to Reyna's 'The No Child Left Behind Act and Scientific Research: A View from Washington, DC'"), Angela M. O'Donnell ("The No Child Left Behind Act: What if it Worked?"), Gary P. Phye ("Educational Science: More Than Research Design"), Michael Pressley ("What Role Should the Government Play in a Science of Education?"), Daniel H. Robinson ("Scientific Research is Programmatic"), and William R. Shadish ("Prudent Inquiry: Conceptual Complexity Versus Practical Simplicity in Knowing What Works"). Reyna's closing contribution ("Federal policy and scientific research") comments on the commentaries.

The target essay for this, the second volume in the series, was prepared by David C. Geary is titled "Educating the Evolved Mind: Reflections and Refinements." Geary's essay presents a comprehensive theory that provides direction for the development of a new, albeit controversial, discipline, *evolutionary educational psychology*. The evolutionary perspective that Geary embraces is based on the understanding of the human brain, mind, and its development and lays the basis for a scientifically grounded approach to children's schooling and, to a lesser degree, to their later occupational interests. By developing a taxonomy of evolved cognitive abilities and providing descriptions of how, from an evolutionary perspective, these abilities are modified and refined during childhood, Geary lays the framework for understanding the relation between evolved abilities, such as language, and nonevolved competencies built from them with schooling. These include reading and mathematics competencies. Integrating his discussion of human intellectual history with cognitive mechanisms, such as working memory, Geary describes how humans are able to transform evolved cognitive abilities into culturally important, school taught competences or what he calls biologically secondary characteristics. Biologically primary abilities are represented by implicit folk knowledge, and, to a large extent, provide the basis for later explicit learning.

Consistent with the purpose of the series, commentaries on Geary's target article were solicited from leading scholars in the field representing varied perspectives on the significance of evolutionary psychology, generally, and the efficacy of applying evolutionary principles to schooling, specifically.

In his commentary, Phillip Ackerman questions the relevance of an evolutionary perspective for education. He voices concern with Geary's emphasis on fluid intelligence (Gf), pointing out that although Gf is important, as is crystallized intelligence (Gc), neither Gf nor Gc (either alone or together) captures the higher-order factors contributing to learning, academic achievement, and, importantly, transfer of acquired knowledge and skills. Ackerman suggests that Geary's evolutionary approach is insufficiently sensitive to cultural factors, including interests, motivations, and orientations to learning that must be taken into consideration to understand individual differences in achievement and the acquisition of domain-specific skills.

Daniel Berch's response to the Geary essay focuses on its educational implications. He suggests that Geary's call for direct and explicit instruction of biologically secondary skills underestimates the potential of guided discovery learning and, particularly, cooperative learning approaches based on principles of situated cognition and distributed learning. Berch argues that it may ultimately prove more beneficial to examine the conditions under which assorted types of pedagogical methods are most effective in promoting the acquisition of differing features of secondary knowledge at varying ages and for diverse ability groups.

David Bjorklund finds much to agree with in Geary's evolutionary approach. He notes that children's early cognitions reflect a natural development of attending to and learning from age-appropriate interactions with the environment. These "intuitive biases" are species specific and age related; they serve as preparation for later learning. In this context, Bjorklund points out the significance of the appropriate "match" between children's developing cognitions and their learning context. He questions the efficacy of direct instructional approaches in early education and early emphasis of areas such as reading. His concern is that children's later interests in and motivation for learning may be impaired. Bjorklund concurs with Geary that direct instruction is important in later domain-specific learning.

Andreas Demetriou evaluates Geary's model on two general levels: the epistemological level, which must specify the general structural and developmental characteristics of human cognition, and the practical level, which must specify how premises about the organization and development of the human mind relates to school learning. At both levels individual differences must be taken into account. Suggesting that phylogenetic theories are too general in scope and too remote from education to be of practical utility, Demetriou argues that Geary's model is both epistemologically and practically weak, offering little added value to what we already know about cognitive development and learning.

Earl Hunt points out that scientific theory must be falsifiable. Noting that the theory of evolution is falsifiable (i.e., it satisfies a "scientific" criterion), he argues that evolutionary psychology is not. He questions how the development of folk knowledge (primary biological abilities) could be traced through evolution and—important for education—how "underconstrained theorizing" of evolutionary psychology could provide a basis for secondary biological knowledge and approaches to education. Hunt suggests that Geary's evolutionary approach underestimates individual differences as well as context- and culture-related malleability of cognitive abilities. Hunt adds that Geary's proposal for educational psychology offers little to what many educational psychologists and educational practitioners already know.

David Klahr's commentary explores the relationship between Geary's model and the development of scientific thinking. He suggests that whereas scientific knowledge is, in Geary's term, biologically secondary, processes of inquiry and exploration are biologically primary. These, he argues, can be observed in both young children's thinking and in the activities of mature and creative scientists. Klahr is in broad agreement with Geary's general perspective that a one-size-fits-all approach to education is inappropriate; variability in human cognitive potential must be taken into consideration and reflected in curriculum and teaching methodology.

John Sweller focuses his comment on the educational relevance of Geary's essay. Noting that biologically primary abilities are not learned consciously, working memory and other cognitive-processing limitations are essentially irrelevant. This is not the case with biologically secondary abilities, however, as the relationships between working memory and long-term memory apply to these cultural and domain-specific acquisitions. Sweller suggests that educational recommendations cannot assume that procedures that work for biologically primary information will work for biologically secondary information as well. This insight, derived from Geary's theory of evolutionary educational psychology, is, in Sweller's view, significant and directly relevant to instructional approaches.

David Geary concludes the volume by responding to the commentators and offering additional grist for his evolutionary educational psychology mill.

The present book series is a continuation (in a different publishing format—a book rather than a journal series) of *Issues in Education: Contributions from Educational Psychology*, first published in 1995 with two issues per volume.

Past volumes of *Issues in Education Contributions from Educational Psychology* include:

- David Share and Keith Stanovich, "Cognitive Processes in Early Reading Development: Accommodating Individual Differences Into a Model of Acquisition." (Volume 1, Number 1)
- Deborah McCutchen, "Cognitive Processes in Children's Writing: Developmental and Individual Differences." (Volume 1, Number 2)
- Steven Yussen and Nihal Ozcan, "The Development of Knowledge About Narratives." (Volume 2, Number 1)
- Earl Hunt and Jim Minstrell, "Effective Instruction in Science and Mathematics: Psychological Principles and Social Constraints." (Volume 2, Number 2)
- Sharon Griffin and Robbie Case, "Re-Thinking the Primary School Math Curriculum: An Approach Based on Cognitive Science." (Volume 3, Number 1)
- D.C. Phillips, "How, Why, What, When, and Where: Perspectives on Constructivism in Psychology and Education." (Volume 3, Number 2)
- Alan Schoenfeld, "Toward a Theory of Teaching-in-Context." (Volume 4, Number 1)
- James Voss, "Issues in the Learning of History." (Volume 4, Number 2)
- Michael Pressley and Richard Allington, "What Should Reading Instructional Research Be the Research Of?" (Volume 5, Number 1)
- Joel Levin and Angela O'Donnell, "What to Do About Educational Research's Credibility Gaps?" (Volume 5, Number 2)
- Scott Paris and colleagues, Five Focus Articles on High-Stakes Testing. (Volume 6, Numbers 1 and 2)
- Lee Swanson and Linda Siegel, "Learning Disabilities as a Working Memory Deficit." (Volume 7, Number 1)
- Robert Sternberg and Elena Grigorenko, "All Testing is Dynamic Testing." (Volume 7, Number 2)
- Diane Halpern, "Sex Differences in Achievement Scores." (Volume 8, Number 1)
- Gregory Schraw and Lori Olafson, "Teachers' Epistemological World Views and Educational Practices." (Volume 8, Number 2)

Readers who wish to purchase the first volume of the book series, *The No Child Left Behind Legislation: Educational Research and Federal Funding*, as well as any of the above-listed issues of *Issues in Education: Contributions from Educational Psychology*, should contact our publishing company, Information Age Publishing, Inc., PO Box 79049, Charlotte, NC 28271. We are grateful to George Johnson at Information Age for encouraging and overseeing both of these projects.

CHAPTER 1

EDUCATING THE EVOLVED MIND

Conceptual Foundations for an Evolutionary Educational Psychology

David C. Geary

It is widely accepted that all children in modern societies will receive formal and extended instruction in a variety of core domains, such as mathematics, and at the very least they will acquire the basic skills, as in being
able to read and write, necessary for employment and day-to-day living in
these societies. Unfortunately, the instructional approaches used to
achieve these goals and in fact the details of the goals themselves are
points of continued and often divisive debate (Hirsch, 1996). At the very
least, these debates date to Rousseau's 1762 publication of *Emile*, and are
framed by basic assumptions about how children learn and how adults
should motivate children to engage in this learning (Rousseau, 1979). At
one extreme is a child-centered approach, whereby adults should come to
understand how children learn and then construct educational goals and
instructional methods around children's learning biases (e.g., McLellan &
Dewey, 1895). At the other extreme is the assumption that adults should

Educating the Evolved Mind: Conceptual Foundations for an
Evolutionary Educational Psychology, pp. 1–99
Copyright © 2007 by Information Age Publishing
All rights of reproduction in any form reserved.

decide the content to be taught in schools, and an accompanying assumption that the methods by which this content is taught should be based on experimental studies of learning, often without much consideration of children's preferences (e.g., Thorndike, 1922). In addition to this lack of consensus about how to approach children's learning, educational goals can be further complicated by attempts to use schools to socialize children in one ideological perspective or another (MacDonald, 1988).

One example of the latter concerns attempts to include the teaching of "intelligent design" along with natural selection in biology courses in some regions of the United States; the former is the argument that the complexity of life implicates a designer and by inference a "God." Research in biology strongly supports the teaching of natural selection, but these mechanisms are at odds with certain religious beliefs, which in turn are the ideological basis for attempts to modify the school curriculum. The use of schools to shape the ideological biases of the next generation is by no means restricted to the United States, and is ironically understandable from an evolutionary perspective (see MacDonald, 1988). The details are not important for the current discussion: My point is that schools present an opportunity for large-scale socialization of children and are thus often used for purposes that have more to do with the best interests of those attempting to influence this socialization than the best educational interests of children. In fact, the history of education in the United States might be viewed as being more strongly driven by ideology and untested assumptions about children's learning than by concerns about the efficacy of schooling vis-à-vis the long-term social and employment interests of children (Ceci & Papierno, 2005; Egan, 2002; Hirsch, 1996).

These ideological debates and the attendant opportunity costs to children's educational outcomes and later employment opportunities will continue well into the twenty-first century, if current attempts to move the field of education to a more solid scientific footing are not successful (Reyna, 2005). With this monograph, I hope to provide a broad and scientifically grounded perspective on these debates by considering how children's schooling and to a lesser degree their later occupational interests can be informed by recent advances in the application of evolutionary theory to the understanding of the human brain, mind, and its development (Bjorklund & Pellegrini, 2002; Cosmides & Tooby, 1994; Geary, 2005; Hirschfeld & Gelman, 1994; Pinker, 1997). I have termed this perspective *evolutionary educational psychology* (Geary, 2002a), but I must emphasize at the outset that this is not a perspective that is ready for direct translation into school curricula. Rather, I will outline the foundations for this discipline, and in doing so I hope to (a) provide a conceptualization of children's learning in school that is less prone to ideological change; (b) consider ways in which this perspective can be used to generate testable empirical hypotheses about this learning; and (c) discuss implications for understanding and ultimately improving educational outcomes.

In the first section, I make a distinction between *biologically primary* folk knowledge and abilities, that is, competencies that are components of evolved cognitive domains, and *biologically secondary* knowledge and abilities, that is, competencies acquired through formal or informal training. In this first section, I focus on primary abilities because these are the foundation for the construction of secondary abilities through formal education. In the second section, I discuss the evolution of general intelligence and how this evolution relates to the primary abilities discussed in the first section. In these first two sections, I provide more detail than might, at first read, seem to be needed. The details are necessary, however, if we are going to make a serious attempt to understand academic learning from an evolutionary perspective and are going to generate explicit and testable hypotheses about the relation between evolved cognitive and social biases and this learning. In the final section, I discuss the historical and schooling-based emergence of secondary abilities, focusing on potential cognitive and social mechanisms involved in the building of secondary competencies, and using reading and scientific reasoning as examples.

COGNITIVE EVOLUTION AND CHILDREN'S DEVELOPMENT

To fully appreciate the enormity of the task of educating millions of children, it is helpful to contrast the abilities and forms of knowledge the human brain is biologically primed to learn and those abilities and forms of knowledge without this advantage but that are needed for successful living in the modern world. The former are termed biologically primary and the culture-specific skills that can be built from these are termed biologically secondary (Geary, 1995). At this point, the distinction between these categories is necessarily fuzzy, but such a distinction is an important first step to approaching children's academic development from an evolutionarily informed perspective. First, I will outline broad distinctions between primary and secondary domains. Next, I describe a taxonomy of primary domains for the human mind, and finally I discuss how children's cognitive development and self-directed activity biases are related to these primary domains.

Primary and Secondary Forms of Cognition

Biologically primary *domains* encompass evolutionary-significant content areas (described below) and are composed of *folk knowledge* (e.g., inferential biases) and *primary abilities* (e.g., language, spatial). Folk knowledge results from the organization of the brain systems that have evolved to process and integrate specific forms of information. These brain regions and associated perceptual and attentional biases focus the individual on these features of the environment and prime the forms of behavioral response that tended to covary with survival or reproductive outcomes during the species' evolutionary history. For many species, there is evidence for specialized systems for detecting features of conspecifics (i.e., members of the same species; Grossman et al., 2000; Kanwisher, McDermott, & Chun, 1997), and different systems for detecting features of typical prey (Barton & Dean, 1993) or predatory (Deecke, Slater, & Ford, 2002) species. These brain, perceptual, and attentional systems are likely to be modularized, that is, they respond to restricted forms of information (e.g., movement of a predator) and prime a restricted class of behavioral response (e.g., predator evasion), but this does not mean the systems cannot be modified based on experience. The extent of any such plasticity is vigorously debated (Clark, Mitra, & Wang, 2001; de Winter & Oxnard, 2001; Finlay, Darlington, & Nicastro, 2001) and, as I describe later, likely varies across modules and development (Geary, 2005; Geary & Huffman, 2002).

In any case, because these perceptual and attentional biases result from the organization of the underlying sensory and brain systems, folk knowledge is largely implicit, that is, the systems operate more or less automatically and below conscious awareness. For these examples, animals of many species behave in ways consistent with an "intuitive" understanding or folk knowledge of how to engage in social interactions with members of their own species and how to hunt and avoid predators (see Gigerenzer, Todd, & ABC Research Group, 1999).

For humans, folk knowledge can sometimes be expressed explicitly and in terms of attributional biases about the behavior of other people (Fiske & Taylor, 1991) or about physical (Clement, 1982) or biological (Atran, 1998) phenomena. Folk knowledge is organized around a constellation of more specialized primary abilities. As an example, the domain of folk psychology includes implicit and sometimes explicit knowledge organized around the self, specific other individuals (e.g., family members), and group-level dynamics, and these knowledge bases are composed of more specific primary abilities. For individual-level folk knowledge, these specific abilities emerge from the brain, perceptual, and cognitive systems that support language, facial processing, gesture processing, and so forth, as described below. The constellation of brain regions that support each of these and related abilities may differ (e.g., Belin, Zatorre, Lafaille, Ahad, & Pike, 2000; Downing, Jiang, Shuman, & Kanwisher, 2001; Kanwisher et al., 1997), but during social discourse they operate in a coordinated manner. The distinction between specific primary abilities is important, because different primary abilities may differentially contribute to the construction of different secondary abilities, as discussed later under the heading Biologically Secondary Learning.

Academic learning involves the modification of primary abilities and explicit attributional biases associated with folk knowledge to create a suite of culture-specific biologically secondary domains, such as mathematics, and biologically secondary abilities and knowledge, such as the ability to phonetically decode written symbols or to understand the base-10 structure of the formal mathematical number system (Geary, 1995, 2002a, 2006). Of course, some secondary abilities are more similar to primary abilities than are others. Spelke (2000), for instance, proposed that learning the mathematical number system involves integrating implicit and primary knowledge of small numbers (e.g., implicitly representing the quantity of small, ≤ 4, sets) and counting principles with another primary ability that enables an analog representation of magnitude, as in the ability to implicitly estimate more than or less than (Pinel, Piazza, Le Bihan, & Dehaene, 2004). Primary knowledge of the numerosity of small collections of objects and the understanding that successive counts increase quantity by one is integrated with the magnitude representation system through a culture-specific system of number words, such that number words come to represent specific quantities outside the range of the primary system. The end result is the ability to represent large quantities verbally or in terms of a formal mathematical number line, that is, to abstractly represent large quantities in a precise manner and in a way that is unique in terms of our evolutionary history. Siegler and Opfer's (2003) research on children's number-line estimation is consistent with this proposal; specifically, when estimating where an Arabic numeral should be placed on a number line, first grade children's estimates conform to predictions of the primary analog magnitude system, but with schooling these estimates eventually conform to the formal secondary mathematical system.

Other features of academic mathematics, such as the base-10 system, are more remote from the supporting primary abilities (Geary, 2002a). Competency in base-10 arithmetic requires a conceptual understanding of the mathematical number line, and an ability to decompose this system into sets of 10 and then to organize these sets into clusters of 100 (i.e., 10, 20, 30, …), 1,000, and so forth. Whereas an implicit understanding of the quantity of small sets of objects is likely to be primary knowledge, the creation of sets around 10 and the superordinate organization of these sets is clearly not. This conceptual knowledge must also be systematically mapped onto the number word system (McCloskey, Sokol, & Goodman, 1986), and integrated with school-taught procedures for solving complex arithmetic problems (Fuson & Kwon, 1992; Geary, 1994). The development of base-10 knowledge thus requires the extension of primary number knowledge to very large numbers; the organization of these number representations in ways that differ conceptually from primary knowledge; and, the learning of procedural rules for applying this new knowledge to the secondary domain of complex, mathematical arithmetic (e.g., to solve 234 + 697).

Evolved Domains of the Human Mind

I assume that primary knowledge and abilities provide the foundation for academic learning. Thus, crucial components for an evolutionary approach to education include knowledge of the organization of primary domains; the extent to which the associated abilities are plastic; and the form and range of species-typical experiences that transform this plasticity into systems well suited to the particulars of the ecology and social group within which children are situated. Unfortunately, we do not yet have all of the pieces of this foundational knowledge, but enough is now known to provide the framework for an evolutionary educational psychology. In the following sections, I provide the cornerstones of this foundation; that is, I: (a) outline a motivation-to-control model that provides a conceptual organization to many levels of evolved traits; (b) describe a taxonomy of primary domains and abilities in humans; and (c) consider the relation between evolution and cognitive development.

Motivation to Control

The brain and mind of all species evolved to attend to and process the forms of information, such as the movement patterns of prey species, which covaried with survival and reproductive prospects during the species' evolutionary history (Geary, 2005). These systems bias implicit decision-making processes and behavioral responses in ways that allow the organism to attempt to achieve access to and control of these outcomes, as in prey capture, or to avoid negative outcomes, as in being captured by a predator (see Gigerenzer et al., 1999). The framework fits well with the general consensus among psychologists that humans have a basic motivation to achieve some level of control over relationships, events, and resources that are of significance in their life (Fiske, 1993; Heckhausen & Schulz, 1995; Shapiro, Schwartz, & Astin, 1996; Thompson, Armstrong, & Thomas, 1998), although there is no consensus as to whether this motivation to control is the result of evolution. My thesis is that the human motivation to control is indeed an evolved disposition, but should not be confused with an explicit goal to control others. Rather, it is a conceptual heuristic for understanding the foci of behavior; that is, the implicit focus of behavior is to attempt to influence social relationships and the behavior of other people in self-serving ways (often masked by self deception; Trivers, 2000), and to gain control of the biological and physical resources that enhance social status and well-being in the local ecology and social group (Geary, 1998, 2005).

The control-related behavioral focus is represented by the apex and adjoining section of Figure 1.1. The bottom of the figure represents the folk modules that in effect result in a bottom-up directing of the individual's attention toward and enable the automatic and implicit processing of social (e.g., facial expressions), biological (e.g., features of hunted species), and physical (e.g., manipulation of objects as tools) information patterns that have tended to be the same across generations and within lifetimes, and have covaried with survival or reproductive prospects during human evolution. The center of the figure represents conscious psychological and cognitive (e.g., working memory) mechanisms that enable more top-down strategic planning and problem solving and that provide affective feedback regarding the effectiveness of actual or mentally simulated control-related behaviors, as described below.

Benefits of Control. If there is indeed an evolved motivation to control, then there should be a relation between achievement of resource control and social influence and survival and reproductive outcomes. In modern societies, some resources are symbolic (e.g., money, stocks) but are important because control of these resources enhances social influence and facilitates control of quality foods, medicines, housing, and so forth. In traditional societies, coalitions of kin cooperate to control local biological (e.g., cows) and physical (e.g., grazing land) resources, and to compete with other coalitions to maintain control of these resources. Although humans have psychological mechanisms that obscure the fact that they often use social relationships and other people for their own ends (Alexander, 1989), use them they do. Other people are resources if they have reproductive potential (e.g., young females; Buss, 1994), social power, or access (e.g., through monetary wealth) to the biological and physical resources that covary with well-being and status in the culture (Irons, 1979). The goal of developing a relationship with an individual who has social power and wealth is fundamentally an attempt to influence the behavior of this individual and through this to achieve access to power and wealth (Fiske, 1993; Geary & Flinn, 2001). In most contexts and for most people, the motivation to control is constrained by formal laws, informal social mores (e.g., enforced through gossip; Barkow, 1992), and by psychological mechanisms (e.g., guilt) that promote social compromise and reciprocal social relationships with members of their in-group (Baron, 1997; Trivers, 1971).

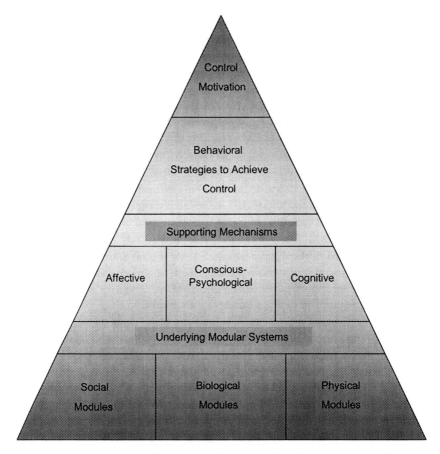

Figure 1.1.   The apex and following section represent the proposal that human behavior is basically driven by a motivation to control the social, biological, and physical resources that have tended to covary survival and reproductive outcomes during human evolution. The midsection shows the supporting affective, conscious psychological (e.g., attributional biases), and cognitive (e.g., working memory) mechanisms that support the motivation to control and operate on the modular systems shown at the base. From "*The origin of mind: Evolution of brain, cognition, and general intelligence,*" by D. C. Geary, p. 74. Copyright 2005 by the American Psychological Association. Reprinted with permission.

Nonetheless, even in resource-rich Western culture, socioeconomic status (SES), that is, control of symbolic (e.g., money) and material resources, is associated with a longer life span and better physical health (e.g., Adler et al., 1994; R. Bradley & Corwyn, 2002), although it is not correlated with happiness or the subjective evaluation of well-being (Diener &

Diener, 1996). The ability to achieve high SES in modern societies is related, in part, to general intelligence (described below) which in turn may moderate the relation between SES and health outcomes (e.g., through better compliance to medical regimes; L. S. Gottfredson, 2004); or, general intelligence may covary directly with overall health (Lubinski & Humphreys, 1992). In any case, in preindustrial and industrializing Western societies, and in traditional societies today (Hill & Hurtado, 1996; United Nations, 1985), SES was considerably more important than it currently is in Western culture (e.g., Hed, 1987; Morrison, Kirshner, & Molho, 1977; Schultz, 1991). In fact, parental SES often influenced which infants and young children would live and which would die. During the 1437-1438 and 1449-1450 epidemics in Florence, Italy, child mortality rates increased 5- to 10-fold and varied with parental SES; higher parental SES was associated with lower mortality (Morrison et al., 1977). In an extensive analysis of birth, death, and demographic records from eighteenth century Berlin, Schultz (1991) found a strong negative correlation ($r = -.74$) between parental SES and infant and child mortality rates. Infant (birth to 1 year) mortality rates were about 10% for aristocrats but more than 40% for laborers and unskilled technicians.

Given these relations, it is not surprising that individual and group-level conflicts of interest are invariably over access to and control of social relationships, the behavior of other people, and the biological and physical resources that covary with survival or reproductive prospects in the local ecology and culture (Alexander, 1979; Chagnon, 1988; Horowitz, 2001; Irons, 1979; Keeley, 1996). Although these relations are often masked by the wealth and low mortality rates enjoyed in Western societies today, the implication is clear: In most human societies and presumably throughout human evolution, gaining social influence and control of biological and physical resources, that is, food, medicine, shelter, land, and so forth, covaried with reproductive opportunity (i.e., choice of mating partner), reproductive success (i.e., the number of offspring surviving to adulthood), and survival prospects. Recent population genetic studies provide strong support for the hypothesis that resource control enhances reproductive prospects (e.g., Zerjal et al., 2003).

A fundamental motivation to control has evolved in humans, because success at achieving control of social, biological, and physical resources very often meant the difference between living and dying. My point is that evolved motivational systems bias children such that they prefer to engage in activities, such as forming social relationships (e.g., Geary, Byrd-Craven, Hoard, Vigil, & Numtee, 2003), that flesh out the primary abilities and knowledge that were the foci of competition for behavioral control and social influence during human evolution, but these activities are often very different from the activities needed to master a biologically secondary academic domain. The contrast between evolved motivational biases and the activities needed for secondary learning has very important implications for children's motivation to learn in school and niche seeking in other evolutionarily novel contexts, such as the work place, as I elaborate in the section Motivation to Learn.

Conscious Psychological Mechanisms. The core psychological mechanism presented in Figure 1.1 is the ability to generate conscious, explicit mental representations of situations that are centered on the self and one's relationship with other people or one's access to biological and physical resources that are of significance in the culture and ecology. The representations are of past, present, or potential future states and might be cast as visual images, in language, or as memories of personal experiences, that is, episodic memories (Tulving, 2002). Of central importance is the ability to create a mental representation of a desired or fantasized state, such as a relationship with another individual, and to compare this to a mental representation of one's current state, such as the nature of the current relationship with this other individual. These are conscious psychological representations of present and potential future states that are of personal significance and are the content on which more explicit and effortful everyday reasoning and problem-solving processes, such as analogy and induction, are applied (Evans, 2002; Holyoak & Thagard, 1997; Stanovich & West, 2000). The goal is to devise and rehearse behavioral strategies that can be used to reduce the difference between the current and desired state (Geary, 2005). Explicit attributions about the self, other people, groups, as well as the behavior of other species or physical phenomena, are also components of these conscious psychological representations, as I describe in the section titled Heuristics and Attributional Biases.

Cognitive Mechanisms. The cognitive mechanisms include working memory, attentional control, and the ability to inhibit automatic processing of folk-related information (e.g., attributional biases) or to inhibit evolved behavioral reactions to this information (Baddeley, 1986; 2000a; Bjorklund & Harnishfeger, 1995; Cowan, 1995), as well as the ability to systematically problem solve and reason about patterns represented in working memory (Newell & Simon, 1972). These cognitive and problem-solving processes are the mechanisms that allow individuals to mentally represent and manipulate information processed by perceptual systems (e.g., sounds and words) and the more complex forms of information that result from the integration of information processed by the social, biological, and physical modules. Working memory, for instance, enables the short-term retention of spoken utterances, which may facilitate vocabulary learning and other specific primary abilities (Baddeley, Gathercole, & Papagno, 1998).

However, my proposal is that the most important evolutionary function concerns the relation between these cognitive and problem-solving mechanisms and the generation and manipulation of conscious psychological representations (Geary, 2005). In other words, working memory and attentional and inhibitory control are the content-free mechanisms that, for instance, enable the integration of a current conscious psychological state with memory representations of related past experiences, and the generation of mental models or simulations of potential future states (Alexander, 1989; Johnson-Laird, 1983). Everyday reasoning and problem solving represent the ways in which these simulations are manipulated in the associated problem space, as individuals generate representations of behavioral or social strategies that will move them from the current state to the desired goal (Newell & Simon, 1972).

Evolutionary Function.   The predicted evolved function of these cognitive and conscious psychological mechanisms is to generate a fantasy representation of how the world "should" operate, that is, a representation of the world that would be most favorable to the individual's reproductive (e.g., fantasy of the "perfect" mate—Whissell, 1996) and survival interests (Geary, 1998, 2005). This mental representation serves as a goal to be achieved and is compared against a mental representation of current circumstances. Working memory serves as the platform, and problem solving (e.g., means-ends analysis; Newell & Simon, 1972) and everyday reasoning processes serve as the means for simulating social and other behavioral strategies that will reduce the difference between the ideal and actual states. If the behavioral strategies are effective, then the difference between the ideal state and the current state will be reduced and the individual will be one step closer to gaining access to and control of social and other resources.

Following Damasio's (2003) distinction, affective mechanisms are separated into emotions, which are observable behaviors (e.g., facial expressions or social withdrawal), and feelings, which are nonobservable conscious representations of an emotional state or other conditions that can potentially influence the individuals' well being. Affective mechanisms can influence behavioral strategies. Emotions provide social feedback (e.g., a frown may automatically signal disapproval) and the associated feelings provide feedback to the individual (Campos, Campos, & Barrett, 1989). The latter provides an indicator of the effectiveness of control-related behavioral strategies. Positive feelings provide reinforcement when strategies are resulting in the achievement of significant goals, or at least a reduction in the difference between the current and desired state, and punishment (negative feelings) and disengagement when behaviors are not resulting in this end (J. A. Gray, 1987).

The supporting brain systems should function, in part, to amplify attention to evolutionarily significant forms of information, such as facial expressions, and produce emotions and feelings and prime corresponding behavioral biases that are likely to reproduce outcomes that have covaried with successful survival or reproduction during human evolution (Damasio, 2003; Lazarus, 1991; Öhman, 2002). For instance, positive affect should function, in part, to maintain the forms of social relationship that are commonly associated with the achievement of survival and reproductive ends, and this appears to be the case. Happiness is strongly related to the strength of reciprocal and romantic relationships (Diener & Seligman, 2002), the former being sources of social support and allies during times of social conflict and the latter obviously related to reproductive goals.

Taxonomy of Biologically Primary Domains

The taxonomy of biologically primary folk domains and abilities shown in Figure 1.2 fleshes out the base of Figure 1.1 (Geary, 2005). At this time, there is vigorous debate regarding the broader question of whether these types of cognitive systems are better conceptualized as inherently modular in organization (Cosmides & Tooby, 1994; Gallistel, 2000; Pinker, 1997; Pinker & Jackendoff, 2005) or as generally plastic, with any modular-like competencies emerging through an interaction between relatively unspecialized brain and perceptual systems and patterns of experience (Elman, Bates, Johnson, Karmiloff-Smith, Parisi, & Plunkett, 1996; Hauser, Chomsky, & Fitch, 2002; Heyes, 2003; Quartz & Sejnowski, 1997). The full implications of and resolutions to these debates will likely be decades in coming, but there are a few points relevant to the current discussion.

First, the cognitive abilities (e.g., reading of facial expressions) associated with the folk domains (e.g., folk psychology) illustrated in Figure 1.2 can be conceptualized as modular in that attentional and information-processing biases and information organization in long-term memory appear to be organized in ways consistent with this taxonomy. However, this organization can be built from multiple lower-level systems, and thus a simple one-to-one correspondence between these cognitive abilities and a specific brain region is not always expected. Although brain regions that differentially respond to evolutionarily significant forms of information, such as the shape of a human face or body, are predicted (Kanwisher et al., 1997; Slaughter, Stone, & Reed, 2004), these regions may also respond to perceptually similar forms of information. Moreover, many primary abilities will involve the coordinated activity of multiple lower-

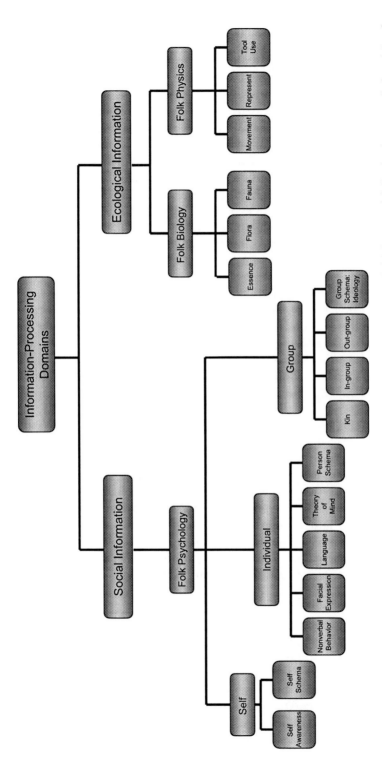

Figure 1.2. Evolved cognitive modules that compose the domains of folk psychology, folk biology, and folk physics. From "*The origin of mind: Evolution of brain, cognition, and general intelligence*," by D. C. Geary, p. 129. Copyright 2005 by the American Psychological Association. Reprinted with permission.

level perceptual systems and thus result in the distribution of activity across multiple brain regions. As I describe in the section titled Cognitive Development and Modular Plasticity, these modular systems are neither strictly inherently modular nor strictly the result of patterns of developmental experience, but rather are predicted to emerge epigenetically from an interaction between inherent perceptual and attentional biases and evolutionarily expectant developmental experiences (Bjorklund & Pellegrini, 2002; Geary & Bjorklund, 2000; Greenough, Black, & Wallace, 1987; Scarr, 1992, 1993). The relative importance of inherent constraints and patterns of developmental experience is predicted to vary from one module to the next (see below), and thus broad generalizations about the contributions of evolution versus development are not appropriate.

Second, I am in agreement with Marcus' (2004) proposal that brain systems that process restricted forms of information, such as angular orientation or object location, might be considered modular at a neural level and serve as building blocks for multiple higher-level perceptual modules, such as perceiving different specific objects. Each perceptual module can be used as a building block for multiple higher-level modules (e.g., a specific object categorized as a tool). In other words, lower-level modular systems can be used as building blocks for multiple higher-level modules, meaning that complex modular skills (e.g., tool use) emerge developmentally and evolutionarily through a template that organizes preexisting lower-level modules but can do so in novel, environmentally contingent ways. From this perspective, a complex cognitive module does not have to evolve de novo, but rather can emerge with an evolutionary duplication or modification of an existing template. The template organizes lower-level systems in a novel way, with no need for evolutionary change in the lower-level systems (Geary, 2005). Marcus' (2004) building blocks imply that basic sensory and perceptual systems have evolved such that they can be configured in many different ways, making them subject to evolutionary and developmental change. The latter contributes to the potential for the "construction" of biologically secondary abilities, within constraints.

Folk Psychology

Folk psychology is composed of the affective, cognitive, and behavioral systems that enable people to negotiate social interactions and relationships. The function of the corresponding primary cognitive abilities is to process and manipulate (e.g., create categories) the forms of social information that have covaried with survival and reproduction during human evolution. The associated domains involve the self, relationships and interactions with other people, and group-level relationships and interactions. These dynamics are supported by the respective primary modular systems corresponding to self, individual, and group shown in the bottom and leftmost sections of Figure 1.2.

Self. Although there is much that remains to be resolved regarding the nature and distinctiveness of self-related cognitions versus those related to other people and the distribution of these representations in the brain (Gillihan & Farah, 2005), people in general often have a self-referenced perspective on social relationships and other matters of significance in their life (Fiske & Taylor, 1991). Self-related cognitions include awareness of the self as a social being and of one's behavior in social contexts (Tulving, 2002), as well as a self schema (Markus, 1977). The self schema is a long-term memory network of information that links together knowledge and beliefs about the self, including positive (accentuated) and negative (discounted) traits (e.g., friendliness), personal memories, self-efficacy in various domains, and so on. Whether implicitly or explicitly represented, self schemas appear to regulate goal-related behaviors—specifically, where one focuses behavioral effort and whether or not one will persist in the face of failure (Sheeran & Orbell, 2000). Self-related regulation results from a combination of implicit and explicit processes that influence social comparisons, self-esteem, valuation of different forms of ability and interests, and the formation of social relationships (Drigotas, 2002).

Individual. The person-related modular competencies function to enable the monitoring and control of dyadic interactions and the development and maintenance of one-on-one relationships. Caporael (1997) and Bugental (2000) have described universal forms of these interactions and relationships, including parent-child attachments and friendships, among others. There are, of course, differences across these dyads, but all of them are supported by the individual-level modules shown in Figure 1.2. These modules include those that enable the reading of nonverbal behavior and facial expressions, language, and theory of mind (e.g., Baron-Cohen, 1995; Brothers & Ring, 1992; Pinker, 1994; Rosenthal, Hall, DiMatteo, Rogers, & Archer, 1979). Theory of mind refers to the ability to make inferences about other people, including their beliefs and motives underlying their behavior, their future intentions, and so forth. The person schema is a long-term memory network that includes representations of other people's physical attributes (age, race, sex), memories for specific behavioral episodes, and more abstract trait information, such as people's sociability (e.g., warm to emotionally distant) and competence (Schneider, 1973). It seems likely that the person schema will also include information related to other people's modular systems, such as theory of mind, as well as people's network of social relationships and kin (Geary & Flinn, 2001). The former would include memories and trait information about how the person typically makes inferences, responds to social cues, and their social and other goals.

Group. A universal aspect of human behavior and cognition is the parsing of the social world into groups (Fiske, 2002). The most common of these groupings are shown in Figure 1.2, and reflect the categorical significance of kin, the formation of in-groups and out-groups, and a group schema. The latter is an ideologically-based social identification, as exemplified by nationality or religious affiliation. The categorical significance of kin is most strongly reflected in the motivational disposition of humans to organize themselves into families of one form or another in all cultures (Brown, 1991). In traditional societies, nuclear families are typically embedded in the context of a wider network of kin (Geary & Flinn, 2001). Individuals within these kinship networks cooperate to facilitate competition with other kin groups over resource control and manipulation of reproductive relationships. As cogently argued by Alexander (1979), coalitional competition also occurs beyond the kin group, is related to social ideology, and is endemic throughout the world (Horowitz, 2001). As with kin groups, competition among ideology-based groups is over resource control. The corresponding selective pressure is the competitive advantage associated with large group size; that is, ideologies enable easy expansion of group size during group-level competition (Alexander, 1989).

Folk Biology and Folk Physics

People living in traditional societies use the local ecology to support their survival and reproductive needs. The associated activities are supported by, among other things, the folk biological and folk physical modules shown in the ecological section of Figure 1.2 (Geary, 2005; Geary & Huffman, 2002). The folk biological modules support the categorizing of flora and fauna in the local ecology, especially species used as food, medicines, or in social rituals (Berlin, Breedlove, & Raven, 1973). Folk biology also includes systems that support an understanding of the essence of these species (Atran, 1998), that is, heuristic-based decisions regarding the likely behavior of these species in contexts relevant to human interests. Essence also includes explicit knowledge about growth patterns and behavior that facilitates hunting and other activities involved in securing and using these species as resources (e.g., food). Physical modules are for guiding movement in three-dimensional physical space, mentally representing this space (e.g., demarcating the in-group's territory), and for using physical materials (e.g., stones, metals) for making tools (Pinker, 1997; Shepard, 1994). The associated primary abilities support a host of evolutionarily significant activities, such as hunting, foraging, and the use of tools as weapons. Finally, there may also be evolved systems for representing small quantities, as noted earlier, and for manipulating these representations by means of counting and simple additions and subtractions (Geary, 1995). On the basis of correlated brain regions (e.g., Dehaene, Spelke, Pinel, Stanescu, & Tsivkin, 1999), these primary quantitative abilities may be aspects of folk physics.

Heuristics and Attributional Biases

In addition to describing "rule of thumb" patterns of behavior (Gigerenzer et al., 1999), heuristics can also include explicit inferential and attributional biases that are integral features of folk knowledge, at least for humans. For instance, people often make attributions about the cause of failures to achieve social influence or other desired outcomes, including academic achievement goals. An attribution of this type might involve an explicit evaluation about the reason for one's failure to achieve a desired outcome—determining, for example, that the failure was due to bad luck—and would function to direct and maintain control-related behavioral strategies in the face of any such failure (Heckhausen & Schultz, 1995). Social attributional biases that favor members of the ingroup and derogate members of out-groups are also well known (Fiske, 2002; W. Stephan, 1985) and facilitate coalitional competition (Horowitz, 2001). The essence associated with folk biology allows people to make inferences (e.g., during the act of hunting) about the behavior of members of familiar species, as well as about the likely behavior of less familiar but related species (Atran, 1998). Attributions about causality in the physical world have also been studied. Children and adults have, as an example, naïve conceptions about motion and other physical phenomena (Clement, 1982).

These biases may often provide good enough explanations for day-to-day living and self-serving explanations for social and other phenomena, but this does not mean all of the explanations are accurate from a scientific perspective. Explicit descriptions of these psychological, physical, and biological phenomena are often times correct, especially for basic relationships (Wellman & Gelman, 1992), but many of these explanations and attributional biases are scientifically inaccurate and may actually interfere with the learning of scientific concepts, as I illustrate in the section titled Academic Learning.

Cognitive Development and Modular Plasticity

With an evolutionary perspective on education, it is important to distinguish cognitive development and academic development (Geary, 1995, 2004). The former is concerned with the evolved function of developmental activities as related to the adaptation of primary abilities to local conditions. Empirically, it is known that for many of the folk abilities (e.g., language) represented by Figure 1.2, plasticity appears to be especially evident during the early developmental period (Kuhl, 1994; Kuhl et al., 1997; Pascalis, de Haan, & Nelson, 2002; Pascalis, Scott, Shannon, Nicholson, Coleman, & Nelson, 2005; Paterson, Brown, Gsödl, Johnson, & Karmiloff-Smith, 1999; Stiles, 2000). Given the potential cost of death before reproductive maturity, the benefits associated with a long developmental period and the presumed corresponding increase in brain and cognitive plasticity must be substantial. In fact, evidence in the fossil record suggests that the human developmental period nearly doubled with the emergence of modern humans (Dean et al., 2001), with particular increases in the length of childhood and adolescence (Bogin, 1999). The extension of the length of the developmental period appears to have coevolved with changes in brain size and organization, among other changes (Flinn, Geary, Ward, 2005; Geary, 2005). One implication is that the increase in the period of immaturity and the attendant increase in the period of brain and cognitive plasticity serves to accommodate greater variation in the conditions in which evolving humans were situated, as I elaborate in the section titled Evolution of General Intelligence.

The mechanisms involved in the experience-driven adaptation of primary modular systems to variation in local conditions are not well understood. At a macro level, and following the lead of R. Gelman (1990), Geary and Huffman (2002) proposed that prenatal brain organization results in inherently constrained features of neural and perceptual modules that guide attention to and processing of stable forms of information (e.g., the general shape of the human face) in the folk domains shown in Figure 1.2. The result is biases in early postnatal attentional, affective, and information-processing capacities, as well as biases in self-initiated behavioral engagement of the environment (Bjorklund & Pellegrini, 2002; Scarr, 1992; Scarr & McCartney, 1983). The latter generate evolutionarily expectant experiences, that is, experiences that provide the social and ecological feedback needed to adjust modular architecture to variation in information patterns in these domains (Bouchard, Lykken, Tellegen, & McGue, 1996; Greenough et al., 1987; MacDonald, 1992). These behavioral biases are expressed as common juvenile activities, such as social play and exploration of the ecology. These experience-expectant processes result in the modification of plastic features of primary modular systems, such that the individual is able to identify and respond to variation (e.g., discriminate one individual from another) within these folk domains, and begin to create the forms of category described above, such as in-groups/out-groups or flora/fauna.

Folk Psychology

As an illustration of the importance of plasticity in a folk domain, consider that the strong bias of human infants to attend to human faces, movement patterns, and speech reflects, in theory, the initial and inherent organizational and motivational structure of the associated folk psychological modules (Freedman, 1974). These biases reflect the evolutionary significance of social relationships (Baumeister & Leary, 1995) and in effect recreate the microconditions (e.g., parent-child interactions) associated with the evolution of the corresponding modules (Caporael, 1997). Attention to and processing of this information also provides exposure to the within-category variation needed to adapt the architecture of these modules to variation in parental faces, behavior, and so forth (R. Gelman & Williams, 1998; Pascalis et al., 2005). It allows the infant to discriminate a parent's voice or face from that of other potential parents with only minimal exposure. Indeed, when human fetuses (gestation age of about 38 weeks) are exposed in utero to human voices, their heart-rate patterns suggest they are sensitive to and learn the voice patterns of their mother, and discriminate her voice from that of other women (Kisilevsky et al., 2003).

Developmental experiences may also facilitate later category formation. Boys' group-level competition (e.g., team sports) provides one example of the early formation of competition based on in-groups and out-groups and the coordination of social activities that may provide the practice for primitive group-level warfare in adulthood (Geary, 1998; Geary et al., 2003). These natural games may provide the practice needed for the skilled formation and maintenance of social coalitions in adulthood, and result in the accumulation of memories for associated activities and social strategies. In other words and in keeping with the comparative analyses of Pellis and Iwaniuk (2000), these games may be more strongly related to learning the skills of other boys and acquiring the social competencies for coordinated group-level activities, as contrasted with learning specific fighting behaviors, such as hitting. These activities and the accompanying effects on brain and cognition are in theory related to the group-level social selection pressures noted earlier, and provide experience with the dynamic formation of in-groups and out-groups.

Folk Biology and Folk Physics

The complexity of hunting and foraging activities varies with the ecology in which the group lives, a situation that should select for plasticity in the associated brain, cognitive, and behavioral systems (S. Gelman, 2003). In theory, children's implicit folk biological knowledge and inherent interest in living things result in the motivation to engage in experiences that automatically create implicit taxonomies of local flora and fauna and result in the accrual of an extensive knowledge base of these species (Wellman & Gelman, 1992). In traditional societies, these experiences include assisting with foraging and play hunting (e.g., Blurton Jones, Hawkes, & O'Connell, 1997). Anthropological research indicates that it often takes many years of engaging in these forms of play and early work to learn the skills (e.g., how to shoot a bow and arrow) and acquire the knowledge needed for successful hunting and foraging (Kaplan, Hill, Lancaster, & Hurtado, 2000), although this is not the case with all hunting and foraging activities (Blurton Jones & Marlowe, 2002).

An example associated with folk physics is provided by the ability to mentally form maplike representations of the large-scale environment, which occurs more or less automatically as animals explore this environment (Gallistel, 1990; Wellman & Gelman, 1992). For humans, the initial ability to form these representations emerges by three years of age (DeLoache, Kolstad, & Anderson, 1991), improves gradually through adolescence, and often requires extensive exploration and exposure to the local environment to perfect (Matthews, 1992). The research of Matthews clearly shows that children automatically attend to geometric features of the large-scale environment and landmarks within this environment and are able to generate a cognitive representation of landmarks and their geometric relations at a later time. Children's skill at generating these representations increases with repeated explorations of the physical environment. Thus, learning about the physical world is a complex endeavor for humans and requires an extended developmental period, in comparison with the more rapid learning that occurs in species that occupy a more narrow range of physical ecologies (Gallistel, 2000). A recent study by Chen and Siegler (2000) suggests that similar processes may occur for tool use. Here, it was demonstrated that 18-month-olds have an implicit understanding of how to use simple tools (e.g., a hooked stick to retrieve a desired toy) and with experience learn to use these tools in increasingly effective ways (Gredlein & Bjorklund, 2005).

EVOLUTION OF GENERAL INTELLIGENCE

In addition to knowledge about folk abilities and knowledge, an evolutionary educational psychology must incorporate the research base on general intelligence (g) and the underlying brain and cognitive systems. This is because performance on measures of g is the best single predictor of grades in school and years of schooling completed (Jensen, 1998; Lubinski, 2000; Walberg, 1984). My goal here is to provide a framework for understanding the evolution of general intelligence and the relation between these systems and the primary folk systems described above; a more complete discussion can be found elsewhere (Geary, 2005). As I discuss in the first section, the interaction between g and folk knowledge and the associated selection pressures provides the key to understanding the uniquely human ability to adapt to variation and novelty within a lifetime and through this the ability to learn in the evolutionarily novel context of school. In the second section, I describe the core mechanisms that appear to underlie performance on measures of g, and thus the mechanisms that may have evolved to enable an experience-driven adaptation to variation in social and ecological conditions during individual lifetimes. Evolved mechanisms that enable humans to adapt to within-lifetime variation are the same mechanisms that likely contribute to the generation of novelty and culture, and that support the learning of secondary knowledge and abilities.

Adapting to Variation

The key to understanding the evolution of g and plasticity in primary modular systems is the pattern of stability and change across generations and within lifetimes in the information patterns that covaried with survival or reproductive outcomes during human evolution (Geary, 2005). As noted above, the three primary categories of evolutionarily significant information are social, biological, and physical and are captured by the respective domains of folk psychology, folk biology, and folk physics. Corresponding examples of these include information patterns generated by the body shape and movement of conspecifics (Blake, 1993; Downing et al., 2001) and by species of predator and prey (Barton & Dean, 1993), as well as by environmental features (e.g., star patterns) used in navigation (Gallistel, 1990), among many other conditions. As emphasized by many evolutionary psychologists, when such information patterns are consistent from one generation to the next and stable within lifetimes, modular brain and cognitive systems that automatically direct attention to and facilitate the processing of these restricted forms of information should evolve, as illustrated by the invariant end of the continuum in Figure 1.3 (Cosmides & Tooby, 1994; Gallistel, 2000).

Built into the organization of many of these systems are implicit (i.e., below the level of conscious awareness) decision-making heuristics (e.g., Gigerenzer & Selten, 2001), that is, behavior-ecology correlations that produce functional outcomes (Simon, 1956). These cognitive "rules of thumb" represent evolved behavioral responses to evolutionarily significant conditions. In some species of bird, for example, parental feeding of chicks can be described as a simple heuristic: "Feed the smallest, if there is plenty of food; otherwise, feed the largest" (Davis & Todd, 2001).

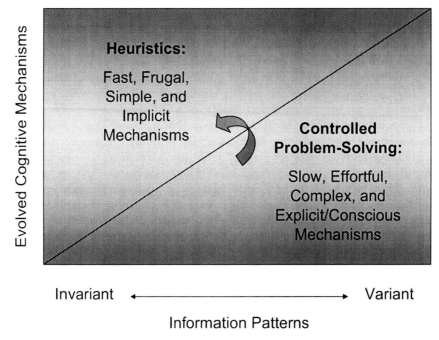

Figure 1.3.   The types of cognitive mechanisms that operate on ecological or social information are predicted to vary with the extent to which that information tended to be invariant (resulting in evolved heuristics) or variant (resulting in evolved problem-solving mechanisms) during the species' evolutionary history and during a typical lifetime. From "*The origin of mind: Evolution of brain, cognition, and general intelligence*," by D. C. Geary, p. 168. Copyright 2005 by the American Psychological Association. Reprinted with permission.

There can also be conditions that influence survival and reproductive prospects but that produce less predictable, or variant, information patterns across generations and within lifetimes. This variation might involve fluctuating climatic conditions (e.g., Potts, 1998), but is most likely to emerge from the behavioral interactions between biological organisms that have competing interests (Maynard Smith & Price, 1973). Host-parasite and predator-prey dynamics, as well as social competition, are central examples of this type of relationship. For humans, variable conditions appear to be largely produced by social dynamics and some dynamics associated with ecological demands, such as hunting. In other words, aspects of social and ecological selection pressures that resulted in the evolution of the folk systems represented in Figure 1.2, also appear to have resulted in conditions that favored the evolution of less modularized, domain-general brain and cognitive systems (Chiappe & MacDonald, 2005; Geary, 2005). As an example, in the context of competitive social relationships, novel behavior or behavioral variability provides an advantage, because it renders implicit, heuristic-based behavioral responses of competitors less effective. As shown at variant end of the continuum in Figure 1.3, these domain-general systems enable the explicit representation of variant information patterns in working memory, and support the controlled problem solving (e.g., mean-ends analysis) needed to cope with these variable conditions.

This is where g meets the motivation to control and integrates with more modularized systems. In particular, I recently proposed that the attentional, working memory, and problem-solving mechanisms that compose g (described below) evolved to support the conscious psychological representations of the perfect world, or at least a better situation, and to enable the simulation of behavioral strategies to reduce the difference between one's current situation and the achievement of this goal (Geary, 2005). The forms of information manipulated in these working memory representations are largely in the domains of folk knowledge—for example, mentally rehearsing a verbal argument to be used at a later time to pursue one's interests. But, variation at this level differs from the within-module variation discussed earlier. The modular-level plasticity evolved to accommodate variation within the restricted classes represented by the bottommost boxes in Figure 1.2 (e.g., facial expression), as in the ability to discriminate one face from another. The working memory simulations, in contrast, evolved to cope with macrolevel variation represented by the higher levels of organization in Figure 1.2 (e.g., individual, folk biology). For example, simulating the potential behavior of a friend in a future but unfamiliar situation can involve pulling together and integrating information from a variety of lower-level stores, including the person schema, and episodic memories of this individual's characteristic facial expressions, language expressions, and so forth (Kahneman & Tversky, 1982). If the interaction between two friends is simulated as they attempt to compromise on competing goals and interests, then the potential for variation in these behavioral dynamics and the potential for change in personal relationships increase substantially.

Variation at this macrolevel cannot be as strongly constrained by inherent mechanisms such as the more modular systems shown in the lower levels of Figure 1.2, because the specifics of this variation (e.g., levels of intergroup hostilities) can change substantively from one generation to the next or within a single lifetime. However, if the ability to mentally anticipate macrolevel variation—to project oneself into the future and simulate potential scenarios in working memory—increased survival or reproductive prospects during human evolution, then brain and cognitive systems that support these mental simulations would evolve. The conditions that would lead to the evolution of these abilities (e.g., mental time travel, complex working memory simulations) are complex, nuanced, and multifaceted and full discussion is beyond the scope of this chapter (see Alexander, 1989; Flinn et al., 2005; Geary, 2005). The gist is that from the viewpoint of the motivation to control, competition with others for control resulted in a within-species arms race (Alexander, 1989; Flinn et al., 2005), possibly beginning with the ability to generate behavioral novelty and thus circumvent the heuristic-based behaviors of competitors (Geary, 2005). The process may have started with *Homo erectus*, but in any event once started it has continued and has driven the evolution of the brain and cognitive systems that enable the creation of novelty and the anticipation of novelty generated by others. My core point here is that this ability to generate and cope with novelty within the life span resulted in the ability to learn and problem solve in evolutionarily novel contexts, including schools.

Components of General Fluid Intelligence

Without an understanding of the evolution of the core mechanisms that enable the generation of cognitive and behavior novelty and adaptation to variation in social and ecological conditions within the life span, we will not have a complete understanding or appreciation of the task of educating children in modern societies. The gist of the following sections is that these core mechanisms substantively overlap with the brain and cognitive systems that compose general intelligence. Because biologically secondary abilities are, by definition, novel from an evolutionary perspective, the brain and cognitive systems that compose general intelligence should be engaged when these abilities are constructed from more modularized domains.

Psychometric Research

Research in this tradition examines individual differences in performance on various forms of paper-and-pencil abilities measures, and began in earnest with Spearman's (1904) classic study. Here, groups of elementary- and high-school students as well as adults were administered a series of sensory and perceptual tasks, and were rated by teachers and peers on their in-school intelligence and out-of-school common sense. Scores on standard exams in classics, French, English, and mathematics were also available for the high-school students. Correlational analyses revealed that above average performance on one task was associated with above average performance on all other tasks, on exam scores, and for ratings of intelligence and common sense. On the basis of these findings, Spearman (1904, p. 285) concluded "that all branches of intellectual activity have in common one fundamental function (or group of functions)." Spearman termed the fundamental function or group of functions general intelligence or *g*.

In a series of important empirical and theoretical works, Cattell and Horn (Cattell, 1963; Horn, 1968; Horn & Cattell, 1966) later argued that the single general ability proposed by Spearman should be subdivided into two equally important but distinct abilities. The first ability is called *crystallized intelligence* (Gc) and is manifested as the result of experience, schooling, and acculturation and is referenced by over-learned skills and knowledge, such as vocabulary. The second ability is called *fluid intelligence* (Gf), and represents a biologically-based ability to acquire skills and knowledge. In fact, human abilities can be hierarchically organized, with processes, such as Gf, that affect performance across many domains at the top of the hierarchy, and processes and knowledge bases that are more restricted, such as computational arithmetic, at the bottom (Carroll, 1993; Thurstone, 1938).

Cognitive Research
Speed of Processing.   Although there are details to be resolved, several important patterns have emerged from studies of the relation between speed of processing simple pieces of information, such as speed of retrieving a word name from long-term memory, and performance on measures of *g* (Hunt, 1978; Jensen, 1998). First, faster speed of cognitive processing is related to higher scores on measures of *g* (Jensen, 1982; Jensen & Munro, 1979) but the strength of the relation is moderate (*r*s ~ 0.3 to 0.4). Second, variability in speed of processing is also related to scores on measures of *g* (*r*s ~ 0.4; Jensen, 1992). The variability measure provides an assessment of the consistency in speed of executing the same process multiple times. Individuals who are consistently fast in executing these processes have the higher scores on measures of *g* than their less consistent peers (Deary, 2000; Jensen, 1998; Neubauer, 1997). Third, the speed with which individuals can identify very briefly (e.g., 50 ms) presented information (e.g., whether ">" is pointed left or right) is moderately correlated with *g* (Deary & Stough, 1996).

These studies suggest that intelligence is related to the speed and accuracy with which information is identified, and then processed by the associated brain and perceptual systems. The processing of this information is often implicit and results in fast and automatic responses to overlearned biologically secondary information (e.g., a written word) and presumably fast and automatic responses to the forms of information (e.g., a facial expression) described in the folk sections above. When this happens, the information is active in short-term memory, but the individual may not be consciously aware of it.

Working Memory. When information cannot be automatically processed by modular and heuristic systems or through access to information stored in long-term memory, the result is an automatic shift in attention to this information (Botvinick, Braver, Barch, Carter, & Cohen, 2001). The focusing of attention results in an explicit representation of this information in working memory, and simultaneous inhibition of irrelevant information (Engle, Conway, Tuholski, & Shisler, 1995). Once represented in working memory and available to conscious awareness, the information is amendable to the explicit, controlled problem solving represented by the rightmost section of Figure 1.3. The attentional system that controls the explicit manipulation of information during problem solving is called the central executive, and the modalities in which the information is represented are called slave systems. The latter include auditory, visual, spatial, or episodic representations of information (Baddeley, 1986, 2000b).

Research on the relation between performance on working-memory tasks and performance on measures of *g* have focused on Gf (Cattell, 1963; Horn, 1968). As Cattell (1963, p. 3) stated: "Fluid general ability ... shows more in tests requiring adaptation to new situations, where crystallized skills are of no particular advantage." In theory then, performance on measures of Gf should be strongly associated with individual differences in working memory and this is indeed the case, whether the measure of Gf is an IQ test (Carpenter, Just, & Shell, 1990; Conway, Cowan, Bunting, Therriault, & Minkoff, 2002; Engle, Tuholski, Laughlin, & Conway, 1999) or scores on psychometric tests of complex reasoning that are highly correlated with IQ scores (Kyllonen & Christal, 1990; Mackintosh & Bennett, 2003). The strength of the relation between performance on working memory tasks and scores on measures of reasoning and Gf range from moderate (*r*s ~ 0.5; Ackerman, Beier, & Boyle, 2005; Mackintosh & Bennett, 2003) to very high (*r*s > 0.8; Conway et al., 2002; Kyllonen & Christal, 1990). On the basis of these patterns, Horn (1988) and other scientists (Carpenter et al., 1990; Stanovich, 1999) have argued that measures of strategic problem solving and abstract reasoning define Gf, and the primary cognitive system underlying problem solving, reasoning, and thus Gf is attention-driven working memory. The relation between speed of processing and working memory is debated (Ackerman et al., 2005; Fry & Hale, 1996) and remains to be resolved (but see below).

Summary. Intelligent individuals identify and apprehend bits of social and ecological information more easily and quickly than do other people; their perceptual systems process this information such that the information is activated in short-term memory more quickly and with greater accuracy than it is for other people. Once active in short-term memory, the information is made available for conscious, explicit representation and manipulation in working memory, but this only happens for that subset of information that becomes the focus of attention; irrelevant information is readily inhibited. Once attention is focused, highly intelligent people are able represent more information in working memory than are other people and have an enhanced ability to consciously manipulate this information. The manipulation in turn is guided and constrained by reasoning and inference making mechanisms (Stanovich, 1999). My argument is that this attention-driven ability to explicitly represent and manipulate information in working memory is a core and evolved component of the human ability to adapt to social and ecological variation within the life span and thus is central to an evolutionarily informed understanding of the learning of biologically secondary knowledge and abilities (Geary, 2005), as I discuss in the section titled Academic Learning.

Neuroscience Research

Brain Size.   Research on the relation between brain volume, as measured by neuroimaging techniques, and performance on measures of g has revealed a modest relation ($r \sim 0.3$ to 0.4); the bigger the better (Deary, 2000; McDaniel, 2005; Rushton & Ankney, 1996). In one of the most comprehensive of these studies, Wickett, Vernon, and Lee (2000) examined the relations between total brain volume and performance on measures of Gf, Gc, short-term memory, and speed of processing. Larger brain volumes were associated with higher fluid intelligence ($r = 0.49$), larger short-term memory capacity ($r = 0.45$), faster speed of processing ($rs \sim 0.4$), but were unrelated to crystallized intelligence ($r = 0.06$). Raz, Torres, Spencer, Millman, Baertschi, and Sarpel (1993) examined the relation between performance on measures of Gf and Gc and total brain volume, and volume of the dorsolateral prefrontal cortex (areas 9 & 46 in both panels of Figure 1.4), portions of the parietal cortex (e.g., areas 39 & 40 in the upper panel), the hippocampus, and several other brain regions. Higher Gf scores were associated with larger total brain volume ($r = .43$), a larger dorsolateral prefrontal cortex ($r = .51$), and more white matter (i.e., neuronal axons) in the prefrontal cortex ($r = .41$), but were unrelated to size of the other brain regions (see also Haier, Jung, Yeo, Head, & Alkire, 2004). Performance on the Gc measure, in contrast, was not related to size of any of these brain regions or to total brain volume.

Regional Activation.   Several studies have examined the brain regions that become activated or deactivated while individuals solve items on measures of Gf (Duncan et al., 2000; J. R. Gray, Chabris, & Braver, 2003; Haier et al., 1988; Prabhakaran, Smith, Desmond, Glover, & Gabrieli,

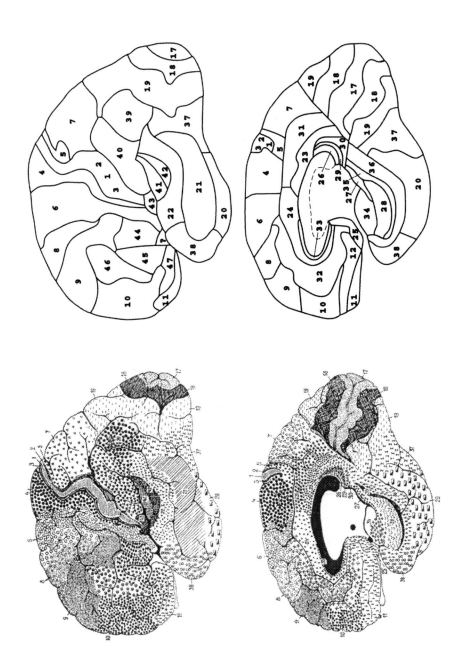

Figure 1.4. To the left, Brodmann's original map of the architectural units of the human neocortex. From *Vergleichende Lokalisationslehre der Grosshirnrinde in ihren Prinzipien dargestellt auf Grund des Zellenbaues* [Comparative localization of the cerebral cortex based on cell composition], p. 131, by K. Brodmann, 1909, Leipzig: Barth. To the right, Mark Dubin's illustration of these same areas. The top section is a lateral (outer) view of the cortex, whereas the bottom section is a medial (center, between the two hemispheres) view. Very generally, areas 1, 2, 3, 5, 31, 39, 40, and 43 are part of the parietal cortex and support a variety of functions including sense of body position, attention, and spatial competencies; Areas 17, 18, and 19 are part of the occipital cortex and support simple and complex visual perception; Areas 22, 41, 42, and subregions of areas 40 and 38 are part of the temporal cortex and support simple and complex auditory and speech perception; Areas 20, 21, 26-28, 34-37 and 52 are also part of the temporal lobe, but support a variety of complex visual competencies; Areas 4, 6, and 8 are involved in complex motor movements and are part of the frontal cortex; Area 44 and subregions of area 45 are involved in speech generation and are part of the frontal cortex; Areas 9, 10, 11, 25, 46, 47, and subregions of 45 are part of the prefrontal cortex and support behavioral control, executive functions, and many complex social competencies; Areas 23, 24, 30, (parts of 31), 32, and 33 are part of the cingulate and support attentional and emotional functions.

1997). These are early and pioneering studies and thus the most appropriate interpretation of their findings is not entirely certain (Deary, 2000). Nonetheless, most of the studies reveal a pattern of activation and deactivation in a variety of brain regions, much of which is likely due to task-specific content of the reasoning measures (e.g., verbal vs. visual information; K. Stephan et al., 2003). Recent studies using the imagining methods most sensitive to regional change in activation/deactivation suggest fluid intelligence may be supported, in part, by the same system of brain regions that the support the working memory, attentional control, and inhibitory control components of the central executive. These areas include the dorsolateral prefrontal cortex, anterior cingulate cortex (area 24 in the lower panel Figure 1.4), and regions of the parietal cortex (Duncan et al., 2000), although size and white matter organization in other brain regions may also contribute to individual differences in Gf.

Other studies suggest that the anterior cingulate cortex is heavily involved in achieving goals that are not readily achieved by means of heuristics (e.g., Miller & Cohen, 2001; Ranganath & Rainer, 2003). The anterior cingulate cortex in particular is activated when goal achievement requires dealing with some degree of novelty, or conflict (e.g., choosing between two alternatives). The result appears to be an automatic attentional shift to the novel or conflicted information and activation of the dorsolateral and other prefrontal areas (Botvinick et al., 2001). These areas in turn enable the explicit, controlled problem solving needed to cope with the novel situation or resolve the conflict (Kerns, Cohen, MacDonald, Cho, Stenger, & Carter, 2004). Botvinick and colleagues' proposal that novelty and conflict result in automatic attentional shifts and activation of executive functions is important, as it addresses the *homunculus* question. The central executive does not activate itself, but rather is automatically activated when heuristic-based processes—those toward the invariant end in Figure 1.3—are not sufficient for dealing with current information patterns or tasks.

Integration

Although definitive conclusions must await further research, brain imaging studies on the whole support the hypothesis that the same brain systems that underlie working memory and explicit controlled problem solving are engaged when people solve items on measures of Gf (Duncan et al., 2000; J. R. Gray et al., 2003; Kane & Engle, 2002). High scores on measures of Gf are associated with activation of the dorsolateral prefrontal cortex, and several brain regions associated with attentional control, including the anterior cingulate cortex and regions of the parietal cortex. These same regions also appear to support the ability to inhibit irrelevant information from intruding into working memory and conscious awareness (Esposito, Kirkby, van Horn, Ellmore, & Berman, 1999). Awareness of information represented in working memory and the ability to mentally manipulate this information may result from a synchronization of the prefrontal brain regions that subserve the central executive and the brain regions that process the specific forms of information (e.g., voice, face, object; Damasio, 1989; Dehaene & Naccache, 2001; Posner, 1994).

An attention-driven synchronization of the activity of dorsolateral prefrontal cortex and the brain regions that support explicit working memory representations of external information or internal mental simulations would be facilitated by faster speed of processing and rich interconnections among these brain regions. The latter are associated with larger brain size and especially a greater volume of white matter (i.e., axons). Speed of processing may be important for the synchronization process: Synchronization appears to occur through neural connections that communicate back and forth between different brain regions, creating feedback cycles. Faster speed of processing would enable more accurate adjustments in synchronization per feedback cycle. With repeated synchronized activity, the result appears to be the formation of a neural network that automatically links the processing of these information patterns (Sporns, Tononi, & Edelman, 2000). In other words, speed of processing and an attention-driven working memory system are not competing explanations of Gf (see Ackerman et al., 2005; Engle, 2002; Kane & Engle, 2002), but rather may be coevolved and complementary mechanisms that support the conscious psychological and cognitive processes (including Gf) that are components of the motivation to control (Geary, 2005).

More generally, I proposed that research on Gf identified many of the core features that support the use of mental simulations as these relate to the ability to anticipate and generate behavioral responses to social and ecological conditions that are toward the variant end of the continuum in Figure 1.3 (Geary, 2005). As noted, the function of a problem-solving based manipulation of mental models is to generate strategies that will reduce the difference between conditions in the real world and those simulated in a perfect world, that is, to generate ways to gain control of important relationships and resources. The problem-solving processes, inference making, and everyday reasoning employed to devise the corresponding social and behavioral strategies are dependent on working memory, attentional control, and the supporting brain systems, along with a sense of self.

In this view, the mechanisms that support an explicit, conscious awareness of information represented in working memory evolved as a result of the same social and ecological pressures that drove the evolution of the ability to generate and use mental models, and Gf. Self awareness is important to the extent that one must cope with the maneuvering of other people, if other people use this same knowledge in their social strategies (Alexander, 1989; Humphrey, 1976). In other words, 100 years of empirical research on g, and especially Gf, has isolated those features of self-centered mental models that are not strongly influenced by content and that enable explicit representations of information in working memory and an attentional-dependent ability to manipulate this information in the service of strategic problem solving to cope with variation and novelty within the life span. These are thus predicted to be core systems engaged in the generation of novelty and biologically secondary knowledge and when learning secondary knowledge generated by others, as illustrated in the section titled Human Intellectual History and the Creation of Culture.

Cattell's (1963) and Horn's (1968) definition of fluid intelligence and subsequent research on the underlying cognitive and brain systems are consistent with this view: There is considerable overlap in the systems that support self-centered mental models and those that support fluid abilities (e.g., Duncan et al., 2000). One important difference between Gf and these mental models is self-awareness, which is a core feature of my proposal but is not assessed on measures of fluid intelligence (Geary, 2005). If Gf evolved to support use of mental simulations and their use was driven in large part by the need to cope with social dynamics, then measures of Gf might be expected to include items that assess social dynamics and awareness of these dynamics vis-à-vis one's self-interest. The reasons for the discrepancy are (a) because the initial development and goal of intelligence tests was to predict academic performance (Binet & Simon, 1916), that is, the ability to learn in the evolutionarily novel context of school, and not to cope with social dynamics. In addition: (b) Gf represents the mechanisms that support content-free problem solving, and thus social items are not necessary.

Modularity and Crystallized Intelligence

In the most comprehensive review of the psychometric literature ever conducted, Carroll (1993, p. 599) concluded that most of the psychometric tests that index Gc "involve language either directly or indirectly." Included among these are tests of vocabulary, listening comprehension, word fluency, reading, and spelling. The two latter skills are taught in school, as are some of the other competencies that index crystallized intelligence, such as arithmetic, and mechanical abilities. General cultural knowledge is also an indicator of Gc, as are some measures of spatial and visual abilities. In total, these tests appear to tap a many of the modular domains shown in Figure 1.2, in particular language and spatial representation. They do not appear to tap all of these domains, but this is potentially because not all of the modular competencies have been assessed. When other modular competencies are measured and correlated with intelligence, there is a relation. Legree (1995), for instance, found that scores on tests of knowledge of social conventions and social judgments are positively correlated with scores on measures of g. In others words, I am suggesting that the inherent knowledge represented in the modular systems defines one class of crystallized intelligence, Gc-primary. The other class is represented by the knowledge (e.g., facts, procedures) learned during a lifetime through formal or informal instruction, or just incidentally, as proposed by Cattell (1963), Gc-secondary.

ACADEMIC LEARNING

My proposal is that the evolution of Gf combined with some degree of plasticity in primary modular systems opened the door to the ability to develop evolutionarily novel, biologically secondary knowledge and abilities in school and in other cultural settings, such as the work place (Geary, 1995; Rozin, 1976). There is, however, a cost to this extraordinary ability to create novel secondary competencies and thus human culture: During the last several millennia, because the cross-generational accumulation of cultural knowledge and artifacts, such as books, has occurred at such a rapid pace (Richerson & Boyd, 2005), the attentional and cognitive biases that facilitate the fleshing out of primary abilities during children's natural activities do not have evolved counterparts to facilitate the learning of secondary abilities. In the first section, I explore the basic implications for schooling and the accumulation of cultural knowledge. In the second and third sections, I provide discussion and hypotheses regarding the potential motivational and cognitive mechanisms, respectively, that may contribute to the acquisition of secondary abilities.

Foundations of Evolutionary Educational Psychology

I begin with the basic premises and principles of evolutionary educational psychology, which are elaborations and refinements of previous work (Geary, 2002a). I then attempt to frame aspects of human intellectual history and the creation of secondary knowledge as this relates to our understanding of primary folk domains. This frame provides a segue into a later discussion of potential motivational and cognitive mechanisms underlying secondary learning.

Premises and Principles

Evolutionary educational psychology is the study of the relation between folk knowledge and abilities and accompanying inferential and attributional biases as these influence academic learning in evolutionarily novel cultural contexts, such as schools and the industrial workplace. The fundamental premises and principles of this discipline are presented in Table 1.1. The premises restate the gist of the previous sections, specifically: that (a) aspects of mind and brain have evolved to draw the individuals' attention to and facilitate the processing of social, biological, physical information patterns that covaried with survival or reproductive outcomes during human evolution (Cosmides & Tooby, 1994; Geary, 2005; R. Gelman, 1990; Pinker, 1997; Shepard, 1994; Simon, 1956); (b) although plastic to some degree, these primary abilities are in part inherently constrained because the associated information patterns tended to be consistent or invariant across generations and within lifetimes (e.g., Caramazza & Shelton, 1998; Geary & Huffman, 2002); (c) other aspects of mind and brain evolved to enable the mental generation of potential future social, ecological, or climatic conditions and enable rehearsal of behaviors to cope with variation in these conditions, and are now known as Gf (including skill at everyday reasoning/problem solving; Chiappe & MacDonald, 2005; Geary, 2005; Mithen, 1996); and (d) children are inherently motivated to learn in folk domains, with the associated attentional and behavioral biases resulting in experiences that automatically and implicitly flesh out and adapt these systems to local conditions (R. Gelman, 1990; R. Gelman & Williams, 1998; S. Gelman, 2003).

The principles in the bottom section of Table 1.1 represent the foundational assumptions for an evolutionary educational psychology. The gist is knowledge and expertise that is useful in the cultural milieu or ecology in which the group is situated will be transferred across generations in the form of cultural artifacts, such as books, or learning traditions, as in apprenticeships (e.g., Baumeister, 2005; Richerson & Boyd, 2005; Flinn, 1997; Mithen, 1996). Across generations, the store of cultural knowledge accumulates and creates a gap between this knowledge base and the forms of folk knowledge and abilities that epigenetically emerge with children's self-initiated activities. There must of course be an evolved potential to learn evolutionarily novel information and an associated bias to seek novelty during the developmental period and indeed throughout the life span; this may be related to the openness to experience dimension of personality (Geary, 1995). However, the cross-generational accumulation of knowledge across cultures, individuals, and domains (e.g., people vs. physics) has resulted in an exponential increase in the quantity of secondary knowledge available in modern

Table 1.1.   Premises and Principles
of Evolutionary Educational Psychology

Premises

1. Natural selection has resulted in an evolved motivational disposition to attempt to gain access to and control of the resources that have covaried with survival and reproductive outcomes during human evolution.

2. These resources fall into three broad categories; social, biological, and physical which correspond to the respective domains of folk psychology, folk biology, and folk physics.

3. Attentional, perceptual, and cognitive systems, including inferential and attributional biases, have evolved to process information in these folk domains and to guide control-related behavioral strategies. These systems process restricted classes of information associated with these folk domains.

4. To cope with variation in social, ecological, or climatic conditions, systems that enabled the mental generation of these potential future conditions and enabled rehearsal of behaviors to cope with this variation evolved and the supporting attentional and cognitive mechanisms are known as general fluid intelligence and everyday reasoning.

5. Children are biologically biased to engage in activities that recreate the ecologies of human evolution; these are manifested as social play, and exploration of the environment and objects. The accompanying experiences interact with the inherent but skeletal folk systems and flesh out these systems such that they are adapted to the local social group and ecology.

Principles

1. Scientific, technological, and academic advances initially emerged from the cognitive and motivational systems that support folk psychology, folk biology, and folk physics. Innovations that enabled better control of ecologies or social dynamics or resulted in a coherent (though not necessarily scientifically accurate) understanding of these dynamics are likely to be retained across generations as cultural artifacts (e.g., books) and traditions (e.g., apprenticeships). These advances result in an ever growing gap between folk knowledge and the theories and knowledge base of the associated sciences and other disciplines (e.g., literature).

2. Schools emerge in societies in which scientific, technological, and intellectual advances result in a gap between folk knowledge and the competencies needed for living in the society.

3. The function of schools is to organize the activities of children such that they acquire the biologically secondary competencies that close the gap between folk knowledge and the occupational and social demands of the society.

4. Biologically secondary competencies are built from primary folk systems and the components of fluid intelligence that evolved to enable individuals to cope with variation and novelty.

5. Children's inherent motivational bias to engage in activities that will adapt folk knowledge to local conditions will often conflict with the need to engage in activities that will result in secondary learning.

6. The need for explicit instruction will be a direct function of the degree to which the secondary competency differs from the supporting primary systems.

societies today. For most people, the breadth and complexity of this knowledge will very likely exceed any biases to learn in evolutionary novel domains.

A related issue concerns the traits that enable the *creation* of biologically secondary knowledge and thus culture and the extent to which these traits overlap with the ability to *learn* knowledge created by others. Stated differently, Is the goal of education to have children recreate the process of discovery, to learn the products of discovery, or some combination? Some educators have advocated a focus on the process of discovery without full consideration of the constellation of traits and opportunity that contribute to the creation of secondary knowledge (e.g., Cobb, Yackel, & Wood, 1992). In fact, research on creative-productive individuals suggests that the full constellation of traits that facilitate the discovery and creation of secondary knowledge is rare and not likely reproducible on a large scale (Simonton, 1999a, 1999b, 2003; Sternberg, 1999; Wai, Lubinski, & Benbow, 2005), although there is likely to be overlap between the traits that enable both the creation and the learning of secondary knowledge. My proposal is that this overlap includes the cognitive and conscious psychological mechanisms that support the motivation to control, that is, the working memory and attentional components of Gf. In the following sections, I hope to illustrate the complexity of the discovery process and at the same time provide suggestions as to how primary folk knowledge may form the foundation for the creation and learning of secondary knowledge, and to provide a contrast of primary and secondary knowledge.

Human Intellectual History and the Creation of Culture

Scientific, technological, and academic domains (e.g., poetry) emerged from an interplay of cultural wealth, opportunity, and a combination of traits in the individuals who made advances in these domains (Murray, 2003; Simonton, 2003). Murray found that historical bursts of creative activity (as with the Renaissance or industrial revolution) tended to emerge in wealthier cultures with mores that did not severely restrict individual freedom and that socially and financially rewarded creative expression. Studies of exceptional accomplishments suggest they tend to be generated by individuals situated in these cultures and with a combination of traits that include high general fluid intelligence, creativity (e.g., ability to make remote associations), an extended period of preparation (about 10 years) in which the basics of the domain are mastered, long work hours (often > 60/week), advantages in certain folk domains, ambition, and sustained output of domain-related products, such as scientific publications (see Ericsson, Krampe, & Tesch-Römer, 1993; Lubinski, 2004; Sternberg, 1999). These components of exceptional accomplishment can be used to illustrate the interplay between folk knowledge, fluid intelligence, motivation, and the generation of secondary knowledge, and to illustrate why children's intuitive folk knowledge and learning biases are not sufficient for secondary learning; implications for understanding individual differences are discussed in the section titled Individual Differences in Secondary Learning.

In other words, I am suggesting that human intellectual history and the emergence of scientific and academic domains, as well as other forms of cultural knowledge (e.g., literature), was possible only after the evolution of the conscious psychological and cognitive mechanisms—components of fluid intelligence—that support the motivation to control. These secondary domains initially coalesced around the areas of folk psychology, folk biology, and folk physics, because these represent areas of inherent interest to human beings and because human beings have built-in biases to organize knowledge in these domains. Academic disciplines in universities, for instance, seem to fall into these three categories, with humanities and the social sciences related to folk psychology; biology, zoology, forestry, and medicine related to folk biology; and, much of mathematics as well as physics and engineering related to folk physics. Of course, at this point in our history the knowledge bases in these domains far exceed knowledge implicit in folk systems, but the interests of individuals who pursue training in these different academic disciplines differ in ways consistent with folk-related motivational biases.

People who pursue careers in the humanities and social sciences tend to be interested in people and social relationships, whereas people who pursue careers in mathematics and the physical sciences tend to be interested in nonliving physical phenomena and abstract theory (Lubinski, 2000; Roe, 1956; Wai et al., 2005), as elaborated in the subsection titled Evolved Interests and Occupational Niches. These may be a reflection of motivational and affective biases that are respective components of folk psychology and folk physics. Consistent with these differences in interests, there may be an accompanying elaboration of associated primary knowledge and abilities. For instance, there is preliminary evidence that some eminent mathematicians and physical scientists may have an enhanced understanding of folk physics, but below average competencies in the domain of folk psychology (Baron-Cohen, Wheelwright, Stone, & Rutherford, 1999). In any case, in the following sections, I illustrate how the creation of secondary knowledge may interact with folk biases, and why the creation of this knowledge may be dependent on the cognitive and conscious psychological representations associated with the motivation to control and Gf.

Scientific Physics and Folk Physics. The scientific domain of physics is one of humanity's most significant intellectual accomplishments and yet is a domain that is remote from the understanding of most of humanity. One reason for this is that people's naïve understanding of certain physical phenomena is influenced by the inferential biases that appear to be an aspect of folk physics but differ from the scientific understanding of the same phenomena (McCloskey, 1983). For instance, when asked about the forces acting on a thrown baseball, most people believe there is a force propelling it forward, something akin to an invisible engine, and a force propelling it downward. The downward force is gravity, but there is in fact no force propelling it forward, once the ball leaves the player's hand (Clement, 1982). The concept of a forward-force, called "impetus", is similar to pre-Newtonian beliefs about motion prominent in the fourteenth to sixteenth centuries. The idea is that the act of starting an object in motion, such as throwing a ball, imparts to the object an internal force— impetus—that keeps it in motion until this impetus gradually dissipates. Although adults and even preschool children often describe the correct trajectory for a thrown or moving object (e.g., Kaiser, McCloskey, & Proffitt, 1986), reflecting their implicit folk competences, their explicit explanations reflect this naïve understanding of the forces acting upon the object.

Careful observation, use of the scientific method (secondary knowledge itself), and use of inductive and deductive reasoning, are necessary to move from an intuitive folk understanding to scientific theory and knowledge. In his masterwork, the *Principia* (1995, p. 13), Newton said as much: "I do not define time, space, place and motion, as being well known to all. Only I must observe, that the vulgar conceive those quantities under no other notions but from the relation they bear to sensible objects." In other words, the "vulgar" among us (myself included) only understand physical phenomena in terms of folk knowledge and Newton intended to and did go well beyond this. Newton corrected the pre-Newtonian beliefs about the forces acting on objects, but still appears to have relied on other aspects of folk physical systems to complete this work. Newton's conceptualization of objects in motion and the gravitational and rectilinear forces underlying the pattern of this motion were based on his ability to explicitly use visuospatial systems to construct geometric representations of motion and then to apply Euclidean geometry and formal logic to mathematically prove the scientific accuracy of these representations. The explicit and exacting use of formal logic is associated with high general fluid intelligence (Stanovich, 1999). In addition, Newton devoted an extended period of sustained effort and attention to this work (e.g., Berlinski, 2000). In fact, Newton has been described as being obsessed with understanding physical phenomena and spent many years thinking about these phenomena and conducting experiments to test his hypotheses, at a cost to social relationships.

Although a functional relation can only be guessed, it is of interest that areas of the neocortex that are typically associated with spatial imagery and other areas of folk physics (i.e., the parietal lobe) were unusually large (area 40 in the upper panel of Figure 1.4) in Albert Einstein's brain (Witelson, Kigar, & Harvey, 1999). In response to a query by Hadamard (1945) as to how he approached scientific questions, Einstein replied:

> The words of the language as they are written or spoken, do not seem to play any role in my mechanism of thought. The psychical entities which seem to serve as elements in thought are certain signs and more or less clear images which can be "voluntarily" reproduced and combined.... There is, of course, a certain connection between those elements and relevant logical concepts. (Hadamard, 1945, p. 142)

Hadamard (1945, p. 143) also noted that Einstein "refers to a narrowness of consciousness," which appears to have referred to sustained attention and the inhibition of distracting information while working on scientific questions, which are components of Gf. Einstein's accomplishments are, of course, unusual, but his descriptions of how he achieved some of his insights are of interest, because they are consistent with an attention-driven use of mental simulations—the conscious psychological systems—and a reliance on the modular systems that support folk physics. It is of interest that a similar pattern of brain morphology and enhanced visuospatial abilities combined with relatively poor language abilities has been identified in an extended family and appears to be heritable (Craggs, Sanchez, Kibby, Gilger, & Hynd, 2006; see also Gohm, Humphreys, & Yao, 1998). In any event, Einstein's discoveries and those of many other twentieth century physicists further widened the gap between folk physics and scientific physics, and in doing so greatly complicated the task of teaching modern physics.

Scientific Biology and Folk Biology. In the eighteenth century, the early and largely accurate (scientifically) classification systems of naturalists, especially that of Linnaeus (i.e., Carl von Linné; cf. Frängsmyr, 1983), were almost certainly based on the same implicit knowledge base and inferential biases that define folk biology, as this Western system for classifying flora and fauna is very similar to the systems found in traditional populations (Berlin et al., 1973). An important difference is that Linnaeus' binomial (genus, species) taxonomy included more than 12,000 plants and animals and was constructed in a *conscious, explicit* (rules for classification were codified) and *systematic* manner in comparison to the more *implicit* organization of folk biological knowledge that is found in people living in natural ecologies (Atran, 1998); the latter is reflected in the way in which individuals of these societies organize examples of different species. Of course, these early scientific taxonomies continue to the expanded and refined, and most recently informed by genetic analyses of the relationships among species (e.g., Liu et al., 2001). Again, the gap between folk and scientific knowledge continues to widen.

Mathematics and Folk Physics.   In an early article (Geary, 1995), I proposed that the development of geometry—the study of space and shape—as a formal discipline might have been initially influenced by early geometers' ability to explicitly represent the intuitive folk physical knowledge implicit in the perceptual and cognitive systems that evolved for navigation in three-dimensional space (Dehaene, Izard, Pica, & Spelke, 2006; Shepard, 1994). For instance, in the refinement and integration of the basic principles of classic geometry, Euclid (1956) formally and explicitly postulated that a straight line can be draw from any point to any point—that is, the intuitive understanding that the fastest way to get from one place to another is to go "as the crow flies" was made explicit in a formal Euclidean postulate. Using a few basic postulates and definitions, Euclid then systematized existing knowledge to form the often complex and highly spatial components of classic geometry. Achievement of this feat must have also required high general intelligence and an exceptional ability to maintain attentional focus. A potentially important difference between geometry and physics is that Euclid's five postulates and 23 definitions are very basic, defining lines, circles, angles, and shapes, and thus not prone to the naïve attributional errors common in people's description of physical phenomena. This difference may help to explain the more than 1,700 year gap between Euclid's *The elements* published circa 30 BC and the 1687 publication of Newton's *Principia*.

Scientific Problem Solving.   The emergence of the biological sciences provides an example of the importance of goal-directed and explicit problem solving, among other factors, for scientific discovery. These examples illustrate the complexity of these tasks, the confluence of experiences and individual traits needed for scientific advances, and the accumulation of secondary knowledge, and they may also inform research and debate on the teaching of the scientific method and scientific reasoning, as I discuss in the section titled Evolution and Science Education. Important differences, for instance, between instruction of science and scientific discovery include the size of the problem space—the operators (e.g., rules for change in the domain) and assumptions that influence how a problem can be solved (Newell & Simon, 1972)—and the ill-structured nature of problems confronting working scientists (Klahr & Simon, 1999). An example of the latter is provided by various attempts to discover the mechanisms responsible for the origin of species (Desmond & Moore, 1994; Raby, 2001). This was an ill structured problem in that the solution required knowledge that spanned many domains (e.g., the fossil and geological records), and the knowledge and operators needed to ultimately solve the problem were not known.

In the first half of the nineteenth century and before this time, most naturalists, such as the renowned paleontologist Owen (1860), assumed the origin of species was driven by some form of divine intervention (Ospovat, 1981). This assumption was crucial because it defined the problem space and the relevant operations and knowledge (e.g., scripture) that could be applied in attempts to solve the problem. Owen's assumption of divine intervention placed legal operators that involved material causes and thus the actual mechanisms involved in the origin of species outside of the problem space and thus rendered the problem unsolvable. Darwin and Wallace, in contrast, assumed the origin of species was due to material causes acting in nature (J. Browne, 2002; Darwin, 1846; Desmond & Moore, 1994; Raby, 2001). The relevant knowledge was not scripture but rather arose, in part, from intuitive folk biological knowledge and motivational biases as these were applied to extensive observations of nature *and* as elaborated by relevant secondary knowledge, including Lyell's (1830) *Principles of geology*. Of particular importance was Lyell's inference regarding patterns in the fossil record (1839, p. 161):

> It appears, that from the remotest periods there has been ever a coming in of new organic forms, and an extinction of those which pre-existed on the earth; some species having endured for a longer, others for a shorter time; but none having ever re-appeared after once dying out. The law which has governed the creation and extinction of species [is not known].

The observations and hypotheses of Malthus (1798) also contributed greatly to Darwin and Wallace's goal-relevant knowledge and to the construction of the mechanisms of natural selection. Malthus' monograph described a pattern of oscillating expansions and contractions of the size of human populations in preindustrial Europe and in other regions of the world. Expansions often continue beyond the carrying capacity of the supporting resources, at which point the population crashes. The crashes represent a sharp increase in mortality, largely due to famine, epidemics, and conflicts with other people (e.g., wars) over control of land and other life-supporting resources, in keeping with the discussion in subsection titled Motivation to Control. The increased mortality reduces the population to a level below carrying capacity, that is, to a point where there are once again excess resources, and thus another cycle of population expansion ensues. With respect to Malthus' description, Wallace noted in a letter written in 1887 and reprinted in Darwin's autobiography (F. Darwin, 2000, pp. 200-201):

> This had strongly impressed me, and it suddenly flashed upon me that all animals are necessarily thus kept down—"the struggle for existence"—while *variations*, on which I was always thinking, must necessarily often be *beneficial*, and would then cause those varieties to increase while the injurious variations diminished. (italics in original)

An illustration of Wallace's *explicit* reasoning about the origin of species before this insight is provided in an 1855 (p. 184) article titled, "On the Law Which Has Regulated the Introduction of New Species." In this article he proposed the following hypothesis, "*Every species has come into existence coincident both in space and time with a pre-existing closely allied species*" (p. 186, italics in original). In other words, new species arise from extant species. Induction—formulating a general principle based on observable facts—played an important part in Wallace's formulation of this conclusion. During his expeditions in the Amazon and throughout Malaysia, Wallace (1855, p. 189) observed that there is a pattern in the geographic distribution of species, "closely allied species in rich groups being found geographically near each other, is most striking and important." He also described how the same pattern is evident in the fossil record. When this pattern was combined with deductions based on a number of premises and facts described in the article, Wallace concluded that related species (e.g., of butterflies) are found in the same geographic location because they all arose from a common ancestor that resided in this location. Wallace further concluded that the creation of new species from existing species "must be the necessary results of some great natural law" (p. 195). Wallace discovered the great natural law—natural selection—3 years later, when he linked Malthus' (1798) observations to the earlier noted favorable and unfavorable variations in traits (Darwin & Wallace, 1858).

In addition to reading Lyell (1830) and Malthus (1798)—cultural artifacts that preserved the insights of earlier generations—Darwin (1846) and Wallace (1855) acquired goal relevant knowledge through their extensive collecting and taxonomically organizing species of many different kinds, and through years of careful observation of these species in natural ecologies. Despite Wallace's statement that the mechanisms of natural selection "suddenly flashed upon me," it is clear that he explicitly formulated the goal of discovering these mechanisms at least 13 years before this insight (Raby, 2001). Similarly, Darwin's understanding of these mechanisms was refined between 1838 and 1856-1857 (Ospovat, 1979, 1981). Nonetheless, it is likely the case that aspects of this process of discovery occurred "unconsciously," that is, through associations that developed implicitly and only at times explicitly entered working memory for conscious evaluation (Simonton, 2004).

My points are that the discovery of the mechanisms of natural selection (a) was built on explicit and biologically secondary knowledge (e.g., documentation of the fossil record) generated by other naturalists and transferred across generations; (b) the knowledge base needed to make this discovery was extensive and required years of study, reflection, and experience; and (c) the discovery of natural selection itself emerged from a confluence of factors interacting with this knowledge base. These factors include the explicit goal of discovering these mechanisms, the ability to explicitly problem solve within an ill-structured problem space, and an intense interest in the natural world. Again, the discovery extended and thus further widened the gap between folk biology and the science of biology.

Implications

One consequence of scientific, technological, and other cultural (e.g., accumulation of literature) advances is a widening of the gap between folk knowledge and abilities and the secondary knowledge and abilities needed to live successfully in the cultures in which these advances emerge. The most basic and critical implication for education is that folk knowledge and abilities, though necessary, are no longer sufficient for occupational and social functioning (e.g., understanding interest on debt) in modern society (Geary, 1995). The educational issues are multifold and not fully understood at this time. In the follow sections, I outline some of the core issues that will confront an evolutionarily informed approach to education, and provide suggestions for future theoretical and empirical research related to these issues. I begin with the issue of children's motivation to learn in school and then proceed to issues related to potential mechanisms involved in transforming primary knowledge and abilities into culturally-useful secondary knowledge and abilities. *The gist is that the cognitive and motivational complexities of the processes involved in the generation of secondary knowledge and the ever widening gap between this knowledge and folk knowledge leads me to conclude that most children will not be sufficiently motivated nor cognitively able to learn all of secondary knowledge needed for functioning in modern societies without well organized, explicit and direct teacher instruction.* (As I discuss in the section titled Individual Differences in Secondary Learning, one exception might be children with high Gf.)

Motivation to Learn

The evolution of Gf and the ability to adapt to social and ecological variation within the life span likely coevolved with the expansion of human childhood and adolescence and with the exquisite human ability to learn during this period of development. The latter is a necessary component of our ability to transfer culturally accumulated knowledge from one generation to the next (Richerson & Boyd, 2005; Flinn, 1997; Henrich & McElreath, 2003; Scarr, 1993). The most fundamental mechanisms of transferring this knowledge include use of stories to convey morals (i.e., cultural rules for social behavior) and other themes relevant to day-to-day living, and apprenticeships, that is, learning culturally important skills (e.g., hunting, tool making) through observation of or direct instruction by more skilled individuals (Brown, 1991). The content of stories and apprenticeships is predicted to be centered on features of social dynamics or the ecology that tend to vary within life spans and for which the ability to adapt to this variation resulted in social or reproductive advantage during human evolution (Geary, 2005). In addition to the mechanisms that support social learning (e.g., observational learning; Bandura, 1986), children's adaptation to this variation is predicted to be dependent on implicit perceptual and affective biases that direct attention to and facilitate the ability to learn in these domains. The latter would include domain-specific abilities, as in quickly and implicitly learning to discriminate one person from another (e.g., Kisilevsky et al., 2003), as well as learning to use Gf to deal with more dynamic situations.

Individual differences in children's and adults' biases toward some aspects of their social or ecological world more than other aspects are also predicted to evolve. These individual differences are common across species (Gosling, 2001), and may be particularly important for species that live in large and complex social groups; these groups are an important context within which evolutionary selection occurs (Alexander, 1989). Among the benefits of individual differences, and the resulting niche specialization and division of labor, are reduced competition and increased reciprocal dependence among members of the in-group (Baumeister, 2005). Moreover, the ability to learn during the lifetime, niche specialization, and the tendency of humans to imitate successful individuals create a social context with several specific benefits. First, at a relatively low cost and by means of social learning many individuals can acquire some of the basic competencies of the most skilled individuals in different niches (e.g., social leadership to tool making). Second, as group size increases and especially as the wealth of the society increases (Murray, 2003), there is opportunity for a small number of very skilled individuals—those having the traits described in the section titled Human Intellectual History and the Creation of Culture—to become creative-productive innovators in their niche (Bjorklund, 2006; Bjorklund &Pellegrini, 2002; Flinn, 1997; Henrich & McElreath, 2003). These are the individuals who provide the most novel solutions to problems that arise from social and ecological variation, solutions that can benefit their group and are imitated by other people.

We are thus confronted with two core issues. The first concerns species-typical biases in children's ability to learn in one domain or another and their corresponding motivational and conative preferences, and the second concerns individual differences within the species-typical range. The implications for how these biases influence learning in school and in other evolutionarily novel contexts are not well articulated at this time.

My goal for the next two sections is to place these conative and motivational biases in an evolutionary perspective; learning biases are addressed in Biologically Secondary Learning. In the first section, I make predictions regarding potential inherent conative and interest biases, and in the second section I discuss these biases in the context of contemporary models of children's academic interests and achievement motivation (Bandura, 1993; Eccles, Wigfield, Harold, & Blumenfeld, 1993; Grant & Dweck, 2003; Wigfield & Eccles, 2000).

Motivation to Control and Folk Domains

It follows from the motivation to control model that all individuals will attempt to organize their world in ways that are most "comfortable" for their phenotype. This statement is keeping with other evolutionary predictions (e.g., Trivers, 1974), and with developmental (e.g., Scarr, 1996; Scarr & McCartney, 1983) and behavioral genetic (Bouchard et al., 1996; Plomin, DeFries, & Loehlin, 1977) theory and research (e.g., Jennings, 1975; Kagan, 1998; Lever, 1978). There are individual differences in children's reactivity to social and other stimuli and in self-directed niche seeking, but all normally developing children attempt to exert some type of control in their social relationships and in other contexts. The difference between my predictions and those of other models are in terms of specificity; that is, children's self-directed activities and interests will coalesce around the social and ecological domains outlined in Figure 1.2. The activities would include, for instance, competitive group formation, formation of dyadic relationships, and object exploration. My goal here is to provide a framework for understanding how these evolved motivational and conative biases might be expressed in the context of modern society. To anchor these biases in society, I start with empirical research on occupational interests and then move to children's activity preferences.

Evolved Interests and Occupational Niches. I began with the assumption that evolved motivational and conative biases, as well as dimensions of personality, influence niche seeking in school and in later occupational choices. If this assumption is correct, then these biases will emerge on measures of occupational interests (e.g., Achter, Lubinski, Benbow, & Eftekhari-Sanjani, 1999; Ackerman, 1996; Ackerman & Heggestad, 1997; Campbell & Holland, 1972; G. D. Gottfredson, Jones, & Holland, 1993; Holland, 1996; Lubinski, 2000; Lubinski & Benbow, 2000; Prediger, 1982; Roe & Klos, 1969; Strong, 1943; Wai et al., 2005). In examining this prediction, I started with Holland's (1966) influential and highly useful hexagon of occupational interests, that is, realistic, investigative, artistic, social, enterprising, and conventional (RIASEC), as shown in Figure 1.5. Factor analytic and other approaches suggest that two more basic dimensions underlie the distribution of these occupational interests, that is, people/things and data/ideas (Lubinski & Benbow, 2000; Prediger, 1982). As shown by the arrows in Figure 1.5, I labeled the latter concrete/abstract to make the dimension less specific to occupational settings. The basic point is that individuals differ in the extent to which they prefer to engage in concrete activities or think about abstract ideas.

I then examined the preferred activities and types of occupations that clustered in different areas of Holland's hexagon and along the people/things, concrete/abstract dimensions (Campbell & Holland, 1972; Harmon, Hansen, Borgen, & Hammer, 1994). Campbell and Holland, for instance, found that Realistic occupations include machinists, tool makers, foresters, and farmers; Investigative occupations include physical scientists, experimental psychologists, mathematicians, biologists, and engineers; Artistic occupations include actors, artists, musicians, and architects; Social occupations include counselors, ministers, secretaries, and teachers; Enterprising occupations include sales people, business managers, and lawyers; and Conventional occupations include bankers, office workers, and accountants. The bias toward people versus things is

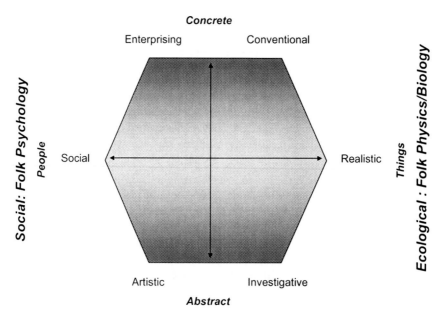

Figure 1.5. Holland's (1996) model of occupational interests, underlying dimensions of basic interests (people/things, concrete/abstract), and potential relation to folk domains. Adapted from "States of excellence" by D. Lubinski & C. P. Benbow, 2000, *American Psychologist, 55*, p. 140.

evident across these occupational clusters and was suggested by Roe and Klos (1969, p. 92) as an "orientation to interpersonal relations vs. natural phenomena." The concrete pole of the concrete/abstract dimension reflects a focus on social (enterprising) or material (conventional) economic activities—those that produce income or other tangible resources (e.g., food in traditional societies)—whereas the abstract pole represents a focus on the symbolic representation and explanation of social and personal experience as well as natural phenomena, as I elaborate below.

Roe and Klos' (1969) casting of the people/things dimension in terms of interpersonal versus natural phenomena maps onto the broad social and ecological domains shown in Figure 1.2 and represented in bold italics in Figure 1.5. In other words, human interests are predicted to map onto the proposed folk domains shown in Figure 1.2, and individual differences in these interests are predicted to span from highly social (folk psychology) to highly interested in how to use objects as tools (folk physics). The prediction of individual differences emerges from the above-noted benefits of niche specialization and a division of labor. If this prediction is correct, then individual differences in niche-related interests and corresponding abilities and personality should co-evolve and cluster in folk domains. One testable empirical prediction is that an interest in things will be associated with enhanced folk physical and folk biological competencies and an interest in people will be associated with enhanced folk psychological competencies, and higher extraversion on measures of personality. Although cause-effect cannot be determined, Ackerman and Heggestad's (1997) analysis of the relations among interests, abilities, and personality provides some supporting evidence (see also L. Larson, Rottinghaus, & Borgen, 2002; Ozer & Benet-Martínez, 2006).

Individuals with strong realistic interests, that is, an interest in things, tend to have good mechanical and spatial abilities, but are often weaker on verbal abilities (Ackerman & Heggestad, 1997; Gohm et al., 1998). Individuals with strong investigative interests tend to be strong on mathematical (i.e., abstract) reasoning, and often have good spatial/mechanical abilities. Individuals with conventional interests tend to have strong perceptual-motor skills, that is, they are fast and efficient on tasks that involve the organization and manual manipulation of physical objects. The enhanced spatial and mechanical interests and abilities of many individuals in realistic and investigative occupations and the working with materials for economic reasons associated with conventional occupations are consistent with the prediction that these have been built upon an evolved folk physics. An interest in nature and in biological occupations also falls in the realistic/investigative area of Holland's hexagon (Harmon et al., 1994), but corresponding abilities in these areas (e.g., for taxonomically organizing species) are not typically assessed psychometrically and thus the relation between these interests and theoretically important abilities was not included in Ackerman and Heggestad's analysis. Nonetheless, these interests are consistent with an evolved folk biology.

The people orientation—associated with social and enterprising interests and to a lesser extent artistic interests—is consistent with an evolved folk psychology. Individuals with artistic interests score highly on measures of verbal and perceptual abilities and highly on the personality dimension of openness, and along with individuals with social and enterprising interests often have relatively poor mechanical abilities, consistent with niche specialization (Ackerman & Heggestad, 1997; Randahl, 1991). Although people with social and enterprising interests tend to be high on the extraversion dimension of personality (Larson et al., 2002), there are some data inconsistent with the prediction that enhanced social interests should correspond with enhanced folk psychological abilities. Ackerman and Heggestad found that verbal abilities, as measured by psychometric tests, were unrelated to social interests and inversely related to enterprising interests.

However, examination of Figure 1.2 reveals that the predicted folk psychological abilities do not map onto verbal psychometric tests, with the exception of language (Carroll, 1993). Even language as used in a natural context to develop social relationships and to influence the behavior of other people is functionally different in many ways than the competencies measured by verbal tests. Moreover, Randahl (1991) found intraindividual variation in abilities across occupational interests. People with strong social and enterprising interests appear to have lower g scores, at least in this college sample ($n = 846$), then people with strong realistic, investigative, and artistic interests, and thus their verbal scores relative to other people are not elevated. However, people with social and enterprising interests are better verbally than they are quantitatively or spatially and thus their social interests (i.e., extraversion) allow them to capitalize on an intraindividual strength.

In any case, testable predictions that follow from my proposal are that individual differences in social, enterprising, and artistic interests should be related to performance differences on measures that capture sensitivity to the meaning of nonverbal behavior and facial expressions, competencies on theory of mind tests, and so forth. A more specific prediction is that individuals with social interests may excel at the individual-level competencies shown in Figure 1.2, and individuals with enterprising interests may excel at the group-level competencies associated with organizing and focusing the behavior of members of their in-group. These interest-ability relations are expected to emerge epigenetically (Bouchard et al., 1996; Scarr, 1993); that is, through interactions between inherent biases to engage in niche-related behaviors (e.g., seeking social relationships and social information), and inherent but nascent attentional and cognitive advantages (e.g., sensitivity to facial expressions). The combination results in practice of the supporting cognitive competencies and their enhancement during development.

The concrete/abstract dimension does not map directly onto the folk domains shown in Figure 1.2, but is consistent with the conscious psychological mechanism of the motivation to control model, that is, the ability to mentally represent and manipulate past, present, or potential future states. These representations would be toward the abstract pole of the concrete/abstract dimension. Use of symbols and other forms of abstract expression are ubiquitous across human societies and are manifested in terms of music, dance, art, poetry, and story telling. These activities express the experiences of the in-group and often serve to increase social cohesion and cooperation (Alcorta & Sosis, 2005; Brown, 1991; Coe, Aiken, & Palmer, 2006). Abstractions are also found in explanations of social (e.g., illness due to witchcraft) and natural (e.g., storms) phenomena that are not well understood by individuals in the culture (Brown, 1991). The latter are commonly expressed in terms of mystical explanations (e.g., gods, witchcraft) and are often accompanied by rituals designed to attempt to control these phenomena (e.g., to cure sickness). Although these folk explanations are not typically scientifically accurate, as Newton railed (1995), they may provide a sense of psychological control and perhaps a means of developing methods of actual utility (e.g., folk medicine) and cross-generational transmission (e.g., stories). More mundane rituals—building fires, gathering food, and so on—are also a universal and necessary feature of day-to-day living in human cultures, and cluster toward the concrete pole of the concrete/abstract dimension.

There are several lines of evidence that support the prediction of inherent and potentially evolved influences on individual differences on the people/things and concrete/abstract dimensions of interest, and thus occupational niche seeking. As with basic dimensions of personality (e.g., extraversion, openness to experience), individual differences in occupational preferences and underlying interests (e.g., in nature) are moderately heritable (Betsworth et al., 1994; Lykken, Bouchard, McGue, & Tellegen, 1993). Sex differences in orientation toward things (males) or interpersonal relationships (females) are predicted from evolutionary theory, as described elsewhere (Geary, 1998, 2002b), and these in turn are related to sex differences in occupational sorting in modern society (e.g., K. R. Browne, 2005; Geary, 2007; Lubinski, 2000). As an example, activities performed exclusively or primarily by men in traditional societies include metal working, weapon making, and working with wood, stone, bone and shells, among other activities (Daly & Wilson, 1983; Murdock, 1981). Across cultures, nearly 92% of those activities that appear to be most similar to the likely tool-making activities of *Homo habilis* and *H. erectus* (i.e., use of wood, stone, bone, and shells) are performed exclusively by men (Gowlett, 1992).

A sex difference, favoring boys and men, is thus predicted and found for interest in working with objects and in corresponding mechanical abilities (Geary, 1998; Hedges & Nowell, 1995). These, in turn, appear to emerge during development through an interaction between the influence of male hormones on activity biases and cognition (Cohen-Bendahan, van de Beek, & Berenbaum, 2005) and object-oriented play and exploration (Gredlein & Bjorklund, 2005). In adulthood, this is expressed in modern societies as a sex difference, favoring men, in realistic interests and work in associated occupations (K. R. Browne, 2005).

Evolved Interests and Children's Development. If social competition was a potent selection pressure during recent human evolutionary history (Alexander, 1989; Geary, 2005; Flinn et al., 2005), then a significant proportion of children's self-directed activities is predicted to be social and to create evolutionarily expectant experiences that flesh out the folk psychological competencies shown in Figure 1.2. Many children are also predicted to engage in activities that will flesh out folk biological and folk physical competencies. Examples of the latter include object-oriented play and exploration of the physical environment (folk physics), as well as the collection and perhaps play hunting of other species (folk biology); Darwin, for instance, was an avid beetle collector in his adolescence (J. Browne, 1995). Indeed, studies of infants' attentional biases and preschool children's nascent and implicit knowledge are often focused on the domains of folk psychology, folk biology, and folk physics (e.g., S. A. Gelman, 2003; Keil, 1992; Keil, Levin, Richman, & Gutheil, 1999; Mandler, 1992; Wellman & Gelman, 1992), although these have not been well linked with observational studies of children's and adolescents' self-directed activities (for discussion see Geary et al., 2003), and the source (inherent bias vs. experience) of these emerging competencies is debated (Au & Romo, 1999). My point is that there is theoretical and empirical research on children's early attentional biases and activity preferences that must be considered in attempts to understand how children's presumably natural preferences are expressed in school settings and how these might relate to later interest biases in other important evolutionarily novel contexts, including the workplace.

Any continuity between children's evolved interests and activities preferences and Holland's (1996) RIASEC model would in theory emerge from the underlying people/things, concrete/abstract dimensions shown in Figure 1.5. Individual variation in specific occupational interests (e.g., physicist vs. lawyer) are predicted to emerge only as children are exposed to opportunities to express their more basic interests within the wider culture (Lykken et al., 1993). In this view, basic interest dimensions (e.g., people/things) are to Holland's occupational taxonomy, as primary folk abilities are to secondary school-taught abilities; the latter is dependent on the former, but the specifics of the latter are also dependent on developmental experiences within a cultural context. In an attempt to directly assess the relation between children's activity preferences and Holland's occupational RIASEC hexagon, Tracey and Ward (1998) developed the *Inventory of Children's Activities* (ICA). The items were developed based on observation of children's activities, and activities that, in theory, capture later occupational interests and the underlying people/things, concrete/abstract (i.e., data/ideas) dimensions. Across two studies, the ICA was administered to elementary school (4th & 5th grade), middle school (6th–8th grade), and college students. The basic RIASEC pattern and the people/things, concrete/abstract dimensions emerged for the college sample, as expected.

For the elementary school sample and for girls and boys respectively, a sex-typed people/things dimension emerged but the abstract/concrete dimension did not. Rather, children's activities varied along an out-of-school (e.g., talking to friends) and in-school (e.g., adding numbers) dimension. The pattern for the middle school students was intermediate between that of the college students and the elementary students. In keeping with the elementary school findings, individual differences in children's self-directed activities along the people/things dimension are found during the preschool years (Golombok & Rust, 1993; Jennings, 1975), and possibly in infancy (Lutchmaya & Baron-Cohen, 2002). These and later individual differences tend to be highly sex-typed (Golombok & Rust, 1993; Tracey & Ward, 1998), but in ways consistent with evolutionary theory (Geary, 1998). As mentioned earlier, men's interest in objects and a corresponding enhancement of mechanical and spatial abilities follow from a likely evolutionary history of greater tool use in our male than in our female ancestors and is preceded by a sex difference in object/tool-related activities and play (Chen & Siegler, 2000; Gredlein & Bjorklund, 2005).

The failure to find to a concrete/abstract dimension in the elementary school samples may indicate that individual variation along this interest dimension emerges later in development than does variation across the people/things dimension. It is certainly the case that children engage in symbolic representation of their experiences, as in sociodramatic play, and use these activities to rehearse commonly observed adult activities (e.g., playing house), many of which would be considered conventional in the RIASEC. In any event, the overall pattern reveals a potential continuity between children's and adolescents' interest and activities biases—the basic people/things dimension and perhaps the concrete/abstract dimension—and interest patterns that emerge across modern occupations. The bottom line is there may be a deep structure to children's and adults' interests that can be organized around folk psychology (interest in people), folk biology (interest in living things), and folk physics (interest in inanimate things). This deep structure also involves use of conscious psychological and working memory systems to create symbolic representations of experiences and a means (e.g., story telling) of conveying these experiences and other forms of knowledge across time and space. The content of these representations is predicted to coalesce around the folk domains and serve social functions (e.g., group cohesion) and utilitarian functions related to the acquisition and control of ecological resources (e.g., hunting strategy or tool construction).

Motivation in School

Evolutionary Biases. The gist of the above argument is that children's natural motivational biases and conative preferences are focused on learning about themselves and other people (folk psychology), other living beings (folk biology), and the physical environment (folk physics). And, that they prefer to engage in this learning through a combination of physical activity (e.g., imitation of hunting) and symbolic representation (i.e., along the concrete/abstract dimension). Children may or may not be explicitly aware of these biases (e.g., as assessed in a survey) but they are nonetheless inferable through children's self-directed activities. Either way, this perspective provides a means of interpreting the finding that many school children value achievement in sports more than achievement in core academic areas (Eccles et al., 1993), and report that in-school activities are a significant source of negative affect (R. Larson & Asmussen, 1991). For a nationally (U.S.) representative sample, Csikszentmihalyi and Hunter (2003) found that the lowest levels of happiness were experienced by children and adolescents while they were doing homework, listening to lectures, and doing mathematics, whereas the highest levels were experienced when they were talking with friends. For high-school students, the weekend is the highlight of their week, largely because they can socialize with their peers (R. Larson & Richards, 1998).

A preference for engagement in peer relationships is a predicted aspect of development for all highly social species (e.g., Joffe, 1997). The finding for sports is not surprising because these games involve ritualized practice of organized in-group/out-group competition and readily maps onto the learning of group-level folk psychological competencies, especially for boys (Geary et al., 2003). The lower valuation of achievement in formal academic areas, such as mathematics and reading (Eccles et al., 1993), and preference for out-of-school social activities (Csikszentmihalyi & Larson, 1987) can be framed in terms of the rapid accumulation of biologically secondary knowledge illustrated in the section titled Human Intellectual History and the Creature of Culture, and the widening gap between this knowledge and people's inherent folk abilities and corresponding motivational and conative biases. The constellation of interest, ability, and motivational traits of the creative-productive individuals who generate this secondary knowledge is rare (Murray, 2003; Simonton, 1999a), and thus it cannot be expected that most children, or even many children, will be motivated or able to easily recreate this knowledge in school settings without formal instruction; intellectually talented youth appear to be an exception (Bleske-Rechek, Lubinski, & Benbow, 2004), as described in the section titled Individual Differences in Secondary Learning.

Indeed, schools are an evolutionarily novel context in which the cross-generational transmission of secondary abilities (e.g., writing) and knowledge (e.g., that a right angle = 90°) is formalized (see the Principles section in Table 1.1). The formalization of schooling is not, however, completely foreign to our evolved learning and motivational biases, because the extended length of childhood and adolescence likely co-evolved with an interest in and ability to transfer culturally important information across generations, as noted earlier (Richerson & Richerson, 2005; Flinn, 1997; Henrich & McElreath, 2003). In other words, a species-typical curiosity about—potentially related to the "openness to experience" dimension of personality (e.g., Komarraju & Karau, 2005)—and an ability to learn evolutionarily novel information is predicted, as are substantive individual differences within the species-typical range. Nonetheless, the rapid cultural accumulation of secondary knowledge over the past several millennia has created a gap between evolved modes of intergenerational knowledge transfer and learning (e.g., story telling, apprenticeships) and between the motivation to engage in the corresponding activities and the forms of activity needed for secondary learning in modern society. If this were not the case, then the activities that produce creative-productive advancements, as illustrated by the processes that contributed to Darwin and Wallace's discovery of natural selection, would be mundane and readily duplicated outside of school. As Pinker (1994) has argued, language is an extraordinary ability that is unique to humans, but its acquisition is mundane and effortless for most children. But, this is not the case for Newtonian physics, classic geometry, and so forth.

Achievement Motivation.   A complete review and integration of the extensive and nuanced literature on children's achievement motivation and related constructs (Ames & Archer, 1988; Barron & Harackiewicz, 2001; Dweck & Leggett, 1988; Eccles et al., 1993; Eccles, Wigfield, & Schiefele, 1998; Grant & Dweck, 2003; Meece, Anderman, & Anderman,

2006; Nicholls, 1984; Weiner, 1985, 1990; Wigfield & Eccles, 2000), as these potentially relate to my evolutionary framework, is beyond the scope of this chapter. These models of achievement motivation include children's understanding of the relation between effort and ability on academic outcomes (Nicholls, 1984); valuation of academic learning in terms of mastery (i.e., intrinsically motivated desire for a deep understanding of the material) or performance (e.g., focus on grades, standing relative to others) goals (Ames & Archer, 1988; Dweck & Leggett, 1988; Grant & Dweck, 2003); academic self efficacy (e.g., Bandura, 1993); and, expectancy of success and attributions regarding the sources of success or failure (e.g. ability vs. bad luck) in achieving academic goals (Eccles et al., 1998; Weiner, 1985; Wigfield & Eccles, 2000).

The perceived value of achievement in one domain or another is also important and this, in turn, is influenced by intrinsic interests and by extrinsic utility; the latter is the usefulness of the academic knowledge for later goals, such as college entrance or employment (Wigfield & Eccles, 2000). Empirical studies indicate that expectancies, values, and so forth become increasingly differentiated across academic domains with schooling (Bong, 2001; Smith & Fouad, 1999), and that variables representing many of these constructs predict academic achievement above and beyond the influence of Gf and various demographic factors (e.g., Duckworth & Seligman, 2005; Gagné & St Père, 2003; Lent, Brown, & Hackett, 1994).

One point of connection between my motivation-to-control model and models of academic motivation is Bandura's (1997) highly influential theory of social and cognitive self efficacy: "People make causal contributions to their own functioning through mechanisms of personal agency. Among the mechanisms of agency, none is more central or pervasive than people's beliefs about their capabilities to exercise control over their own level of functioning and over events that affect their lives" (Bandura, 1993, p. 118). Self efficacy is an aspect of this personal agency and at its core is a self-referenced appraisal regarding the likelihood of success in various domains and through this influences, among other things, the pursuit of achievement in these domains and persistence in the face of failure. Bandura emphasizes one's explicit appraisal of efficacy and attributions regarding associated outcomes (e.g., cause of failure), and these in turn map onto the folk psychological domains of self awareness, self schema, and the ability to explicitly represent associated information in the conscious psychological component of control-related mental models. The content of mental models will include attributional biases, expectancies, and other social learning mechanisms that can influence evaluations of future goals and behavioral persistence in attempts to achieve these goals (Geary, 2005).

In other words, Bandura's (1993, 1997) model of self-efficacy is highly consistent with an evolutionary perspective, but with different points of emphasis regarding children's academic motivations and corresponding self evaluations. One area in which my evolutionary model differs from social learning theory is with my assumption of domain-specific and inherent learning and motivational biases associated with folk knowledge (Figure 1.2), but not academic knowledge, such as mathematics. Further, the core of the self schema is predicted, from an evolutionary perspective, to be referenced in terms of one's standing vis-à-vis peers and particularly for traits that have an evolutionary history, including physical abilities (greater importance for boys than girls), physical attractiveness (greater importance for girls than boys), social influence, and family status (Geary, 1998). These are predicted to be universal and implicit influences on the development of self schemas and self evaluations, whereas culturally specific activities, such as schooling, are predicted to be important in these cultures but less central to most children's and adolescents' emerging self schemas and evaluations. In keeping with this view is the finding that self awareness and the emerging self schema are embedded in a web of social relationships and that the best predictor of global self esteem from childhood to adulthood is perceived physical attractiveness (Harter, 1998) and not, for instances, grades in high school mathematics classes.

From an evolutionary perspective, the valuation of academic achievement and the relation between achievement and self-esteem is predicted to be highly variable across and within cultures, and to be heavily dependent on explicit parental and cultural valuation of associated activities and outcomes (e.g., grades; Stevenson & Stigler, 1992), and heavily influenced by peers' valuation of academic achievement (Harris, 1995). From a social learning perspective (Bandura, 1986), many children will imitate parents and teachers who engage in academic activities (e.g., reading); many will come to focus on these activities because they provide access to culturally valuable resources, such as a job and income; and, many will come to enjoy these activities in their own right, developing a mastery orientation (Winner, 2000). Children and adolescents will also develop a sense of academic self efficacy. These outcomes also follow from an evolutionary perspective that includes evolved modes of cross-generational knowledge transmission. The crucial difference comparing these theoretical views is with respect to specificity of predictions: With successive grade levels, academic content will increasingly diverge from its evolved foundation, as was illustrated in the seciton titled Primary and Secondary Forms of Cognition, and thus academic learning is predicted to become more difficult and any motivation to engage in this learning is predicted to decrease, and this is the case (Eccles et al., 1993). Social living also becomes more complex and nuanced as people mature into adulthood, but motivational disengagement from social life is predicted to be far less common than disengagement from academic life.

Thus, if the goal is to educate nearly all children and adolescents in academic domains that are of a recent cultural origin and remote from folk domains, then there may be a need to *explicitly* highlight the utility of these skills in the culture and perhaps focus on the intellectual and academic accomplishments of creative-productive individuals, that is, show that these individuals are socially valued (Stevenson & Stigler, 1992). In other words, children's and adolescent's explicit valuation of academic learning, the perceived utility of academic skills, and the centrality of self efficacy in these areas to their overall self esteem are predicted to be highly dependent on sociocultural valuation of academic competencies, such as explicit rewards for academic achievement (e.g., honor rolls) and valuation of cultural innovators (e.g., Edison). In contrast, the children's and adolescent's valuation of and perceived efficacy related to their physical traits or social relationships are an implicit features of their evolved folk psychology, contrary to current assumptions regarding the source of the focus on these traits (e.g. Harter, 1998).

Biologically Secondary Learning

Biologically secondary learning is the acquisition of culturally important information and skills (Gc-secondary) by means of the evolved mechanisms, including Gf, that enable people to cope with novelty and change and that enable the cross-generational transfer of cultural knowledge. Evidence for the importance of Gf for learning in novel contexts, such as school and the workplace, is well known and documented (L. Gottfredson, 1997; Jensen, 1998; Walberg, 1984). In contrast, the importance of specific abilities for success in school or at work is often hypothesized (Gardner, 1983; Kalbleisch, 2004; Sternberg, 2000; Winner, 2000), as it is here (see below), but the empirical evidence for their importance, above and beyond the influence of Gf, has been found for only a few academic domains and occupations (Baron-Cohen et al., 1999; Humphreys, Lubinski, & Yao, 1993; Shea, Lubinski, & Benbow, 2001). In the first section, I attempt to elaborate on the mechanisms underlying the relation between Gf and the ability to acquire evolutionarily novel competencies, and in the second I discuss ways in which Gf and specific folk abilities might interact in the acquisition of biologically secondary abilities and knowledge. In the final section, I discuss individual differences in secondary learning and accompanying educational implications.

Fluid Intelligence and Secondary Learning

The correlation between performance on measures of Gf and ease of learning in evolutionarily novel contexts does not inform us as to how fluid intelligence actually affects the learning process. In the following sections, I review research on the mechanisms that appear to relate Gf to secondary learning, and discuss applied examples in Folk Systems and Secondary Learning.

Inhibition of Folk Biases.   One of the principles of evolutionary educational psychology (see Table 1.1) states that children are biased to engage in activities that will adapt folk knowledge to local conditions, and these biases will often conflict with the need to engage in the activities needed for secondary learning. The principle follows from the rapid (and accelerating) cross-generational accumulation of secondary knowledge over the past several millennia. One implication is that evolved folk attributional (e.g., the folk physical concept of "impetus," as I described earlier) and behavioral (e.g., preference for peer activities over mathematics homework) biases will often need to be inhibited before secondary learning will occur. Indeed, educational research supports the importance of inhibitory control for school-based learning (Duckworth & Seligman, 2005; Fabes, Martin, Hanish, Anders, & Madden-Derdich, 2003) and is consistent with empirical research on the cognitive components of Gf; specifically, attentional focus and an ability to inhibit irrelevant information from entering working memory (Engle, 2002; Engle et al., 1999; Kane & Engle, 2002).

Engagement of these inhibitory mechanisms is predicted to be effortful and to occur in evolutionarily novel contexts and for information the individual explicitly determines to be useful in terms of meeting control-related goals. In the case of schooling and culturally evolving secondary knowledge, however, it cannot be expected that children will understand which forms of secondary knowledge will be necessary for successful living as an adult. For that matter, in cultures with rapid changes in secondary knowledge, educators cannot fully know what is necessary for their students' long-term employment and cultural needs. Even in these cultures there are core skills (e.g., reading) that must be taught and learned, and it is adults, not children, who must determine these core skills and what is culturally-important knowledge.

Process of Secondary Learning.   Ackerman (1988) proposed the mechanisms that relate Gf to learning can be divided into three stages, cognitive, perceptual-speed, and psychomotor (see also Anderson, 1982). The gist is that different abilities are related to individual differences in academic and job-related performance at different points in the learning process. For school-based and job-related learning, the cognitive stage refers to the relation between Gf and initial task performance. The prediction is that novel and complex tasks will require an attention-driven, explicit representation of task goals and information patterns in working memory. During this phase, the task goals and the sequence of steps needed to perform the task are learned, and memorized. With enough practice, the eventual result is the automatic, implicit processing of task features and automatic behavioral responses to these features. These phases of learning represent the shift from explicit representations and controlled problem solving to automatic, implicit and heuristic-based processing of and responding to the task, as illustrated by the arrow in the center of Figure 1.3. Ackerman's model can be readily integrated with the folk systems shown in Figure 1.2, if we assume that one core difference between biologically primary competencies and biologically secondary competencies is the need for the cognitive phase of learning. The inherent constraints associated with evolved competencies can be understood as putting them at Ackerman's second or third phase of learning—resulting in their implicit operation—without the need for the explicit learning associated with this first phase.

A work-related example is provided by tasks that simulate the demands of an air traffic controller, which is clearly an evolutionarily novel demand. One task involves learning the rules that govern decision making, such as whether to keep a plane in a holding pattern or allow it to land based on air traffic, wind, and so forth. Another task involves the especially complex demands of tracking and making decisions based on constantly changing information patterns (e.g., multiple plane icons) represented on dynamic radar screens (Ackerman & Cianciolo, 2000, 2002). Performance on these tasks is indexed by the number of properly routed flights and speed of making routing decisions. Ease of initial rule learning is moderately correlated with Gf ($rs \sim 0.4$ to 0.5), and remains so even after six hours of practice ($r \sim 0.3$). Performance on the radar task is moderately to highly correlated with Gf ($rs \sim 0.4$ to 0.8), and remains so throughout training. A causal relation between performance and Gf was experimentally demonstrated by manipulating the number of planes the individual needed to simultaneously monitor. As the number of planes increased, the importance of Gf increased.

Cognitive and Brain Mechanisms. On the basis of work described in the section titled Evolution of General Intelligence, the initial learning of evolutionarily novel academic and job-related competencies, as illustrated by Ackerman's (1988) research, is driven by the ability to control attention, inhibit irrelevant information (both Gc-primary and Gc-secondary), simultaneously represent multiple pieces of information in working memory, and logically piece this information together to meet problem-solving goals (e.g., Embretson, 1995; Fry & Hale, 2000; Kane & Engle, 2002). In many cases, the drawing of inferences about information represented in working memory will be facilitated if the information is made available to conscious awareness, although pattern learning can occur without awareness (Stadler & Frensch, 1997). For explicit learning and problem solving, the supporting brain regions appear to be the dorsolateral prefrontal cortex (areas 47, 9 in both panels of Figure 1.4), the anterior cingulate cortex (area 24 in the lower panel), and the posterior attentional systems of the parietal cortex (area 40 in the upper panel; e.g., Duncan, 2001; Duncan & Owen, 2000). Other areas are also active when people are engaged in these tasks, and there are, of course, different patterns of brain activity associated with learning one type of skill or another (e.g., McCandliss, Posner, & Givón, 1997). Additional research is needed, but current evidence suggests the dorsolateral prefrontal cortex and anterior cingulate cortex are primarily engaged during Ackerman's (1988) first phase of learning (Raichle, Fiez, Videen, MacLeod, Pardo, & Petersen, 1994). Thereafter, brain activation is associated with the particular type of stimulus (e.g., visual vs. auditory) and the specifics of task demands.

There are only a few studies that have combined learning and brain imaging with assessments of Gf (e.g., Gevins & Smith, 2000; Haier, Siegel, Tang, Abel, & Buchsbaum, 1992). Haier et al. assessed the brain's use of glucose during the learning of a novel spatial problem-solving task. Individuals with high IQ scores learned the task more quickly than their less-intelligent peers, and showed more rapid declines in glucose metabolism across learning trials. Using electrophysiological methods, Gevins and Smith found the dorsolateral prefrontal cortex was initially engaged during the learning of a complex task that required working memory and attentional control, but engagement of this region declined as individuals learned the task. The decline was especially pronounced for intelligent individuals, who in turn appeared to shift the processing of task requirements to more posterior regions of the brain.

At this point, it appears that one function of the dorsolateral prefrontal cortex, the anterior cingulate cortex, and the posterior attentional system is to ensure the synchronized activity of other brain regions, such that anatomical and functional links are formed among these regions; see the description in the section titled Neuroscience Research. When couched in terms of Gf, it appears that the associated ability to focus attentional resources and inhibit the activation of task-irrelevant information (Kane & Engle, 2002) results in the ability to synchronize only those brain regions needed for secondary learning. The result would be lower glucose use and faster learning for individuals high in Gf, because fewer unneeded brain regions are activated and thus fewer regions are anatomically linked. Functionally, the result would be a sharper representation and better understanding of the new competency, because irrelevant information and concepts would not be linked to this competency. Once formed, an evolutionarily novel, biologically secondary cognitive competency emerges. The more fundamental issue concerns *how* these components of Gf and supporting brain systems create competencies that do not have an evolutionary history.

Folk Systems and Secondary Learning

The attentional and working memory components of Gf are engaged during the initial phase of biologically secondary learning, but the fully developed secondary competencies reside in a network of cognitive and brain systems that differ from those that support Gf (Gevins & Smith, 2000; Raichle et al., 1994). These networks represent the two earlier noted classes of crystallized intelligence (Cattell, 1963), that is, Gc-primary and Gc-secondary. In effect, the components of Gf are used to modify plastic Gc-primary abilities to create Gc-secondary abilities. As described in the section Cognitive Development and Modular Plasticity, there is evidence for plasticity in many primary modules, as well as an evolutionary logic as to why such plasticity is expected. However, limits on the plasticity of Gc-primary modules implies these systems can be modified to create secondary competencies only to the extent this novel information is similar to the forms of information the system evolved to process (Sperber, 1994), and to the extent independent modular systems can be interconnected to form unique neural networks and functional competencies (Garlick, 2002; Sporns et al., 2000). In the first section, I discuss how the transformation from Gc-primary to Gc-secondary might occur in the domain of reading, and in the second I focus on the more complex domain of scientific reasoning.

Folk Psychology and Reading

As noted in the section Human Intellectual History and the Creation of Culture, I assume there are functional, motivational, cognitive, and neural links between secondary abilities and the primary folk systems from which they are built, although the "remoteness" of many of these links increases with the cross-generational accumulation of secondary knowledge and across school grade levels (Geary, 2002a). If this assumption is correct, then empirical links between basic secondary abilities and knowledge—those that tend to be taught in the early years of schooling—and one or several of the primary domains shown in Figure 1.2 should be found. The most crucial mechanisms of cross-generational knowledge transfer in modern societies, that is, reading and writing, are included among these secondary abilities. In terms of cultural history, these systems must have initially emerged from the motivational disposition to communicate with and influence the behavior of other people (e.g., morals in the Bible), and are predicted to engage at least some of the social communication systems shown in Figure 1.2, that is, components of folk psychology. In fact, it has been suggested many times that reading is built on evolved language systems (e.g., Mann, 1984; Rozin, 1976). My goal here is describe the basic relations between language processing and processing in other folk psychological domains and reading, and by doing so provide directions as to how this form of analysis might be used more generally with an evolutionary educational psychology.

Cognitive Mechanisms.   Research on the cognitive predictors of children's reading acquisition, the effectiveness of various types of reading instruction, and sources of individual differences in ease of learning to read provide solid support for the prediction that the core components of reading competency are dependent on primary language skills (Bradley & Bryant, 1983; Connor, Morrison, & Petrella, 2004; Hindson, Byrne, Shankweiler, Fielding-Barnsley, Newman, & Hine, 2005; Lovett, Lacerenza, Borden, Frijters, Steinbach, & De Palma, 2000; Mann, 1984; Moats & Foorman, 1997; Stevens, Slavin, & Farnish, 1991; Vukovic & Siegel, 2006; Wagner & Torgesen, 1987; Wagner, Torgesen, & Rashotte, 1994). The crucial components in early reading acquisition include an explicit awareness of distinct language sounds, that is, phonemic awareness, and the ability to decode unfamiliar written words into these basic sounds. Decoding requires an *explicit* representation of the sound (e.g., *ba, da, ka*) in phonemic working memory and the association of this sound, as well as blends of sounds, with corresponding visual patterns, specifically letters (e.g., *b, d, k*) and letter combinations (Bradley & Bryant, 1983). Phonetic working memory has also been proposed as the mechanism that supports vocabulary acquisition during natural language learning (Baddeley et al., 1998; Mann, 1984), but this form of word learning occurs quickly (sometimes with one exposure) and the associated mechanisms operate *implicitly* (Lenneberg, 1969; Pinker, 1994).

Wagner et al. (1994) found individual differences in the fidelity of kindergarten children's phonological processing systems to be strongly predictive of the ease with which basic word decoding skills are acquired in first grade. Children who show a strong explicit awareness of basic language sounds are more skilled than are other children at associating these sounds with the symbol system of the written language. The majority of children acquire these competencies most effectively with systematic, organized, and teacher-directed explicit instruction on phoneme identification, blending, and word decoding (e.g., Connor et al., 2004; Hindson et al., 2005; Lovett et al., 2000; Stevens et al., 1991). Other components of skilled reading include fluency and text comprehension. Fluency is the fast and automatic retrieval of word meanings as they are read, which is related in part to frequency with which the word has been encountered or practiced in the past (e.g., Sereno & Rayner, 2003). Text comprehension involves coming to understand the meaning of the composition and involves a number of component skills, such as locating main themes and distinguishing highly relevant from less relevant passages. Unlike comprehension of spoken language (Pinker, 1994), explicit instruction in the use of these strategies for understanding written text is needed for many children (Connor et al., 2004; Stevens et al., 1991).

Brain Mechanisms. The neuroanatomy of basic language abilities has been understood for more than 100 years (e.g., Martin, 2005; Poldrack, Wagner, Prull, Desmond, Glover, & Gabrieli, 1999; Price, 2000), and has substantive overlap with the brain regions that support the acquisition of basic phonological decoding, reading fluency, and text comprehension (Paulesu et al., 2001; Price & Mechelli, 2005; Pugh et al., 1997; Temple, 2002; Turkeltaub, Eden, Jones, & Zeffiro, 2002; Turkeltaub, Gareau, Flowers, Zeffiro, & Eden, 2003). In a thorough review of neuropsychological and brain imaging research on language processing, Price (2000) concluded (and I have simplified here) that passive processing of language sounds occurs in the traditional Wernicke's area (posterior region of area 22 in the upper panel of Figure 1.4); speech production involves Broca's area (area 44 in the lower panel) and areas that support word articulation (e.g., area 6 in both panels); and, the representations of the meaning of spoken and heard utterances is distributed across the temporal (e.g., areas 21, 38 in both panels), and parietal (areas 39, 40 in the upper panel) cortices. Prefrontal working memory areas related to language (areas 45, 47 in the upper panel) are engaged when the speaker or listener has to make active decisions about the utterances (Poldrack et al., 1999). Although there is a left-hemispheric bias for much of this processing, the corresponding regions in the right-hemisphere are often engaged as well.

Brain imaging studies of individuals with normal reading acquisition and those with reading disability are beginning to provide insights into the areas of convergence and divergence comparing reading and natural language processing, and the brain regions that support core reading abilities. Among other regions, tasks that tap phonological awareness or involve phonological decoding engage Wernicke's and Broca's areas (Paulesu et al., 2001; Turkeltaub et al., 2003), as do tasks that involve the reading of single words (Pugh et al., 1997; Turkeltaub et al., 2002). Word reading also engages areas in the temporal (e.g., area 21 in the upper panel) and parietal (e.g., area 39 in the upper panel) cortices that support the comprehension of spoken utterances (Price & Mechelli, 2005). Early research on the comprehension of the syntax and the basic meaning of read sentences suggested engagement of the same brain regions that support the production and comprehension of spoken utterances, including Broca's and Wernicke's areas, although both hemispheres were involved in sentence reading (Just, Carpenter, Keller, Eddy, & Thulborn, 1996). Subsequent studies are generally consistent with this finding, but also suggest involvement of additional regions of the temporal cortex (e.g., areas 38, 21) and part of the parietal cortex (area 39), areas also involved in language comprehension (Caplan, 2004; Price, 2000).

There are also important differences between language processing and reading. Areas at the junction of the temporal and occipital lobes (e.g., area 37) are more likely to be engaged during reading than during natural language processing. An intriguing exception might be natural object naming, which engages this same temporal/occipital area (Price & Mechelli, 2005). Basically, learning to read and skilled reading in adulthood involve the integration of the visual systems that process the orthography of written symbols and those that translate these images into the language-based sounds that support the comprehension and production (e.g., reading aloud) of the read material (Simos, Fletcher, Francis, Castillo, Pataraia, & Denton, 2005; Paulesu et al., 2001).

Summary and Integration.   As noted, the argument that reading and reading acquisition are built on language systems is by no means novel (Mann, 1984; Rozin, 1976; for a related argument on writing see Karmiloff-Smith, 1992). However, I hope an evolutionarily informed analysis of the associated cognitive and brain links will provide a more nuanced understanding of the specific relation between reading/language and, more generally, an example of how this type of analysis can be used to better understand the learning of other secondary abilities. Text that is read aloud or silently engages the same network of brain regions and results in the same types of cognitive representations (i.e., language sounds) involved in generating or listening to natural language, in keeping with the prediction that there will be a close relation between secondary abilities and the primary systems from which they are built (Sperber, 1994). Moreover, this tight relation is in keeping with the view that the cultural construction and development of written symbols was to socially communicate; in other words, reading and writing may tap the same underlying motivational systems that are components of folk psychology, unlike secondary abilities (e.g., geometry) built on folk physical or folk biological systems.

For most children, learning how to phonemically decode words and to use text comprehension strategies is facilitated by explicit, teacher-organized instruction (Connor et al., 2004; Hindson et al., 2005). The necessity of teacher and curriculum organization of secondary material follows logically, if one assumes that much of this material has been generated in the past several generations or millennia of human history and that children therefore do not have built-in attentional, cognitive, or motivational mechanisms that will drive child-centered learning in these domains. The need for explicit instruction also follows from my proposal that the ability to generate and learn evolutionarily novel content and abilities, such as written text and reading, are dependent on the systems that evolved to generate and cope with social and ecological conditions that tend to vary during the human life span (Geary, 2005). The mechanisms are associated with Gf; specifically, the ability to inhibit primary heuristics and explicitly represent, through attentional control, variation in social or ecological conditions in working memory and then use problem solving to devise behavioral strategies to cope with these dynamics.

For instance, during the initial phases of reading acquisition, attentional focus on the relation between the sound and written letter (when decoding) or word (when reading) should, in theory, result in the amplification of the activity of the brain regions that process these auditory and visual forms of information, and their simultaneous representation in working memory. This may involve the integration of brain areas involved in object naming (e.g., area 37 in both panels in Figure 1.4) and those involved in phonetic (Wernicke's area) and semantic (e.g., areas 38, 39 in both panels) language processing (Price & Mechelli, 2005). The synchronization and integration of these normally distinct systems would initially involve the attentional and working memory systems of the dorsolateral prefrontal cortex (e.g., areas 9, 46 in the upper panel), but with sufficient practice the formation of a learned association between the sound and letter or word should occur. In this view, the reading of printed words involves integration of two biologically primary systems. The first supports the naming and description of visually processed objects in the real world and the second involves the access to concepts associated with these utterances. With extended practice, the association becomes represented in long-term memory and thus becomes implicit knowledge, representing Ackerman's (1988) final stages of learning. When this is achieved, the association between the sound and letter, or letter combination and word sound, is automatically triggered when the letter string is processed during the act of reading and thus no longer engages the prefrontal cortex and no longer requires Gf. In keeping with this prediction, one potential source of reading disability is a poor white-matter connection between these object naming and phonetic/semantic brain regions, even for children with average or better IQ scores (Paulesu et al., 2001; Simos et al., 2005; Temple, 2002).

A more novel evolution-based prediction is that reading comprehension will also be dependent on theory of mind and other folk psychological domains, at least for literary stories, poems, dramas, and other genre that involve human relationships (Geary, 1998). Most of these stories involve the recreation of social relationships, more complex patterns of social dynamics, and even elaborate person schema knowledge for main characters. The theme of many of the most popular genre involves the dynamics of mating relationships (e.g., romance novels) and intrasexual competition for over mates (e.g., Whissell, 1996), and often involves the social scenario building that Alexander (1989), myself (Geary, 2005), and others (e.g., Flinn et al., 2005; Humphrey, 1976) have argued is a competency that evolved as the result of intense social competition. In other words, once people learn to read, they engage in this secondary activity because it allows for the representation of more primary themes, particularly the mental representation and rehearsal of social dynamics. In addition to social relationships, the RIASEC model (Holland, 1996; Lubinski & Benbow, 2000) and the underlying people/things dimension of interests indicates that some people will be interested in reading about mechanical things (e.g., the magazine *Popular Mechanics)* and biological phenomena (e.g., the magazine *Natural History*). For instance, the content of children's literature also includes other living things, such as dinosaurs, and thus may capture an inherent interest in folk biology. These individual differences, as well as the more fundamental desire to exert some level of personal control, suggest that children should be given some choice in the literature they read, but only once basic skills are acquired.

Evolution and Science Education

The learning of phonemic decoding and other basic reading skills is a relatively simple task, but illustrates how the processes may work for the learning of more complex biologically secondary skills. The core difference across task complexity involves the length of the first phase of learning, to use Ackerman's (1988) model. More precisely, complexity is predicted to be related to the extent to which the task is evolutionarily novel (granted, a system for making this determination remains to be fully articulated); the amount of information that must be identified and processed to deal with task demands; and, the extent to which this information changes across time. As each of these features increases in complexity, there is an accompanying increase in the need for sustained attention, working memory, and the ability to reason and make inferences, that is, an increased reliance on Gf. Scientific reasoning is one of the most complex tasks in modern societies today (L. Gottfredson, 1997) and—as illustrated by earlier discussion of Euclid (1956), Newton (1995), and Darwin (1859)—the results are among humanity's greatest accomplishments (Murray, 2003). Today, the scientific enterprise and the insights of individual scientists and teams of scientists are engines of cultural innovation, technological change, and generation of secondary knowledge. Yet, the ability to reason rationally and scientifically does not come naturally to most people (Stanovich, 1999; Stanovich & West, 2000), and in fact the scientific method is itself a cultural innovation and thus an understanding of this method is not expected to come easily to most people.

The literature on the cognitive mechanisms involved in scientific and mathematical reasoning and the use of experimentation to test naïve hypotheses includes the seminal studies by Piaget and his colleagues (e.g., Inhelder & Piaget, 1958; Piaget, Inhelder, Szeminska, 1960), and more recent studies that have approached these issues from an information-processing or neonativist (i.e., in terms of folk knowledge) perspective (e.g., Capon & Kuhn, 2004; Carey, 2001; Carey & Spelke, 1994; Chen & Klahr, 1999; Hunt & Minstrell, 1994; Klahr & Dunbar, 1988; Klahr & Nigam, 2004; Klahr & Simon, 1999; Koslowski, 1996; Kuhn, 1989, 2005; Kuhn & Dean, 2005; Shtulman, 2005; Williams, Papierno, Makel, & Ceci, 2004). An exhaustive review of this literature is not my goal and nor is it necessary, as excellent and recent reviews of this and related literatures are available elsewhere (Klahr, 2000; Klahr & Simon, 1999; Strauss, 1998; Zimmerman, 2000, 2005). Rather, in the first two respective sections, I highlight some of the research on the cognitive and brain mechanisms related to scientific reasoning and its development. In the final section, I discuss how these themes may potentially inform and be informed by an evolutionary educational psychology.

Cognitive Mechanisms. As described for Darwin and Wallace's (1858) discovery of natural selection, the achievement of scientific goals involves problem solving within an ill-defined problem space. The process is based on assumptions and prior knowledge that define the problem space, the use of experimentation and observation to generate and test hypotheses, and evaluation of experimental results related to these hypotheses. Similarly, the cognitive processes and knowledge bases around which naïve children's and adults' scientific reasoning and problem solving coalesce are the reciprocal interactions between theory-hypothesis generation, experimental testing, and evaluation of experimental results vis-à-vis generated hypotheses (Klahr & Dunbar, 1988; Klahr & Simon, 1999; Kuhn, 1989). Klahr and Dunbar's dual-space model of scientific reasoning has been particularly influential (see Zimmerman, 2000, 2005), as has the assumption that scientific reasoning and problem solving are developed from the same mechanisms (e.g., analogy, induction) used in everyday problem solving (Klahr & Simon, 1999). The dual spaces include an *hypothesis space*—the set of hypotheses related to the phenomena in question—derived from prior knowledge, assumptions, and observations, and an *experiment space*—the set of procedures available to generate or test hypotheses. The hypothesis space and associated knowledge bases will often differ across content domains, such as evolutionary biology and Newtonian physics, but aspects of the experiment space and the evaluation processes will be domain general (e.g., the empirical testing of hypotheses).

Wallace's (1855) conclusion that related species are found in the same geographic location because they all arose from a common ancestor that resided in this location was part of his hypothesis space and was related to his goal of discovering the natural law that resulted in the emergence of new species. Darwin, of course, had the same hypothesis, and spent many years explicitly testing this and related hypotheses. One example was the use of selective breeding (artificial selection) to produce different breeds of, for instance, pigeon (Darwin, 1859). The tests were drawn from his experiment space and the results were used to evaluate hypotheses about natural selection and potential refutations of these hypotheses (J. Browne, 1995). Darwin (and Wallace), nonetheless, made mistakes. Darwin's pangenesis theory of how traits were transmitted from parents to children was incorrect, but he resisted changing the theory even in the face of strong contradictory evidence (J. Browne, 2002). Even Newton spent many years engaged in unsuccessful alchemy experiments (White, 1998).

And so it is with all people: As described in the section titled Cognitive Development and Modular Plasticity, children and adults have naïve folk beliefs about people, other livings beings, and the physical word that provide a sense of coherence and control in their daily life, are often functional, and sometimes scientifically accurate (Wellman & Gelman, 1992). These folk beliefs and mental models of how the world works, however, are often scientifically inaccurate or incomplete. These misconceptions are nonetheless part of the a priori beliefs that influence children's and adult's scientific reasoning and their understanding of and ability to learn scientific concepts (Carey, 2001; Clement, 1982; Kuhn, 1989; McCloskey, 1983; Shtulman, 2006). In addition to priori and often incorrect beliefs, children and many naïve adults have difficulty separating the hypothesis and experiment spaces. There is a tendency to focus on observations and experimental results that confirm existing hypotheses (confirmation bias), and to ignore or discount disconfirming results. Many people view evidence as an example of an existing theory (and thus a confirmation), rather than viewing the theory "as an object of cognition, that is, [thinking] about the theory rather than with it" (Kuhn, 1989, p. 679).

Kuhn's (1989) conclusion and that of others (Klahr & Dunbar, 1989; Klahr & Simon, 1999) suggests that the adaptation of everyday reasoning for use in scientific endeavors does not come easily. Indeed, the skilled use of everyday reasoning (e.g., analogy) in scientific contexts, separation of the hypothesis and experiment spaces, and acquiring appropriate rules of evidence for evaluating the relation between experimental results and hypotheses are highly dependent on formal instruction. At this time, there is no agreed upon instructional approach to bring about these ends. Research groups differ in the focus of their work (e.g., on the experiment space or hypothesis space) (Capon & Kuhn, 2004; Klahr & Nigam, 2004;

Williams et al., 2004), and often disagree on the most effective instructional methods (e.g., Klahr, 2005; Kuhn, 2005). Klahr and colleagues (Chen & Klahr, 1999; Klahr & Nigam, 2004), for instance, have demonstrated that explicit, teacher-directed instruction is more effective than child-directed discovery for learning how to control variables during experimental manipulations. Kuhn and Dean (2005) argued this approach may not promote effective transfer across domains and that conceptual learning may be more effectively achieved with a problem-based, discovery approach (e.g., Capon & Kuhn, 2002).

Although we await definitive results, in a very recent review of this literature Zimmerman (2005) concluded that some of the debate is definitional and perhaps less substantive than it appears; direct instruction often includes a "hands-on" component, and discovery is often guided (e.g., by prompts, questions) by teachers or experimenters. In any case, Zimmerman's review indicates that an unguided self discovery approach is ineffective for teaching scientific reasoning to the vast majority of children before the fifth grade, and even for older individuals it is not sufficient; for instance, students often fail to develop experiments that would disconfirm their hypotheses. In short, most children and adults do not develop the full repertoire of skills related to the use of the scientific method without formal instruction that is extended over many years. Without solid instruction, children do not: (a) learn many basic scientific concepts, such as natural selection (Shtulman, 2006); (b) effectively separate and integrate the hypothesis and experiment spaces; (c) effectively generate experiments that include all manipulations needed to fully test and especially to disconfirm hypotheses; and (d) learn all of the rules of evidence for evaluating experimental results as these relate to hypothesis testing. In addition, they: (e) are often reluctant to give up naïve folk beliefs, even when faced with contradictory evidence (Zimmerman, 2005).

Brain Mechanisms. Brain imaging research on scientific reasoning and problem solving as related to science education is in its infancy and thus strong conclusions cannot yet be reached. Nonetheless, early studies and related research have provided intriguing insights into the potential brain systems that govern the inductive and deductive reasoning associated with scientific discovery and the processes involved in the generation and evaluation of hypotheses (Acuna, Eliassen, Donoghue, & Sanes, 2002; Dunbar & Fugelsang, 2005; Fugelsang & Dunbar, 2005; Goel & Dolan, 2000; Goel, Gold, Kapur, & Houle, 1998; Goel, Makale, & Grafman, 2004).

Fugelsang and Dunbar (2005) examined the brain regions involved in interpreting data that are either congruent or incongruent with a plausible or implausible mechanism governing the relation between use of psychotropic drugs and patient mood. There was more bilateral activation of the left- (areas 45, 47 in the upper panel of Figure 1.4) and right- (area 9 in both panels) prefrontal areas when adults evaluated data related to a plausible versus an implausible mechanism, suggesting that plausible mechanisms are more thoroughly evaluated. When participants evaluated data *inconsistent* with a plausible mechanism, there was even wider activation of the left dorsolateral prefrontal area (area 9 in both panels), as well as activation of the anterior cingulate cortex (areas 24, 32 in the lower panel). Dunbar, Fugelsang, and Stein (in press) examined the brain activity of naïve adults and physics students as they watched two videos on the motion of falling objects. The first video presented scientifically incorrect patterns of object motion consistent with naïve folk physical conceptions. The second video presented object motion consistent with Newtonian physics. When naïve adults watched the video of correct Newtonian motion, their dorsolateral prefrontal cortices were active, whereas only areas associated with memory were active for the physics students. The opposite pattern emerged for the video based on folk physical conceptions of motion.

The results suggest the cortical areas associated with attentional control, working memory, and conflict resolution are engaged only when presented with information inconsistent with current conceptual models of the phenomena; folk models for the naïve adults, and Newtonian models for the physics students. In keeping with this conclusion, Stavy, Goel, Critchley, and Dolan (2006) found that several areas of the occipital and parietal cortices (e.g., areas 18, 40 in both panels in Figure 1.4) are engaged when adults process intuitive, folk physical information associated with the area and perimeter of shapes. When judgments require access to formally taught geometric knowledge that conflicts with this folk knowledge, areas of the prefrontal cortex (e.g., 11, 47 in both panels) are engaged. For several of their participants, Dunbar et al. (2006) also found a disconnection between explicit statement of theory and brain activation; specifically, several naïve adults who explicitly stated the correct pattern of Newtonian motion showed brain activation patterns similar to that found with naïve adults who did not understand Newtonian motion. The results are consistent with cognitive models of concept development, namely that "deep" conceptual understanding and explicit statements of concepts are not the same thing (Kuhn, 1989).

In a series of related studies, Goel and colleagues have found that the systems of brain regions that support inductive and deductive reasoning differ and vary with whether the focus of reasoning involves familiar or unfamiliar information and easy or difficult judgments. Making difficult inductive inferences—generating an abstract rule based on examples and observations—engages several areas of the right prefrontal cortex (areas 47, 11 in both panels in Figure 1.4; Goel & Dolan, 2000). Drawing difficult deductive conclusions about familiar concepts—making a judgment about an outcome based on whether it logically follows from stated premises—often engages distributed areas within the left hemisphere; in particular: Broca's area (area 45 in the upper panel), other prefrontal regions (e.g., areas 46, 47 in the upper panel), as well as several temporal areas (e.g., 22 in the upper panel) associated with concept representation (Goel et al., 1998). In contrast, deductive problems that involve unfamiliar geometric relations seem to be more dependent on the bilateral spatial-parietal systems than on the language systems (Goel et al., 2004).

The combination suggests that deductive problems involving familiar content are solved by means of attentional and working memory representations of preexisting concepts that tend to be explicitly cast in terms of language, whereas some deductive problems with unfamiliar geometric relations engage the bilateral visuospatial attentional and working memory systems. The solving of inductive problems also involves attentional control and working memory but is not dependent on language or access to preexisting concepts. The results for deductive problems are consistent with an explicit representation and manipulation of the processed information in working memory, but in these studies inductive tasks did not require explicit statement of the principles that bound together the presented examples and thus could have been solved implicitly. Of course, scientific discovery involves explicit statement of hypotheses and mechanisms, although implicit inductions may sometimes precede this: As stated earlier, Wallace's statement that the mechanisms of natural selection "suddenly flashed upon me" (F. Darwin, 2000), was preceded by 13 years of observations and attempts to induce these mechanisms.

On the one hand, it is not surprising that scientific reasoning and evaluation of data engage areas of the prefrontal cortex associated with attentional control, working memory, and conflict resolution. On the other hand, there are several findings emerging from this literature that are important for science education and an emerging evolutionary educational psychology. It is important to know that different brain regions are involved in inductive and deductive reasoning; plausible mechanisms are evaluated more closely than implausible mechanisms; and data that conflict with predictions derived from plausible mechanisms are especially likely to trigger brain regions associated with cognitive conflict and working memory. The latter finding suggests that relevant aspects of the hypothesis space may need to be explicitly articulated and explicitly compared to relevant data derived from the experiment space for a thorough evaluation of concepts.

Summary and Integration.   From an evolutionary perspective, science emerged from recent cultural innovations that were driven by a small fraction of humanity (Murray, 2003), and therefore there is not a suite of biologically primary cognitive systems or motivational biases to facilitate the teaching and learning of modern day science. As suggested in the section titled Human Intellectual History and the Creation of Culture, early scientists likely developed scientific concepts and experimental methods based on evolved cognitive and motivational systems associated with folk domains, but were able to inhibit these biases and use more general, if everyday, reasoning (e.g., analogy, induction) to construct increasingly accurate models of physical, biological, and social phenomena. These conceptual and methodological advances must be reconstructed for each and every generation, or they will be lost. The reconstruction is through science education. Science learning in modern societies requires, among other things that children come to understand (a) core concepts (e.g., natural selection, gravity) and experimental findings for many specific fields; (b) how scientists develop hypotheses from theory and observation and use experiments to test these hypotheses; (c) how to systematically develop their own experimental tests and to thoroughly relate experimental results to hypotheses; and (d) the rules of evidence for accepting and especially for disconfirming hypotheses (Klahr, 2000; Klahr & Dunbar, 1988; Kuhn 1989; Kuhn & Dean, 2005; Zimmerman, 2000, 2005).

From an evolutionary perspective, children are predicted to bring to the science classroom conceptual and attributional biases in the domains of folk psychology, folk biology, and folk physics (Wellman & Gelman, 1992). These constitute core aspects of their initial hypothesis space, which at times may facilitate the learning of associated scientific concepts and at other times will interfere with this learning (Kuhn, 1989; Zimmerman, 2005). One goal of an evolutionary educational psychology is to better integrate research on children's core knowledge and conceptual development in these domains (e.g., S. Gelman, 2003) into a coherent framework for guiding research on science education and learning in other academic domains. The integration will include knowledge about how and what children understand in these core domains and where this knowledge is consistent with or inconsistent with our scientific understanding of the same phenomena. As an example, on the basis of intense social competition, human folk psychological domains (see Figure 1.2) are predicted to be more fully articulated and biased than are folk biological or folk physical domains, and the associated biases are predicted to be self serving and function to guide attempts at behavioral control (Geary, 2005). A corresponding prediction is that more conceptual and attributional biases interfere with the scientific study and learning of social phenomena than of biological or physical phenomena, and this appears to be the case (Zimmerman, 2005). There are clear biases in folk biology and folk physics that influence learning in the biological and physical sciences, respectively, but biases in folk psychology may result in even greater interference in learning the social sciences. Although people are inherently motivated to understand people and social relationships, this is not the same as understanding these phenomena scientifically. In fact, people are likely to be especially resistant to research results that "undermine" their sense of personal agency and control.

For an example of how folk knowledge might interfere with scientific learning in a key area of biology, consider Shtulman's (2006) study of high school and college students' conceptual understanding of natural selection. The students' understanding was assessed in terms of their knowledge and integration of the basic mechanisms (e.g., within-species variation, inheritance) that result in natural selection. The same measures were administered to a contrast group of three evolutionary biologists. The latter, of course, understood each of the specific concepts (e.g., speciation) and had them integrated into a coherent mental model of the actual mechanisms of natural selection. Although the majority of high school and college students stated they were familiar with Darwin's theory (76%), and agreed that natural selection was the best explanation of how species change over time (69%), the majority did not actually understand how natural selection works. They did, however, have a coherent theory of cross-generational change in species, albeit a theory that is not scientifically accurate. For instance, most of these individuals assumed that each species had its own essence that resulted in trivial within-species variation. Cross-generational change occurs at the level of the species' essence and is driven by adaptive need, and not selection acting on heritable variation. Their knowledge seemed to be a mix of folk biology and misunderstood or poorly taught school biology.

In addition to misconceptions regarding species' essence, there are several others ways in which such naïve folk biological concepts and biases might interfere with learning the mechanisms of natural selection. First, one inferential folk bias results in a focus on *similarities* across members of the same, and related, species (Atran, 1998). This bias facilitates the functional goal of being able to predict the behavior (e.g., growth patterns) of these plants and animals, as related to procuring food and medicines. At the same time, the focus on within-species similarities runs counter to the insight that within-species differences, or variability, provide the grist for natural selection. Second, folk biological knowledge is also implicitly focused on the behavior of flora and fauna at different points in a single life span (e.g., maturity of a plant, relative to when it is best to harvest) and not the cross-generational time scale over which natural selection operates. In other words, people are biased to think about and understand the biological world in ways that are functional in natural settings and have been beneficial during our evolutionary history, but these biases also interfere with understanding the mechanisms of natural selection.

Research in evolutionary educational psychology will focus on identifying such biases, generating explicit comparisons between these biases and scientific concepts in the same domain, and assessing alternative instructional approaches to correcting these naïve beliefs (e.g., Hunt & Minstrel, 1994).

The reliance on the brain and cognitive systems supporting attentional control, working memory, and conflict resolution during scientific reasoning and when comparing experimental data with conceptual models can be integrated into my motivation to control model. More precisely, the historical emergence of science and the ability to learn science in the modern classroom is predicted to be dependent upon the conscious psychological and cognitive systems that evolved to cope with variant social and ecological dynamics. As described in the section Motivation to Control, the combination allows for the explicit generation of mental models of past, present, and potential future states in working memory. These representations are predicted to be centered on social (e.g. group conflict), ecological (e.g., hunting), or physical (e.g., climate change) conditions and to access folk knowledge in the respective domains of psychology, biology, and physics. Everyday problem solving (e.g., use of analogy, induction) represents the constraints and biases in how mental models of these situations are manipulated in the problem space to generate control-related behavioral solutions to novel, dynamic situations (Geary, 2005).

In other words, because scientific knowledge and the scientific method are evolutionarily novel cultural innovations, the brain and cognitive systems that evolved to cope with novelty—including a bias to construct mental models that include mechanisms (often incorrect) of how and why the phenomena of interest operates in the world—are predicted to be engaged in the generation of scientific knowledge and in the learning of this knowledge. If this is correct, then an understanding of these conscious psychological mental models might provide insights into how naïve folk knowledge is represented and manipulated in working memory when children and adults construct models of the world and how these same mechanisms might be used to modify naïve concepts and better teach the corresponding scientific concept. As noted, naïve folk biological knowledge may include construction of mental (or explicitly represented) models of species' change but these changes tend to be constrained to individual lifetimes and to minimize individual differences (Shtulman, 2006; Wellman & Gelman, 1992). To understand the mechanisms of natural selection, these mental models need to be expanded to include individual variation within and change across lifetimes. In this way, the teaching of natural selection involves modification of existing, naïve concepts.

If learning of evolutionarily novel information, including components of natural selection, involves use of explicit mental models, attentional control, and working memory, then several predictions follow: (a) children's conceptual understanding will be facilitated if they are able to construct a mental model of how and why the phenomena of interest operates; (b) construction of any such models will be initially based on folk knowledge and modifications of these concepts will be facilitated if folk assumptions are made explicit and directly compared and contrasted with the corresponding scientific concept; and (c) conceptual change will require repeated exposures to the new concepts, especially for concepts that conflict with folk beliefs. Included among the latter are beliefs about human agency, origins, social motives, and so forth; scientific knowledge that contradicts evolved folk psychological biases are predicted to be especially difficult to teach.

Individual Differences in Secondary Learning

Individual differences in the ease of secondary learning are well known and often a source of educational and political debate (Benbow & Lubinski, 1996; Benbow & Stanley, 1996; Ceci & Papierno, 2005). The source of these individual differences is multifold, and includes many of the traits associated with eminent achievement noted in the section titled Human Intellectual History and the Creation of Culture, including individual differences in Gf, motivation, hours worked, and opportunity (Lubinski, 2004). Variation in these traits is expected from an evolutionary perspective, and thus individual differences in secondary learning are expected as well. The central educational and political debate centers on this variation and whether the variation is consistent with the cultural more of "equality." The nuances of this debate are lucidly addressed by Ceci and Papierno, and thus do not need attention here. Rather, I wish to echo the concerns raised by Benbow and Lubinski regarding the consequence of attempts to achieve equity in educational outcomes. More precisely, the focus on attempts to reduce individual differences in educational outcomes, that is, individual differences in secondary abilities and knowledge acquired in school and elsewhere, have focused on improving the learning of low achieving students. From an evolutionary perspective, these are exactly the students who are predicted to need well-organized, explicit and often teacher driven instruction for efficient secondary learning. But, the focus on the learning needs of these children and the implicit goal of achieving equality of outcomes has come at a cost to the educational and long-term occupational potential of many children who are toward the high end (> 90th percentile) on measures of Gf.

Indeed, if the evolved function of Gf is to cope with and learn about evolutionarily novel information patterns, then children and adults who are high in Gf should require less formal instruction then other people to achieve the same level of secondary abilities and knowledge. This is because learning in school is all about acquiring evolutionarily novel abilities and knowledge, and because individuals who are high in Gf have an enhanced—and evolved—ability to learn novel information rapidly and on their own. Not only is the rate of secondary learning of these children accelerated, the experiences that result in the achievement of their full educational potential differs in important ways from that of other children (see Benbow & Lubinski, 1996; Bleske-Rechek et al., 2004). For instance, the finding that phonemic and word decoding skills are most effectively acquired through explicit and teacher directed instruction (Hindson et al., 2005; Wagner & Torgesen, 1987), does not apply to many intellectually gifted children. Many of these children show greater school-year gains in reading when allowed to work independently (e.g., silent reading), presumably because they have acquired basic phonemic and decoding skills earlier than most other children (Connor et al., 2004). Because children high in Gf learn novel information more rapidly then other children, it follows that full engagement of these gifted children in schooling and to achieve their full educational potential will require acceleration through the typical curriculum as well as a more complex curriculum (Bleske-Rechek et al., 2004).

From the perspective I have outlined here, facilitating the educational and occupational achievement of these individuals is important for any culture, because scientific, technological, and other cultural innovations are disproportionately produced by these individuals. On the basis of historical patterns (Murray, 2003), cultures that facilitate the ability of these individuals to learn complex cultural innovations (e.g., become physicians, lawyers) and to create new innovations will be advantaged relative to other cultures. In other words, attempts to achieve within-culture "equity" may come at a long-term cost in terms of the ability to compete with other cultures.

CONCLUSION

In modern societies today, there are formal institutions, such as research universities and commercial laboratories, that are designed to be engines of cultural, artistic, and scientific innovation and for the generation of new knowledge. When viewed from the lens of human evolution, these cultural institutions and the resulting explosion of biologically secondary knowledge are unique and very recent phenomena. Although these advances have resulted in extraordinary benefits (e.g., reduced infant and child mortality), they have also created equally extraordinary demands on our ability to fully understand and cope with this new knowledge. One of the changes that has emerged in these cultures is an accompanying need for other formal institutions, especially schools, that function to prepare children for the evolutionarily novel demands of living and succeeding in these societies. In fact, the need to educate children for these demands is going to accelerate, because more and more institutions of knowledge generation are likely to emerge in coming decades and will result in an exponential increase in secondary knowledge. Because formal schooling and the need to teach recent cultural innovations to children are themselves evolutionarily novel, adults are not expected to intuitively understand how to best proceed with this endeavor (Geary, 1995). As part of their folk psychological repertoire, adults may intuitively know how to use stories and modeling to impart to children knowledge and competencies that have been useful in more natural environments and in kin-based social groups. But, this intuitive repertoire is no longer sufficient and because of this, considerable confusion, conflict, and derision among competing educational approaches is predicted and found (e.g., Hirsch, 1996; Loveless, 2001; Egan, 2003).

By placing the field of education on a more scientific foundation, an evolutionary approach will reduce these conflicts. Evolutionary developmental psychology and accompanying insights into children's cognitive development and motivational biases will provide the first level of this foundation (Bjorklund, 2006; Geary & Bjorklund, 2000). From this perspective, cognitive development is an inherent feature of the human life span, and represents the fleshing out of the plastic features of modularized folk domains such that these brain and cognitive systems become sensitive to nuances in the local social, biological, and physical ecologies (Geary, 2004). The experiences needed to adjust these folk systems to these ecologies are generated by children's natural social play, exploratory activities, and adult-child interactions. The result of these activities is the effortless and automatic adaptation of folk systems such that the child easily makes discriminations among different people and learns about their personality and behavioral dispositions; forms categories of local plants and animals and learns about their essence; and, develops mental maps of the group's physical territory, among many other cognitive changes (Wellman & Gelman, 1992). These cognitive competencies are biologically primary, that is, the human mind is inherently biased to acquire knowledge in these domains and to do so with little effort.

Academic development, in contrast, involves the experience-driven acquisition of nonevolved, or biologically secondary cognitive competencies (Geary, 1995). The acquisition of these competencies is dependent on plasticity in modularized folk domains, and the existence of domain-general mechanisms that evolved to enable the adaptation of these folk systems to evolutionarily novel information. An example of the latter was provided with my discussion of how associations among language sounds and visual patterns are formed to create the ability to read and write. Although not typically approached from an evolutionary perspective, research in experimental psychology has identified these domain general systems; specifically, general fluid intelligence (Kane & Engle, 2002). Fluid intelligence is composed of the attentional and working memory systems that enable people to explicitly represent and manipulate information that has tended to be variable during human evolutionary history, and thus is to some extent evolutionarily novel. It appears that the explicit representation of information in working memory and the reasoned manipulation of this information are at the heart of the human ability to construct non-evolved cognitive competencies (Ackerman, 1988) and thus are the core cognitive mechanisms underlying the maintenance and generation of human culture.

From an evolutionary perspective there are several key points: First, secondary learning is predicted to be heavily dependent on teacher- and curriculum-driven selection of content, given that this content may change across and often within lifetimes. Second, for biologically primary domains, there are evolved brain and perceptual systems that automatically focus children's attention on relevant features (e.g., eyes) and result in a sequence of attentional shifts (e.g., face scanning) that provide goal-related information, as needed, for example, to recognize other people (Schyns, Bonnar, & Gosselin., 2002). Secondary abilities do not have these advantages and thus a much heavier dependence on the explicit, conscious psychological mechanisms of the motivation-to-control model—Ackerman's (1988) cognitive stage of learning—is predicted to be needed for the associated learning. Third, children's inherent motivational biases and conative preferences are linked to biologically primary folk domains and function to guide children's fleshing out of the corresponding primary abilities (see Figure 1.2). In many cases, these biases and preferences are likely to conflict with the activities needed for secondary learning.

Although these conclusions might seem obvious to some readers and not in need of an evolutionary framework, such a framework might have obviated the often rancorous debate on how to most effectively teach children, for instance, how to read (e.g., Loveless, 2001). These debates have waxed and waned without resolution for nearly 250 years, since Rousseau's 1762 publication of *Emile*. Of course, Rousseau and other philosophers of education did not have an evolutionary theory in place to guide their thinking about these issues. But, this is no longer the case. My point here is that we do not have to repeat this contentious process for each and every academic domain, if there are foundational principles in place for understanding secondary learning in general.

ACKNOWLEDGMENTS

I thank Jason Bessey for suggested readings, and Mary Hoard, David Lubinski, and Brian Rudrick for comments on an earlier draft. Preparation of this chapter was supported, in part, by grants R01 HD38283 from the National Institute of Child Health and Human Development (NICHD), and R37 HD045914 cofunded by NICHD and the Institute for Education Sciences.

REFERENCES

Achter, J. A., Lubinski, D., Benbow, C. P., & Eftekhari-Sanjani, H. (1999). Assessing vocational preferences among gifted adolescents adds incremental validity to abilities: A discriminant analysis of educational outcomes over a 10-year interval. *Journal of Educational Psychology, 91*, 777-786.

Ackerman, P. L. (1988). Determinants of individual differences during skill acquisition: Cognitive abilities and information processing. *Journal of Experimental Psychology: General, 117*, 288-318.

Ackerman, P. L. (1996). A theory of adult intellectual development: Process, personality, interests, and knowledge. *Intelligence, 22*, 227-257.

Ackerman, P. L., Beier, M. E., & Boyle, M. O. (2005). Working memory and intelligence: The same or different constructs? *Psychological Bulletin, 131*, 30-60.

Ackerman, P. L., & Cianciolo, A. T. (2000). Cognitive, perceptual-speed, and psychomotor determinants of individual differences in skill acquisition. *Journal of Experimental Psychology: Applied, 6*, 259-290.

Ackerman, P. L., & Cianciolo, A. T. (2002). Ability and task constraint determinants of complex task performance. *Journal of Experimental Psychology: Applied, 8*, 194-208.

Ackerman, P. L., & Heggestad, E. D. (1997). Intelligence, personality, and interests: Evidence for overlapping traits. *Psychological Bulletin, 121*, 219-245.

Acuna, B. D., Eliassen, J. C., Donoghue, J. P., & Sanes, J. N. (2002). Frontal and parietal lobe activation during transitive inference in humans. *Cerebral Cortex, 12*, 1312-1321.

Adler, N. E., Boyce, T., Chesney, M. A., Cohen, S., Folkman, S., Kahn, R. L., & Syme, S. L. (1994). Socioeconomic status and health: The challenge of the gradient. *American Psychologist, 49*, 15-24.

Alcorta, C. S., & Sosis, R. (2005). Ritual, emotion, and sacred symbols: The evolution of religion as an adaptive complex. *Human Nature, 16*, 323-359.

Alexander, R. D. (1979). *Darwinism and human affairs*. Seattle, WA: University of Washington Press.

Alexander, R. D. (1989). Evolution of the human psyche. In P. Mellars & C. Stringer (Eds.), *The human revolution: Behavioural and biological perspectives on the origins of modern humans* (pp. 455-513). Princeton, NJ: Princeton University Press.

Ames, C., & Archer, J. (1988). Achievement goals in the classroom: Students' learning strategies and motivation processes. *Journal of Educational Psychology, 80*, 260-267.

Anderson, J. R. (1982). Acquisition of cognitive skill. *Psychological Review, 89*, 369-406.

Atran, S. (1998). Folk biology and the anthropology of science: Cognitive universals and cultural particulars. *Behavioral and Brain Sciences, 21*, 547-609.

Au, T. K. -F., & Romo, L. F. (1999). Mechanical causality in children's "folkbiology." In D. L. Medin & S. Atran (Eds.), *Folkbiology* (pp. 355-401). Cambridge, MA: MIT Press/Bradford Book.

Baddeley, A. D. (1986). *Working memory.* Oxford: Oxford University Press.

Baddeley, A. (2000a). Short-term and working memory. In E. Tulving & F. I. M. Craik (Eds.), *The Oxford handbook of memory* (pp. 77-92). New York: Oxford University Press.

Baddeley, A. (2000b). The episodic buffer: A new component of working memory? *Trends in Cognitive Sciences, 4*, 417-423.

Baddeley, A., Gathercole, S., & Papagno, C. (1998). The phonological loop as a language learning device. *Psychological Review, 105*, 158-173.

Bandura, A. (1986). *Social foundations of thought and action: A social cognitive theory.* Englewood Cliffs, NJ: Prentice-Hall.

Bandura, A. (1993). Perceived self-efficacy in cognitive development and functioning. *Educational Psychologist, 28*, 117-148.

Bandura, A. (1997). *Self-efficacy: The exercise of control.* San Francisco: Freeman.

Barkow, J. H. (1992). Beneath new culture is old psychology: Gossip and social stratification. In J. H. Barkow, L. Cosmides, & J. Tooby (Eds.), *The adapted mind: Evolutionary psychology and the generation of culture* (pp. 627-637). New York: Oxford University Press.

Baron, J. (1997). The illusion of morality as self-interest: A reason to cooperate in social dilemmas. *Psychological Science, 8*, 330-335.

Baron-Cohen, S. (1995). *Mindblindness: An essay on autism and theory of mind.* Cambridge, MA: MIT Press/Bradford Books.

Baron-Cohen, S., Wheelwright, S., Stone, V., & Rutherford, M. (1999). A mathematician, a physicist and a computer scientist with Asperger syndrome: Performance on folk psychology and folk physics tests. *Neurocase, 5*, 475-483.

Barron, K. E., & Harackiewicz, J. M. (2001). Achievement goals and optimal motivation: Test multiple goals models. *Journal of Personality and Social Psychology, 80*, 706-722.

Barton, R. A., & Dean, P. (1993). Comparative evidence indicating neural specialization for predatory behaviour in mammals. *Proceedings of the Royal Society of London B, 254*, 63-68.

Baumeister, R. F. (2005). *The cultural animal: Human nature, meaning, and social life.* New York: Oxford University Press.

Baumeister, R. F., & Leary, M. R. (1995). The need to belong: Desire for interpersonal attachment as a fundamental human motive. *Psychological Bulletin, 117*, 497-529.

Belin, P., Zatorre, R. J., Lafaille, P., Ahad, P., & Pike, B. (2000, January 20). Voice-selective areas in human auditory cortex. *Nature, 403*, 309-312.

Benbow, C. P., & Lubinski, D. (Eds.) (1996). *Intellectual talent: Psychometric and social issues*. Baltimore, MD: Johns Hopkins University Press.

Benbow, C. P., & Stanley, J. C. (1996). INEQUITY IN EQUITY: How "equity" can lead to inequity for high-potential students. *Psychology, Public Policy, and Law, 2,* 249-292.

Berlin, B., Breedlove, D. E., & Raven, P. H. (1973). General principles of classification and nomenclature in folk biology. *American Anthropologist, 75,* 214-242.

Berlinski, D. (2000). *Newton's gift*. New York: Touchstone.

Betsworth, D. G., Bouchard, T. J. Jr., Cooper, C. R., Grotevant, H. D., Hansen, J. -I. C., Scarr, S., et al. (1994). Genetic and environmental influences on vocational interests assessed using adoptive and biological families and twins reared apart and together. *Journal of Vocational Behavior, 44,* 263-278.

Binet. A., & Simon, T. (1916). *The development of intelligence in children*. Baltimore, MD: Williams & Wilkins.

Bjorklund, D. F. (2006). Mother knows best: Epigenetic inheritance, maternal effects, and the evolution of human intelligence. *Developmental Review*.

Bjorklund, D. F., & Pellegrini, A. D. (2002). *The origins of human nature: Evolutionary developmental psychology*. Washington, DC: American Psychological Association.

Bjorklund, D. F., & Harnishfeger, K. K. (1995). The evolution of inhibition mechanisms and their role in human cognition and behavior. In F. N. Dempster & C. J. Brainerd (Eds.), *New perspectives on interference and inhibition in cognition* (pp. 141-173). New York: Academic Press.

Blake, R. (1993). Cats perceive biological motion. *Psychological Science, 4,* 54-57.

Bleske-Rechek, A., Lubinski, D., & Benbow, C. P. (2004). Meeting the educational needs of special populations: Advanced placement's role in developing exceptional human capital. *Psychological Science, 15,* 217-224.

Blurton Jones, N. G., Hawkes, K., & O'Connell, J. F. (1997). Why do Hadza children forage? In N. L. Segal, G. E. Weisfeld, & C. C. Weisfeld (Eds.), *Uniting psychology and biology: Integrative perspectives on human development* (pp. 279-313). Washington, DC: American Psychological Association.

Blurton Jones, N., & Marlowe, F. W. (2002). Selection for delayed maturity: Does it take 20 years to learn to hunt and gather? *Human Nature, 13,* 199-238.

Bogin, B. (1999). Evolutionary perspective on human growth. *Annual Review of Anthropology, 28,* 109-153.

Bong, M. (2001). Between- and within-domain relations of academic motivation among middle and high school students: Self-efficacy, task-value, and achievement goals. *Journal of Educational Psychology, 93,* 23-34.

Botvinick, M. M., Braver, T. S., Barch, D. M., Carter, C. S., & Cohen, J. D. (2001). Conflict monitoring and cognitive control. *Psychological Review, 108,* 624-652.

Bouchard, T. J., Jr., Lykken, D. T., Tellegen, A., & McGue, M. (1996). Genes, drives, environment, and experience. In C. P. Benbow & D. Lubinski (Eds.), *Intellectual talent: Psychometric and social issues* (pp. 5-43). Baltimore: Johns Hopkins University Press.

Bradley, L., & Bryant, P. E. (1983, February 3). Categorizing sounds and learning to read—A causal connection. *Nature, 301,* 419-421.

Bradley, R. H., & Corwyn, R. F. (2002). Socioeconomic status and child development. *Annual Review of Psychology, 53*, 371-399.

Brodmann, K. (1909). *Vergleichende Lokalisationslehre der Grosshirnrinde in ihren Prinzipien dargestellt auf Grund des Zellenbaues* [Comparative localization of the cerebral cortex based on cell composition]. Leipzig: Barth.

Brothers, L., & Ring, B. (1992). A neuroethological framework for the representation of minds. *Journal of Cognitive Neuroscience, 4*, 107-118.

Brown, D. E. (1991). *Human universals*. Philadelphia, PA: Temple University Press.

Browne, J. (1995) *Charles Darwin: Voyaging*. London, Jonathan Cape.

Browne, J. (2002). *Charles Darwin: The power of place*. New York: Knopf.

Browne, K. R. (2005). Evolved sex differences and occupational segregation. *Journal of Organizational Behavior, 26*, 1-20.

Bugental, D. B. (2000). Acquisition of the algorithms of social life: A domain-based approach. *Psychological Bulletin, 126*, 187-219.

Buss, D. M. (1994). *The evolution of desire: Strategies of human mating*. New York: Basic Books.

Campbell, D. P., & Holland, J. L. (1972). A merger in vocational interest research: Applying Holland's theory to Strong's data. *Journal of Vocational Behavior, 2*, 353-376.

Campos, J. J., Campos, R. G., & Barrett, K. C. (1989). Emergent themes in the study of emotional development and emotion regulation. *Developmental Psychology, 25*, 394-402.

Caplan, D. (2004). Functional neuroimaging studies of written sentence comprehension. *Scientific Studies of Reading, 8*, 225-240.

Caporael, L. R. (1997). The evolution of truly social cognition: The core configurations model. *Personality & Social Psychology Review, 1*, 276-298.

Capon, N., & Kuhn, D. (2004). What's so good about problem-based learning? *Cognition and Instruction, 22*, 61-79.

Caramazza, A., & Shelton, J. R. (1998). Domain-specific knowledge systems in the brain: The animate-inanimate distinction. *Journal of Cognitive Neuroscience, 10*, 1-34.

Carey, S. (2001). Science education as conceptual change. *Journal of Applied Developmental Psychology, 21*, 13-19.

Carey, S., & Spelke, E. (1994). Domain-specific knowledge and conceptual change. In L. A. Hirschfeld & S. A. Gelman (Eds.), *Mapping the mind: Domain specificity in cognition and culture* (pp. 169-200). New York: Cambridge University Press.

Carroll, J. B. (1993). *Human cognitive abilities: A survey of factor-analytic studies*. New York: Cambridge University Press.

Carpenter, P. A., Just, M. A., & Shell, P. (1990). What one intelligence test measures: A theoretical account of processing in the Raven Progressive Matrices Test. *Psychological Review, 97*, 404-431.

Cattell, R. B. (1963). Theory of fluid and crystallized intelligence: A critical experiment. *Journal of Educational Psychology, 54*, 1-22.

Ceci, S. J., & Papierno, P. B. (2005). The rhetoric and reality of gap closing: When the "have-nots" gain but the "haves" gain even more. *American Psychologist, 60*, 149-160.

Chagnon, N. A. (1988, February 26). Life histories, blood revenge, and warfare in a tribal population. *Science, 239*, 985-992.

Chen, Z, & Klahr, D. (1999). All other things being equal: Acquisition and transfer of the control of variables strategy. *Child Development, 70*, 1098-1120.

Chen, Z., & Siegler, R. S. (2000). Across the great divide: Bridging the gap between understanding toddlers' and older children's thinking. *Monographs of the Society for Research in Child Development, 65* (No 2, serial no. 261).

Chiappe, D., & MacDonald, K. (2005). The evolution of domain-general mechanisms in intelligence and learning. *Journal of General Psychology, 132*, 5-40.

Clark, D. A., Mitra, P. P., & Wang, S. S. -H. (2001, May 10). Scalable architecture in mammalian brains. *Nature, 411*, 189-193.

Clement, J. (1982). Students' preconceptions in introductory mechanics. *American Journal of Physics, 50*, 66-71.

Cobb, P., Yackel, E., & Wood, T. (1992). A constructivist alternative to the representational view of mind in mathematics education. *Journal for Research in Mathematics Education, 23*, 2-33.

Coe, K., Aiken, N. E., & Palmer, C. T. (2006). Once upon a time: Ancestors and the evolutionary significance of stories. *Anthropological Forum, 16*, 21-40.

Cohen-Bendahan, C. C. C., van de Beek, C., & Berenbaum, S. A. (2005). Prenatal sex hormone effects on child and adult sex-typed behavior: Methods and findings. *Neuroscience and Biobehavioral Reviews, 29*, 353-384.

Connor, C. M., Morrison, F. J., & Petrella, J. N. (2004). Effective reading comprehension instruction: Examining child X instruction interactions. *Journal of Educational Psychology, 96*, 682-698.

Conway, A. R. A., Cowan, N., Bunting, M. F., Therriault, D. J., & Minkoff, S. R. B. (2002). A latent variable analysis of working memory capacity, short-term memory capacity, processing speed, and general fluid intelligence. *Intelligence, 30*, 163-183.

Cosmides, L., & Tooby, J. (1994). Origins of domain specificity: The evolution of functional organization. In L. A. Hirschfeld & S. A. Gelman (Eds.), *Mapping the mind: Domain specificity in cognition and culture* (pp. 85-116). New York: Cambridge University Press.

Cowan, N. (1995). *Attention and memory: An integrated framework*. New York: Oxford University Press.

Craggs, J. G., Sanchez, J., Kibby, M. Y., Gilger, J. W., & Hynd, G. W. (2006). Brain morphology and neuropsychological profiles in a family displaying dyslexia and superior nonverbal intelligence. *Cortex, 42*, 1107-1118.

Csikszentmihalyi, M., & Hunter, J. (2003). Happiness in everyday life: The uses of experience sampling. *Journal of Happiness Studies, 4*, 185-199.

Csikszentmihalyi, M., & Larson, R. (1987). Validity and reliability of the experience-sampling method. *Journal of Nervous and Mental Disease, 175*, 526-536.

Daly, M., & Wilson, M. (1983). *Sex, evolution and behavior* (2nd ed.). Boston: Willard Grant.

Damasio, A. R. (1989). Time-locked multiregional retroactivation: A systems-level proposal for the neural substrates of recall and recognition. *Cognition, 33*, 25-62.

Damasio, A. (2003). *Looking for Spinoza: Joy, sorrow, and the feeling brain*. Orlando, FL: Harcourt.

Darwin, C. (1846). *Journal of researches into the geology and natural history of the various countries visited by H. M. S. Beagle*. New York: Harper & Brothers.

Darwin, C. (1859). *The origin of species by means of natural selection*. London: John Murray.

Darwin, C., & Wallace, A. (1858). On the tendency of species to form varieties, and on the perpetuation of varieties and species by natural means of selection. *Journal of the Linnean Society of London, Zoology, 3*, 45-62.

Darwin, F. (Ed.). (2000). *The autobiography of Charles Darwin*. Amherst, NY: Prometheus Books. (Original work published 1893)

Davis, J. N., & Todd, P. M. (1999). Parental investment by simple decision rules. In G. Gigerenzer, P. M. Todd, & the ABC Research Group (Eds.), *Simple heuristics that make us smart* (pp. 309-324). New York: Oxford University Press.

Dean, C., Leakey, M. G., Reid, D., Schrenk, F., Schwartz, G. T., Stringer, C., et al. (2001, December 6). Growth processes in teeth distinguish modern humans from *Homo erectus* and earlier hominins. *Nature, 414*, 628-631.

Deary, I. J. (2000). *Looking down on human intelligence: From psychophysics to the brain*. Oxford, United Kingdom: Oxford University Press.

Deary, I. J., & Stough, C. (1996). Intelligence and inspection time: Achievements, prospects, and problems. *American Psychologist, 51*, 599-608.

Deecke, V. B., Slater, P. J. B., & Ford, J. K. B. (2002, November 14). Selective habituation shapes acoustic predator recognition in harbour seals. *Nature, 420*, 171-173.

Dehaene, S., & Naccache, L. (2001). Towards a cognitive neuroscience of consciousness: Basic evidence and a workspace framework. *Cognition, 79*, 1-37.

Dehaene, S., Izard, V., Pica, P., & Spelke, E. (2006, January 20). Core knowledge of geometry in an Amazonian indigene group. *Science, 311*, 381-384.

Dehaene, S., Spelke, E., Pinel, P., Stanescu, R., & Tsivkin, S. (1999, May 7). Sources of mathematical thinking: Behavioral and brain-imaging evidence. *Science, 284*, 970-974.

DeLoache, J. S., Kolstad, D. V., & Anderson, K. N. (1991). Physical similarity and young children's understanding of scale models. *Child Development, 62*, 111-126.

Desmond, A., & Moore, J. (1994). *Darwin: Life of a tormented evolutionist*. New York: Norton.

Dweck, C. S., & Leggett, E. L. (1988). A social–cognitive approach to motivation and personality. *Psychological Review, 95*, 256-273.

de Winter, W., & Oxnard, C. E. (2001, February 8). Evolutionary radiations and convergences in the structural organization of mammalian brains. *Nature, 409*, 710-714.

Diener, E., & Diener, C. (1996). Most people are happy. *Psychological Science, 7*, 181-185.

Diener, E., & Seligman, E. P. (2002). Very happy people. *Psychological Science, 13*, 81-84.

Downing, P. E., Jiang, Y., Shuman, M., & Kanwisher, N. (2001, September 28). A cortical area selective for visual processing of the human body. *Science, 293*, 2470-2473.

Drigotas, S. M. (2002). The Michelangelo phenomenon and personal well-being. *Journal of Personality, 70*, 59-77.

Duckworth, A. L., & Seligman, M. E. P. (2005). Self-discipline outdoes IQ in predicting academic performance of adolescents. *Psychological Science, 16*, 939-944.

Dunbar, K., & Fugelsang, J. (2005). Scientific thinking and reasoning. In K. J. Holyoak & R. G. Morrison (Eds.), *The Cambridge handbook of thinking and reasoning* (pp. 705-725). New York: Cambridge University Press.

Dunbar, K. N., Fugelsang, J. A., & Stein, C. (in press). Do naïve theories ever go away? Using brain and behavior to understand changes in concepts. In P. Shah & M. Lovett (Eds.), *Thinking about data: 33rd Carnegie symposium on cognition*. Hillsdale, NJ: Erlbaum.

Duncan, J. (2001). An adaptive coding model of neural function in prefrontal cortex. *Nature Reviews: Neuroscience, 2*, 820-829.

Duncan, J., & Owen, A. M. (2000). Common regions of the human frontal lobe recruited by diverse cognitive demands. *Trends in Neurosciences, 23*, 475-483.

Duncan, J., Rüdiger, J. S., Kolodny, J., Bor, D., Herzog, H., Ahmed, A., et al. (2000, July 21). A neural basis for general intelligence. *Science, 289*, 457-460.

Eccles, J., Wigfield, A., Harold, R. D., & Blumenfeld, P. (1993). Age and gender differences in children's self- and task perceptions during elementary school. *Child Development, 64*, 830-847.

Eccles, J. S., Wigfield, A., & Schiefele, U. (1998). Motivation to succeed. In N. Eisenberg (Vol. Ed.), *Social, emotional, and personality development, Vol 3* (pp. 1017-1095). W. Damon (Gen. Ed.), *Handbook of child psychology* (5th ed.). New York: John Wiley & Sons.

Egan, K. (2002). *Getting it wrong from the beginning: Our progressive inheritance from Herbert Spencer, John, Dewey, and Jean Piaget*. New Haven, CT: Yale University Press.

Elman, J. L., Bates, E. A., Johnson, M. H., Karmiloff-Smith, A., Parisi, D., & Plunkett, K. (1996). *Rethinking innateness: A connectionist perspective on development*. Cambridge, MA: Bradford Books/MIT Press.

Embretson, S. E. (1995). The role of working memory capacity and general control processes in intelligence. *Intelligence, 20*, 169-189.

Engle, R. W. (2002). Working memory capacity as executive attention. *Current Directions in Psychological Science, 11*, 19-23.

Engle, R. W., Conway, A. R. A., Tuholski, S. W., & Shisler, R. J. (1995). A resource account of inhibition. *Psychological Science, 6*, 122-125.

Engle, R. W., Tuholski, S. W., Laughlin, J. E., & Conway, A. R. A. (1999). Working memory, short-term memory, and general fluid intelligence: A latent-variable approach. *Journal of Experimental Psychology: General, 128*, 309-331.

Ericsson, K. A., Krampe, R. T., & Tesch-Römer, C. (1993). The role of deliberate practice in the acquisition of expert performance. *Psychological Review, 100*, 363-406.

Esposito, G., Kirkby, B. S., van Horn, J. D., Ellmore, T. M., & Berman, K. F. (1999). Context-dependent, neural system-specific neurophysiological concomitants of ageing: Mapping PET correlates during cognitive activation. *Brain, 122,* 963-979.

Euclid (1956). *The thirteen books of the elements* (Vol. 1, T. L. Heath, Trans.). New York: Dover. (Original published circa 300 BC)

Evans, J. St. B. T. (2002). Logic and human reasoning: An assessment of the deduction paradigm. *Psychological Bulletin, 128,* 978-996.

Fabes, R. A., Martin, C. L., Hanish, L. D., Anders, M. C., & Madden-Derdich, D. A. (2003). Early school competence: The roles of sex-segregated play and effortful control. *Developmental Psychology, 39,* 848-858.

Finlay, B. L., Darlington, R. B., & Nicastro, N. (2001). Developmental structure in brain evolution. *Behavioral and Brain Sciences, 24,* 263-308.

Fiske, S. T. (1993). Controlling other people: The impact of power on stereotyping. *American Psychologist, 48,* 621-628.

Fiske, S. T. (2002). What we know now about bias and intergroup conflict, the problem of the century. *Current Directions in Psychological Science, 11,* 123-128.

Fiske, S. T., & Taylor, S. E. (1991). *Social cognition* (2nd ed.). New York: McGraw-Hill.

Frängsmyr, T. (Ed.) (1983). *Linnaeus: The man and his work.* Berkeley, CA: University of California Press.

Freedman, D. G. (1974). *Human infancy: An evolutionary perspective.* New York: John Wiley & Sons.

Flinn, M. V. (1997). Culture and the evolution of social learning. *Evolution and Human Behavior, 18,* 23-67.

Flinn, M. V., Geary, D. C., & Ward, C. V. (2005). Ecological dominance, social competition, and coalitionary arms races: Why humans evolved extraordinary intelligence. *Evolution and Human Behavior, 26,* 10-46.

Fry, A. F., & Hale, S. (1996). Processing speed, working memory, and fluid intelligence: Evidence for a developmental cascade. *Psychological Science, 7,* 237-241.

Fugelsang, J. A., & Dunbar, K. N. (2005). Brain-based mechanisms underlying complex causal thinking. *Neuropsychologia, 43,* 1204-1213.

Fuson, K. C., & Kwon, Y. (1992). Korean children's understanding of multidigit addition and subtraction. *Child Development, 63,* 491-506.

Gagné, F., & St Père, F. (2003). When IQ is controlled, does motivation still predict achievement? *Intelligence, 30,* 71-100.

Gallistel, C. R. (1990). *The organization of learning.* Cambridge, MA: MIT Press/Bradford Books.

Gallistel, C. R. (2000). The replacement of general-purpose learning models with adaptively specialized learning modules. In M. S. Gazzaniga (editor-in-chief.), *The new cognitive neurosciences* (2nd ed.) (pp. 1179-1191). Cambridge, MA: Bradford Books/MIT Press.

Gardner, H. (1983). *Frames of mind: The theory of multiple intelligences.* New York: Basic Books.

Garlick, D. (2002). Understanding the nature of the general factor of intelligence: The role of individual differences in neural plasticity as an explanatory mechanism. *Psychological Review, 109*, 116-136.

Geary, D. C. (1994). *Children's mathematical development: Research and practical applications.* Washington, DC: American Psychological Association.

Geary, D. C. (1995). Reflections of evolution and culture in children's cognition: Implications for mathematical development and instruction. *American Psychologist, 50*, 24-37.

Geary, D. C. (1998). *Male, female: The evolution of human sex differences.* Washington, DC: American Psychological Association.

Geary, D. C. (2002a). Principles of evolutionary educational psychology. *Learning and Individual Differences, 12*, 317-345.

Geary, D. C. (2002b). Sexual selection and sex differences in social cognition. In A. V. McGillicuddy-De Lisi & R. De Lisi (Eds.), *Biology, society, and behavior: The development of sex differences in cognition* (pp. 23-53). Greenwich, CT: Ablex/Greenwood.

Geary, D. C. (2004). Evolution and cognitive development. In R. Burgess & K. MacDonald (Eds.), *Evolutionary perspectives on human development* (pp. 99-133). Thousand Oaks, CA: Sage.

Geary, D. C. (2005). *The origin of mind: Evolution of brain, cognition, and general intelligence.* Washington, DC: American Psychological Association.

Geary, D. C. (2006). Development of mathematical understanding. In D. Kuhl & R. S. Siegler (Vol. Eds.), *Cognition, perception, and language, Vol 2* (pp. 777-810). W. Damon (Gen. Ed.), *Handbook of child psychology* (6th ed.). New York: John Wiley & Sons.

Geary, D. C. (2007). An evolutionary perspective on sex differences in mathematics and the sciences. In S. J. Ceci & W. Williams (Eds.), *Are sex differences in cognition responsible for the underrepresentation of women in scientific careers?* (pp. 173-188). Washington, DC: American Psychological Association.

Geary, D. C., & Bjorklund, D. F. (2000). Evolutionary developmental psychology. *Child Development, 71*, 57-65.

Geary, D. C., Byrd-Craven, J., Hoard, M. K., Vigil, J., & Numtee, C. (2003). Evolution and development of boys' social behavior. *Developmental Review, 23*, 444-470.

Geary, D. C., & Flinn, M. V. (2001). Evolution of human parental behavior and the human family. *Parenting: Science and Practice, 1*, 5-61.

Geary, D. C., & Huffman, K. J. (2002). Brain and cognitive evolution: Forms of modularity and functions of mind. *Psychological Bulletin, 128*, 667-698.

Gelman, R. (1990). First principles organize attention to and learning about relevant data: Number and animate-inanimate distinction as examples. *Cognitive Science, 14*, 79-106.

Gelman, R., & Williams, E. M. (1998). Enabling constraints for cognitive development and learning: Domain-specificity and epigenesis. In D. Kuhl & R. S. Siegler (Vol. Eds.), *Cognition, perception, and language, Vol 2* (pp. 575-630). W. Damon (Gen. Ed.), *Handbook of child psychology* (5th ed.). New York: John Wiley & Sons.

Gelman, S. A. (2003). *The essential child: Origins of essentialism in everyday thought.* New York: Oxford University Press.

Gevins, A., & Smith, M. E. (2000). Neurophysiological measures of working memory and individual differences in cognitive ability and cognitive style. *Cerebral Cortex, 10,* 829-839.

Gigerenzer, G., & Selten, R. (Eds.) (2001). *Bounded rationality: The adaptive toolbox.* Cambridge, MA: MIT Press.

Gigerenzer, G., Todd, P. M., & and ABC Research Group. (Eds.). (1999). *Simple heuristics that make us smart.* New York: Oxford University Press.

Gillihan, S. J., & Farah, M. J. (2005). Is self special? A critical review of evidence from experimental psychology and cognitive neuroscience. *Psychological Bulletin, 131,* 76-97.

Goel, V., & Dolan, R. J. (2000). Anatomical segregation of component processes in an inductive inference task. *Journal of Cognitive Neuroscience, 12,* 110-119.

Goel, V., Gold, B., Kapur, S., & Houle, S. (1998). Neuroanatomical correlates of human reasoning. *Journal of Cognitive Neuroscience, 10,* 293-302.

Goel, V., Makale, M., & Grafman, J. (2004). The hippocampal system mediates logical reasoning about familiar spatial environments. *Journal of Cognitive Neuroscience, 16,* 654-664.

Gohm, C. L., Humphreys, L. G., & Yao, G. (1998). Underachievement among spatially gifted students. *American Educational Research Journal, 35,* 515-531.

Gottfredson, G. D., Jones, E. M., & Holland, J. L. (1993). Personality and vocational interests: The relation of Holland's six interest dimensions to five robust dimensions of personality. *Journal of Counseling Psychology, 40,* 518-524.

Gottfredson, L. (1997). Why g matters: The complexity of everyday life. *Intelligence, 24,* 79-132.

Gottfredson, L. S. (2004). Intelligence: Is it the epidemiologists' elusive "fundamental cause" of social class inequalities in health? *Journal of Personality and Social Psychology, 86,* 174-199.

Golombok, S., & Rust, J. (1993). The pre-school activities inventory: A standardized assessment of gender role in children. *Psychological Assessment, 5,* 131-136.

Gosling, S. D. (2001). From mice to men: What can we learn about personality from animal research? *Psychological Bulletin, 127,* 45-86.

Gowlett, J. A. J. (1992). Tools—The Paleolithic record. In S. Jones, R. Martin, & D. Pilbeam (Eds.), *The Cambridge encyclopedia of human evolution* (pp. 350-360). New York: Cambridge University Press.

Grant, H., & Dweck, C. S. (2003). Clarifying achievement goals and their impact. *Journal of Personality and Social Psychology, 85,* 541-553.

Gray, J. A. (1987). Perspectives on anxiety and impulsivity: A commentary. *Journal of Research in Personality, 21,* 493-509.

Gray, J. R., Chabris, C. F., & Braver, T. S. (2003). Neural mechanisms of general fluid intelligence. *Nature Neuroscience, 6,* 316-322.

Gredlein, J. M., & Bjorklund, D. F. (2005). Sex differences in young children's use of tools in a problem-solving task. *Human Nature, 16,* 211-232.

Greenough, W. T., Black, J. E., & Wallace, C. S. (1987). Experience and brain development. *Child Development, 58,* 539-559.

Grossman, E., Donnelly, M., Price, R., Pickens, D., Morgan, V., Neighbor, G., et al. (2000). Brain areas involved in perception of biological motion. *Journal of Cognitive Neuroscience, 12*, 711-720.

Hadamard, J. (1945). *The psychology of invention in the mathematical field*. New York: Dover.

Haier, R. J., Siegel, B. V., Jr., Nuechterlein, K. H., Hazlett, E., Wu, J. C., Paek, J., et al. (1988). Cortical glucose metabolic rate correlates of abstract reasoning and attention studied using positron emission tomography. *Intelligence, 12*, 199-217.

Haier, R. J., Jung, R. E., Yeo, R. A., Head, K., & Alkire, M. T. (2004). Structural brain variation and general intelligence. *NeuroImage, 23*, 425-433.

Haier, R. J., Siegel, B., Tang, C., Abel, L., & Buchsbaum, M. S. (1992). Intelligence and changes in regional cerebral glucose metabolic rate following learning. *Intelligence, 16*, 415-426.

Harmon, L. W., Hansen, J. -I. C., Borgen, F. H., & Hammer, A. L. (1994). *Strong interest inventory: Applications and technical guide*. Palo Alto, CA: Consulting Psychologists Press.

Harris, J. R. (1995). Where is the child's environment? A group socialization theory of development. *Psychological Review, 102*, 458-489.

Harter, S. (1998). The development of self representations. In N. Eisenberg (Vol. Ed.), *Social, emotional, and personality development, Vol. 3* (pp. 1017-1095). W. Damon (Gen. Ed.), *Handbook of child psychology* (5th ed.). New York: John Wiley & Sons.

Hauser, M. D., Chomsky, N., & Fitch, W. T. (2002, November 22). The faculty of language: What is it, who has it, and how did it evolve? *Science, 298*, 1569-1579.

Heckhausen, J., & Schulz, R. (1995). A life-span theory of control. *Psychological Review, 102*, 284-304.

Hed, H. M. E. (1987). Trends in opportunity for natural selection in the Swedish population during the period 1650-1980. *Human Biology, 59*, 785-797.

Hedges, L. V., & Nowell, A. (1995, July 7). Sex differences in mental scores, variability, and numbers of high-scoring individuals. *Science, 269*, 41-45.

Henrich, J., & McElreath, R. (2003). The evolution of cultural evolution. *Evolutionary Anthropology, 12*, 123-135.

Heyes, C. (2003). Four routes of cognitive evolution. *Psychological Review, 110*, 713-727.

Hindson, B., Byrne, B., Shankweiler, D., Fielding-Barnsley, R., Newman, C., & Hine, D. W. (2005). Assessment and early instruction of preschool children at risk for reading disability. *Journal of Educational Psychology, 97*, 687-704.

Hill, K., & Hurtado, A. M. (1996). *Ache life history: The ecology and demography of a foraging people*. New York: Aldine de Gruyter.

Hirsch, E. D., Jr. (1996). *The schools we need and why we don't have them*. New York: Doubleday.

Hirschfeld, L. A., & Gelman, S. A. (Eds.) (1994), *Mapping the mind: Domain specificity in cognition and culture*. New York: Cambridge University Press.

Holland, J. L. (1996). Exploring careers with typology: What we have learned and some new directions. *American Psychologist, 51*, 397-406.

Holyoak, K. J., & Thagard, P. (1997). The analogical mind. *American Psychologist, 52*, 35-44.

Horn, J. L. (1968). Organization of abilities and the development of intelligence. *Psychological Review, 75*, 242-259.

Horn, J. L., & Cattell, R. B. (1966). Refinement and test of the theory of fluid and crystallized general intelligence. *Journal of Educational Psychology, 57*, 253-270.

Horowitz, D. L. (2001). *The deadly ethnic riot.* Berkeley, CA: University of California Press.

Humphrey, N. K. (1976). The social function of intellect. In P. P. G. Bateson & R. A. Hinde (Eds.), *Growing points in ethology* (pp. 303-317). New York: Cambridge University Press.

Humphreys, L. G., Lubinski, D., & Yao, G. (1993). Utility of predicting group membership and the role of spatial visualization in becoming an engineer, physical scientist, or artist. *Journal of Applied Psychology, 78*, 250-261.

Hunt, E. (1978). Mechanics of verbal ability. *Psychological Review, 85*, 109-130.

Hunt, E., & Minstrell, J. (1994). A cognitive approach to the teaching of physics. In K. McGilly (Ed.), *Classroom lessons: Integrating cognitive theory and classroom practice* (pp. 51-74). Cambridge, MA: MIT Press.

Inhelder, B., & Piaget, J. (1958). *The growth of logical thinking from childhood to adolescence.* New York: Basic Books.

Irons, W. (1979). Cultural and biological success. In N. A. Chagnon & W. Irons (Eds.), *Natural selection and social behavior* (pp. 257-272). North Scituate, MA: Duxbury Press.

Jennings, K. D. (1975). People versus object orientation, social behavior, and intellectual abilities in preschool children. *Developmental Psychology, 11*, 511-519.

Jensen, A. R. (1982). Reaction time and psychometric g. In H. J. Eysenck (Ed.), *A model for intelligence* (pp. 93-132). New York: Springer-Verlag.

Jensen, A. R. (1992). The importance of intraindividual variation in reaction time. *Intelligence, 13*, 869-881.

Jensen, A. R. (1998). *The g factor: The science of mental ability.* Westport, CT: Praeger.

Jensen, A. R., & Munro, E. (1979). Reaction time, movement time, and intelligence. *Intelligence, 3*, 121-126.

Joffe, T. H. (1997). Social pressures have selected for an extended juvenile period in primates. *Journal of Human Evolution, 32*, 593-605.

Johnson-Laird, P. N. (1983). *Mental models.* Cambridge, England: Cambridge University Press.

Just, M. A., Carpenter, P. A., Keller, T. A., Eddy, W. F., & Thulborn, K. R. (1996, October 4). Brain activation modulated by sentence comprehension. *Science, 274*, 114-116.

Kagan, J. (1998). Biology and the child. In N. Eisenberg (Vol. Ed.), *Social, emotional, and personality development, Vol 3* (pp. 177-235). W. Damon (Gen. Ed.), *Handbook of child psychology* (5th ed.). New York: John Wiley & Sons.

Kahneman, D., & Tversky, A. (1982). The simulation heuristic. In D. Kahneman, P. Slovic, & A. Tversky (Eds.), *Judgment uncertainty: Heuristics and biases* (pp. 201-208). Cambridge, London: Cambridge University Press.

Kaiser, M. K., McCloskey, M., & Proffitt, D. R. (1986). Development of intuitive theories of motion: Curvilinear motion in the absence of external forces. *Developmental Psychology, 22*, 67-71.

Kalbleisch, M. L. (2004). Functional neural anatomy of talent. *The Anatomical Record, 277B*, 21-36.

Kane, M. J., & Engle, R. W. (2002). The role of prefrontal cortex in working-memory capacity, executive attention, and general fluid intelligence: An individual-differences perspective. *Psychonomic Bulletin & Review, 9*, 637-671.

Kaplan, H., Hill, K., Lancaster, J., & Hurtado, A. M. (2000). A theory of human life history evolution: Diet, intelligence, and longevity. *Evolutionary Anthropology, 9*, 156-185.

Kanwisher, N., McDermott, J., & Chun, M. M. (1997). The fusiform face area: A module in human extrastriate cortex specialized for face perception. *Journal of Neuroscience, 17*, 4302-4311.

Karmiloff-Smith, A. (1992). *Beyond modularity: A developmental perspective on cognitive science*. Cambridge, MA: Bradford Books/MIT Press.

Keeley, L. H. (1996). *War before civilization: The myth of the peaceful savage*. New York: Oxford University Press.

Keil, F. C. (1992). The origins of an autonomous biology. In M. R. Gunnar & M. Maratsos (Eds.), *Modularity and constraints in language and cognition: The Minnesota symposia on child psychology* (Vol. 25, pp. 103-137). Hillsdale, NJ: Erlbaum.

Keil, F. C., Levin, D. T., Richman, B. A., & Gutheil, G. (1999). Mechanism and explanation in the development of biological thought: The case of disease. In D. L. Medin & S. Atran (Eds.), *Folkbiology* (pp. 285-319). Cambridge, MA: MIT Press/Bradford Book.

Kerns, J. G., Cohen, J. D., MacDonald, A. W., III, Cho, R. Y., Stenger, V. A., & Carter, C. S. (2004, February 13). Anterior cingulate conflict monitoring and adjustments in control. *Science, 303*, 1023-1026.

Kisilevsky, B. S., Hains, S. M. J., Lee, K., Xie, X., Huang, H., Ye, H. H., et al. (2003). Effects of experience on fetal voice recognition. *Psychological Science, 14*, 220-224.

Klahr, D. (2000). *Exploring science: The cognition and development of discovery processes*. Cambridge, MA: MIT Press.

Klahr, D. (2005). Early science instruction: Addressing fundamental issues. *Psychological Science, 16*, 871-872.

Klahr, D., & Dunbar, K. (1988). Dual space search during scientific reasoning. *Cognitive Science, 12*, 1-48.

Klahr, D., & Nigam, M. (2004). The equivalence of learning paths in early science instruction: Effects of direct instruction and discovery learning. *Psychological Science, 15*, 661-667.

Klahr, D., & Simon, H. A. (1999). Studies of scientific discovery: Complementary approaches and convergent findings. *Psychological Bulletin, 125*, 524-543.

Koslowski, B. (1996). *Theory and evidence: The development of scientific reasoning*. Cambridge, MA: MIT Press.

Komarraju, M., & Karau, S. J. (2005). The relationship between the big five personality traits and academic motivation. *Personality and Individual Differences, 39*, 557-567.

Kuhl, P. K. (1994). Learning and representation in speech and language. *Current Opinion in Neurobiology, 4*, 812-822.

Kuhl, P. K., Andruski, J. E., Chistovich, I. A., Chistovich, L. A., Kozhevnikova, E. V., Ryskina, V. L., et al. (1997, August 1). Cross-language analysis of phonetic units in language addressed to infants. *Science, 277*, 684-686.

Kuhn, D. (1989). Children and adults as intuitive scientists. *Psychological Review, 96*, 674-689.

Kuhn, D. (2005). What needs to be mastered in mastery of scientific method? *Psychological Science, 16*, 873-874.

Kuhn, D., & Dean, D., Jr. (2005). Is developing scientific thinking all about learning to control variables? *Psychological Science, 16*, 866-870.

Kyllonen, P. C., & Christal, R. E. (1990). Reasoning ability is (Little more than) working-memory capacity?! *Intelligence, 14*, 389-433.

Larson, L. M., Rottinghaus, P. J., & Borgen, F. H. (2002). Meta-analyses of big six interests and big five personality factors. *Journal of Vocational Behavior, 61*, 217-239

Larson, R., & Asmussen, L. (1991). Anger, worry, and hurt in early adolescence: An enlarging world of negative emotions. In M. E. Colten & S. Gore (Eds.), *Adolescent stress: Causes and consequences* (pp. 21-41). New York: Aldine de Gruyter.

Larson, R., & Richards, M. (1998). Waiting for the weekend: Friday and Saturday night as the emotional climax of the week. *New Directions for Child and Adolescent Development, 82*, 37-51.

Lazarus, R. S. (1991). *Emotion and adaptation*. New York: Oxford University Press.

Legree, P. J. (1995). Evidence for an oblique social intelligence factor established with a Likert-based testing procedure. *Intelligence, 21*, 247-266.

Lenneberg, E. H. (1969, May 9). On explaining language. *Science, 164*, 635-643.

Lent, R. W., Brown, S. D., & Hackett, G. (1994). Toward a unifying social cognitive theory of career and academic interest, choice, and performance. *Journal of Vocational Behavior, 45*, 79-122.

Lever, J. (1978). Sex differences in the complexity of children's play and games. *American Sociological Review, 43*, 471-483.

Liu, F. -G. R., Miyamoto, M. M., Freire, N. P., Ong, P. Q., Tennant, M. R., Young, T. S., et al. (2001, March 2). Molecular and morphological supertrees for eutherian (placental) mammals. *Science, 291*, 1786-1789.

Loveless, T. (Ed.). (2001) *The great curriculum debate: How should we teach reading and math?* Washington, DC: Brookings Institute.

Lovett, M. W., Lacerenza, L., Borden, S. L., Frijters, J. C., Steinbach, K. A., & De Palma, M. (2000). Components of effective remediation for developmental reading disabilities: Combining phonological and strategy-based instruction to improve outcomes. *Journal of Educational Psychology, 92*, 263-283.

Lubinski, D. (2000). Scientific and social significance of assessing individual differences: "Sinking shafts at a few critical points." *Annual Review of Psychology, 51*, 405-444.

Lubinski, D. (2004). Introduction to the special section on cognitive abilities: 100 years after Spearman's (1904) "'general intelligence,' objectively determined and measured". *Journal of Personality and Social Psychology, 86*, 96-111.

Lubinski, D., & Benbow, C. P. (2000). States of excellence. *American Psychologist, 55*, 137-150.

Lubinski, D., & Humphreys, L. G. (1992). Some bodily and medical correlates of mathematical giftedness and commensurate levels of socioeconomic status. *Intelligence, 16*, 99-115.

Lutchmaya, S., & Baron-Cohen, S. (2002). Human sex differences in social and non-social looking preferences, at 12 months of age. *Infant Behavior & Development, 25*, 319-325.

Lyell, C. (1830). *Principles of geology: An attempt to explain the former changes of the earth's surface*. London. John Murray.

Lyell, C. (1839). *Elements of geology*. Philadelphia, PA: James Kay, Jun., and brother.

Lykken, D. T., Bouchard, T. J., Jr., McGue, M., & Tellegen, A. (1993). Heritability of interests: A twin study. *Journal of Applied Psychology, 78*, 649-661.

MacDonald, K. (1988). *Social and personality development: An evolutionary synthesis*. New York: Plenum.

MacDonald, K. (1992). Warmth as a developmental construct: An evolutionary analysis. *Child Development, 63*, 753-773.

Mackintosh, N. J., & Bennett, E. S. (2003). The fractionation of working memory maps onto different components of intelligence. *Intelligence, 31*, 519-531.

Malthus, T. R. (1798). *An essay on the principle of population as it affects the future improvement of society with remarks on the speculations of Mr. Godwin, M. Condorcet, and other writers*. London: Printed for J. Johnson, in St. Paul's church-yard.

Mann, V. A. (1984). Reading skill and language skill. *Developmental Review, 4*, 1-15.

Maynard Smith, J., & Price, G. R. (1973). The logic of animal conflict. *Nature, 246*, 15-18.

Mandler, J. M. (1992). How to build a baby: II. Conceptual primitives. *Psychological Review, 99*, 587-604.

Marcus, G. (2004). *The birth of the mind: How a tiny number of genes creates the complexities of human thought*. New York: Basic Books.

Markus, H. (1977). Self-schemata and processing information about the self. *Journal of Personality and Social Psychology, 35*, 63-78.

Martin, R. C. (2005). Components of short-term memory and their relation to language processing: Evidence from neuropsychology and neuroimaging. *Current Directions in Psychological Science, 14*, 204-208.

Matthews, M. H. (1992). *Making sense of place: Children's understanding of large-scale environments*. Savage, MD: Barnes & Noble Books.

Maynard Smith, J., & Price, G. R. (1973, November 2). The logic of animal conflict. *Nature, 246*, 15-18.

McCandliss, B. D., Posner, M. I., & Givón, T. (1997). Brain plasticity in learning visual words. *Cognitive Psychology, 33*, 88-110.

McCloskey, M. (1983). Intuitive physics. *Scientific American, 248*, 122-130.

McCloskey, M., Sokol, S. M., & Goodman, R. A. (1986). Cognitive processes in verbal-number production: Inferences from the performance of brain-damaged subjects. *Journal of Experimental Psychology: General, 115*, 307-330.

McDaniel, M. A. (2005). Big-brained people are smarter: A meta-analysis of the relationship between in vivo brain volume and intelligence. *Intelligence, 33,* 337-346.

McLellan, J. A., & Dewey, J. (1895). *The psychology of number and its applications to methods of teaching arithmetic.* New York: D. Appleton.

Meece, J. L., Anderman, E. M., & Anderman, L. H. (2006). Classroom goal structure, student motivation, and academic achievement. *Annual Review of Psychology, 57,* 487-503.

Miller, E. K., & Cohen, J. D. (2001). An integration of theory of prefrontal cortex function. *Annual Review of Neuroscience, 24,* 167-202.

Mithen, S. (1996). *The prehistory of the mind: The cognitive origins of art and science.* New York: Thames and Hudson.

Moats, L. C., & Foorman, R. B. (1997). Components of effective reading instruction. *Scientific Studies of Reading, 1,* 187-189.

Morrison, A. S., Kirshner, J., & Molho, A. (1977). Life cycle events in 15th century Florence: Records of the *Monte Delle Doti. American Journal of Epidemiology, 106,* 487-492.

Murdock, G. P. (1981). *Atlas of world cultures.* Pittsburgh, PA: University of Pittsburgh Press.

Murray, C. (2003). *Human accomplishment: The pursuit of excellence in the arts and sciences, 800 B.C. to 1950.* New York: HarperCollins.

Neubauer, A. C. (1997). The mental speed approach to the assessment of intelligence. In J. Kingma & W. Tomic (Eds.), *Advances in cognition and education: Reflections on the concept of intelligence* (pp. 149-173). Greenwich, CT: JAI Press.

Newell, A., & Simon, H. A. (1972). *Human problem solving.* Englewood Cliffs, NJ: Prentice-Hall.

Newton, I. (1995). *The principia* (A. Motte, Trans.). Amherst, NY: Prometheus Books. (Original work published in 1687).

Nicholls, J. G. (1984). Achievement motivation: Conceptions of ability, subjective experience, task choice, and performance. *Psychological Review, 91,* 328-346.

Öhman, A. (2002). Automaticity and the amygdala: Nonconscious responses to emotional faces. *Current Directions in Psychological Science, 11,* 62-66.

Ospovat, D. (1979). Darwin after Malthus. *Journal of the History of Biology, 12,* 211-230.

Ospovat, D. (1981). *The development of Darwin's theory: Natural history, natural theology, and natural selection, 1838-1859.* Cambridge, United Kingdom: Cambridge University Press.

Owen, R. (1860). Darwin on the origin of species. *Edinburgh Review, 3,* 487-532.

Ozer, D. J., & Benet-Martínez, V. (2006). Personality and the prediction of consequential outcomes. *Annual Review of Psychology, 57,* 401-421.

Pascalis, O., de Haan, M., & Nelson, C. A. (2002, May 17). In face processing species-specific during the first year of life? *Science, 296,* 1321-1323.

Pascalis, O., Scott, L. S., Shannon, R. W., Nicholson, E., Coleman, M., & Nelson, C. A. (2005). Plasticity of face processing in infancy. *Proceedings of the National Academy of Sciences USA, 102,* 5297-5300.

Paterson, S. J., Brown, J. H., Gsödl, M. K., Johnson, M. H., & Karmiloff-Smith, A. (1999, December 17). Cognitive modularity and genetic disorders. *Science, 286*, 2355-2358.

Paulesu, E., Démonet, J. -F., Fazio, F., McCrory, E., Chanoine, V., Brunswick, N., et al. (2001, March 16). Dyslexia: Cultural diversity and biological unity. *Science, 291*, 2165-2167.

Pellis, S. M., & Iwaniuk, A. N. (2000). Adult-adult play in primates: Comparative analyses of its origin, distribution and evolution. *Ethology, 106*, 1083-1104.

Piaget, J., Inhelder, I., & Szeminska, A. (1960). *The child's conception of geometry.* London: Routledge and Kegan Paul.

Pinel, P., Piazza, D., Le Bihan, D., & Dehaene, S. (2004). Distributed and overlapping cerebral representations of number, size, and luminance during comparative judgments. *Neuron, 41*, 1-20.

Pinker, S. (1994). *The language instinct.* New York: William Morrow.

Pinker, S. (1997). *How the mind works.* New York: W. W. Norton & Co.

Pinker, S., & Jackendoff, R. (2005). The faculty of language: What's special about it? *Cognition, 95*, 201-236.

Plomin, R., DeFries, J. C., & Loehlin, J. C. (1977). Genotype-environment interaction and correlation in the analysis of human behavior. *Psychological Bulletin, 84*, 309-322.

Poldrack, R. A., Wagner, A. D., Prull, M. W., Desmond, J. E., Glover, G. H., & Gabrieli, J. D. E. (1999). Functional specialization for semantic and phonological processing in the left inferior prefrontal cortex. *NeuroImage, 10*, 15-35.

Posner, M. I. (1994). Attention: The mechanisms of consciousness. *Proceedings of the National Academy of Sciences USA, 91*, 7398-7403.

Potts, R. (1998). Variability selection in hominid evolution. *Evolutionary Anthropology, 7*, 81-96.

Prabhakaran, V., Smith, J. A. L., Desmond, J. E., Glover, G. H., & Gabrieli, J. D. E. (1997). Neural substrates of fluid reasoning: An fMRI study of neocortical activation during performance of the Raven's progressive matrices test. *Cognitive Psychology, 33*, 43-63.

Price, C. J. (2000). The anatomy of language: Contributions from functional neuroimaging. *Journal of Anatomy, 197*, 335-359.

Price, C. J., & Mechelli, A. (2005). Reading and reading disturbance. *Current Opinion in Neurobiology, 15*, 231-238.

Pugh, K. R., Shaywitz, B. A., Shaywitz, S. E., Shankweiler, D. P., Katz, L., Fletcher, J. M., et al. (1997). Predicting reading performance from neuroimaging profiles: The cerebral basis of phonological effects in printed word identification. *Journal of Experimental Psychology: Human Perception and Performance, 23*, 299-318.

Prediger, D. J. (1982). Dimensions underlying Holland's hexagon: Missing link between interests and occupations? *Journal of Vocational Behavior, 21*, 259-287.

Quartz, S. R., & Sejnowski, T. J. (1997). The neural basis of cognitive development: A constructivist manifesto. *Behavioral and Brain Sciences, 20*, 537-596.

Raby, P. (2001). *Alfred Russel Wallace: A life.* Princeton, NJ: Princeton University Press.

Raichle, M. E., Fiez, J. A., Videen, T. O., MacLeod, A. M. K., Pardo, J. V., & Petersen, S. E. (1994). Practice-related changes in human brain functional anatomy during non-motor learning. *Cerebral Cortex, 4*, 8-26.

Randahl, G. J. (1991). A typology analysis of the relations between measured vocational interests and abilities. *Journal of Vocational Behavior, 38*, 333-350.

Ranganath, C., & Rainer, G. (2003). Neural mechanisms for detecting and remembering novel events. *Nature Reviews: Neuroscience, 4*, 193-202.

Raz, N., Torres, I. J., Spencer, W. D., Millman, D., Baertschi, J. C., & Sarpel, G. (1993). Neuroanatomical correlates of age-sensitive and age-invariant cognitive abilities: An *In Vivo* MRI investigation. *Intelligence, 17*, 407-422.

Reyna, V. F. (2005). The No Child Left Behind Act and scientific research: A view from Washington, DC. In J. S. Carlson & J. R. Levin (Eds.), *The No Child Left Behind Act Legislation: Educational research and federal funding* (pp. 1-25). Greenwich, CT: Information Age Publishing.

Richerson, P. J., & Boyd, R. (2005). *Not by genes alone: How culture transformed human evolution*. Chicago: University of Chicago Press.

Roe, A. (1956). *Psychology of occupations*. New York: John Wiley & Sons.

Roe, A., & Klos, D. (1969). Occupational classification. *Counseling Psychologist, 1*, 84-92.

Rosenthal, R., Hall, J. A., DiMatteo, M. R., Rogers, P. L., & Archer, D. (1979). *Sensitivity to nonverbal communication: The PONS test*. Baltimore: The Johns Hopkins University Press.

Rousseau, J. -J. (1979). *Emile: Or, on education* (A. Bloom, Trans.). New York: Basic Books. (Original work published 1762).

Rozin, P. (1976). The evolution of intelligence and access to the cognitive unconscious. In J. M. Sprague & A. N. Epstein (eds.), *Progress in psychobiology and physiological psychology* (Vol. 6, pp. 245-280). New York: Academic Press.

Rushton, J. P., & Ankney, C. D. (1996). Brain size and cognitive ability: Correlations with age, sex, social class, and race. *Psychonomic Bulletin & Review, 3*, 21-36.

Scarr, S. (1992). Developmental theories of the 1990s: Developmental and individual differences. *Child Development, 63*, 1-19.

Scarr, S. (1993). Biological and cultural diversity: The legacy of Darwin for development. *Child Development, 64*, 1333-1353.

Scarr, S. (1996). How people make their own environments: Implications for parents and policy makers. *Psychology, Public Policy, and Law, 2*, 204-228.

Scarr, S., & McCartney, K. (1983). How people make their own environments: A theory of Genotype → environment effects. *Child Development, 54*, 424-435.

Schneider, D. J. (1973). Implicit personality theory: A review. *Psychological Bulletin, 79*, 294-309.

Schultz, H. (1991). Social differences in mortality in the eighteenth century: An analysis of Berlin church registers. *International Review of Social History, 36*, 232-248.

Schyns, P. G., Bonnar, L., & Gosselin, F. (2002). Show me the features! Understanding recognition from the use of visual information. *Psychological Science, 13*, 402-409.

Sereno, S. C., & Rayner, K. (2003). Measuring word recognition in reading: Eye movements and event-related potentials. *Trends in Cognitive Sciences, 7,* 489-493.

Shapiro, D. H., Jr., Schwartz, C. E., & Astin, J. A. (1996). Controlling ourselves, controlling our world: Psychology's role in understanding positive and negative consequences of seeking and gaining control. *American Psychologist, 51,* 1213-1230.

Shea, D. L., Lubinski, D., & Benbow, C. P. (2001). Importance of assessing spatial ability in intellectually talented young adolescents: A 20-year longitudinal study. *Journal of Educational Psychology, 93,* 604-614.

Sheeran, P., & Orbell, S. (2000). Self-schemas and the theory of planned behaviour. *European Journal of Social Psychology, 30,* 533-550.

Shepard, R. N. (1994). Perceptual-cognitive universals as reflections of the world. *Psychonomic Bulletin & Review, 1,* 2-28.

Shtulman, A. (2006). Qualitative differences between naïve and scientific theories of evolution. *Cognitive Psychology, 52,* 170-194.

Siegler, R. S., & Opfer, J. (2003). The development of numerical estimation: Evidence for multiple representations of numerical quantity. *Psychological Science, 14,* 237-243.

Simon, H. A. (1956). Rational choice and the structure of the environment. *Psychological Review, 63,* 129-138.

Simonton, D. K. (1999a). Talent and its development: An emergenic and epigenetic model. *Psychological Review, 106,* 435-457.

Simonton, D. K. (1999b). *Origins of genius: Darwinian perspective on creativity.* New York: Oxford University Press.

Simonton, D. K. (2003). Scientific creativity as constrained stochastic behavior: The integration of product, person, and process perspectives. *Psychological Bulletin, 129,* 475-494.

Simonton, D. K. (2004). *Creativity in science: Chance, logic, genius, and zeitgeist.* Cambridge, England: Cambridge University Press

Simos, P. G., Fletcher, J. M., Francis, D. J., Castillo, E. M., Pataraia, E., & Denton, C. (2005). Early development of neurophysiological processes involved in normal reading and reading disability: A magnetic source imaging study. *Neuropsychology, 19,* 787-798.

Slaughter, V., Stone, V. E., & Reed, C. (2004). Perception of faces and bodies. *Current Directions in Psychological Science, 13,* 219-223.

Smith, P. L., & Fouad, N. A. (1999). Subject-matter specificity of self-efficacy, outcome expectancies, interests, and goals: Implications for the social–cognitive model. *Journal of Counseling Psychology, 46,* 461-471.

Spearman, C. (1904). General intelligence, objectively determined and measured. *American Journal of Psychology, 15,* 201-293.

Spelke, E. S. (2000). Core knowledge. *American Psychologist, 55,* 1233-1243.

Sperber, D. (1994). The modularity of thought and the epidemiology of representations. In L. A. Hirschfeld & S. A. Gelman (Eds.), *Mapping the mind: Domain specificity in cognition and culture* (pp. 39-67). New York: Cambridge University Press.

Sporns, O., Tononi, G., & Edelman, G. M. (2000). Connectivity and complexity: The relationship between neuroanatomy and brain dynamics. *Neural Networks, 13,* 909-922.

Stadler, M. A., & Frensch, P. A. (Eds.) (1997). *Handbook of implicit learning.* Thousand Oaks, CA: Sage.

Stanovich, K. E. (1999). *Who is rational? Studies of individual differences in reasoning.* Mahwah, NJ: Erlbaum.

Stanovich, K. E., & West, R. F. (2000). Individual differences in reasoning: Implications for the rationality debate? *Behavioral and Brain Sciences, 23,* 645-726.

Stavy, R., Goel, V., Critchley, H., & Dolan, R. (2006). Intuitive interference in quantitative reasoning. *Brain Research, 1073/1074,* 383-388.

Stephan, K. E., Marshall, J. C., Friston, K. J., Rowe, J. B., Ritzl, A., Zilles, K., et al. (2003, July 18). Lateralized cognitive processes and lateralized task control in the human brain. *Science, 301,* 384-386.

Stephan, W. G. (1985). Intergroup relations. In G. Lindzey & E. Aronson (Eds.), *Handbook of social psychology: Vol II. Special fields and applications* (pp. 599-658). New York: Random House.

Sternberg, R. J. (Ed.). (1999). *Handbook of creativity.* Cambridge, United Kingdom: Cambridge University Press.

Sternberg, R. J. (2000, July 21). The holey grail of general intelligence. *Science, 289,* 399-401.

Stevens, R. J., Slavin, R. E., & Farnish, A. M. (1991). The effects of cooperative learning and direct instruction in reading comprehension strategies on mean idea identification. *Journal of Educational Psychology, 83,* 8-16.

Stevenson, H. W., & Stigler, J. W. (1992). *The learning gap: Why our schools are failing and what we can learn from Japanese and Chinese education.* New York: Summit Books.

Stiles, J. (2000). Neural plasticity and cognitive development. *Developmental Neuropsychology, 18,* 237-272.

Strauss, S. (1998). Cognitive development and science education: Toward a middle level model. In I. E. Sigel & A. Renninger (Vol. Eds), *Child psychology in practice, Vol 4* (pp. 357-399). W. Damon (Gen. Ed.), *Handbook of child psychology* (5th ed.). New York: John Wiley & Sons.

Strong, E. K., Jr. (1943). *Vocational interests of men and women.* Stanford, CA: Stanford University Press.

Temple, E. (2002). Brain mechanisms in normal and dyslexic readers. *Current Opinion in Neurobiology, 12,* 178-183.

Thompson, S. C., Armstrong, W., & Thomas, C. (1998). Illusions of control, underestimations, and accuracy: A control heuristic explanation. *Psychological Bulletin, 123,* 143-161.

Thorndike, E. L. (1922). *The psychology of arithmetic.* New York: MacMillan.

Thurstone, L. L. (1938). Primary mental abilities. *Psychometric Monographs* (No. 1).

Tracey, T. J. G., & Ward, C. C. (1998). The structure of children's interests and competence perceptions. *Journal of Counseling Psychology, 45,* 290-303.

Trivers, R. L. (1971). The evolution of reciprocal altruism. *Quarterly Review of Biology, 46,* 35-57.

Trivers, R. L. (1974). Parent-offspring conflict. *American Zoologist, 14,* 249-264.

Trivers, R. L. (2000). The elements of a scientific theory of self-deception. *Annals of the New York Academy of Sciences, 907*, 114-131.

Tulving, E. (2002). Episodic memory: From mind to brain. *Annual Review of Psychology, 53*, 1-25.

Turkeltaub, P. E., Eden, G. F., Jones, K. M., & Zeffiro, T. A. (2002). Meta-analysis of the functional neuroanatomy of single-word reading: Method and validation. *NeuroImage, 16*, 765-780.

Turkeltaub, P. E., Gareau, L., Flowers, D. L., Zeffiro, T. A., & Eden, G. F. (2003). Development of neural mechanisms for reading. *Nature Neuroscience, 6*, 767-773.

United Nations. (1985). *Socio-economic differentials in child mortality in developing countries*. New York: Author.

Vukovic, R. K., & Siegel, L. S. (2006). The double-deficit hypothesis: A comprehensive analysis of the evidence. *Journal of Learning Disabilities, 39*, 25-47.

Wai, J., Lubinski, D., & Benbow, C. P. (2005). Creativity and occupational accomplishments among intellectually precocious youths: An age 13 to age 33 longitudinal study. *Journal of Educational Psychology, 97*, 484-492.

Wagner, R. K., & Torgesen, J. K. (1987). The nature of phonological processing and its causal role in the acquisition of reading skills. *Psychological Bulletin, 101*, 192-212.

Wagner, R. K., Torgesen, J. K., & Rashotte, C. A. (1994). Development of reading-related phonological processing abilities: New evidence of bidirectional causality from a latent variable longitudinal study. *Developmental Psychology, 30*, 73-87.

Walberg, H. J. (1984). Improving the productivity of America's schools. *Educational Leadership, 41*, 19-27.

Wallace, A. R. (1855). On the law which has regulated the introduction of new species. *Annals and Magazine of Natural History, 16*, 184-196.

Weiner, B. (1985). An attributional theory of achievement motivation and emotion. *Psychological Review, 92*, 548-573.

Weiner, B. (1990). History of motivational research in education. *Journal of Educational Psychology, 82*, 616-622.

Wellman, H. M., & Gelman, S. A. (1992). Cognitive development: Foundational theories of core domains. *Annual Review of Psychology, 43*, 337-375.

Whissell, C. (1996). Mate selection in popular women's fiction. *Human Nature, 7*, 427-447.

White, M. (1998). *Newton: The last sorcerer*. Reading, MA: Perseus Books.

Wickett, J. C., Vernon, P. A., & Lee, D. H. (2000). Relationships between factors of intelligence and brain volume. *Personality and Individual Differences, 29*, 1095-1122.

Wigfield, A., & Eccles, J. S. (2000). Expectancy-value theory of achievement motivation. *Contemporary Educational Psychology, 25*, 68-81.

Williams, W. M., Papierno, P. B., Makel, M. C., & Ceci, S. J. (2004). Thinking like a scientist about real-world problems: The Cornell institute for research on children science education program. *Applied Developmental Psychology, 25*, 107-126.

Winner, E. (2000). The origins and ends of giftedness. *American Psychologist, 55*, 159-169.

Witelson, S. F., Kigar, D. L., & Harvey, T. (1999). The exceptional brain of Albert Einstein. *Lancet, 353*, 2149-2153.

Zerjal, T., Xue, Y., Bertorelle, G., Wells, R. S., Bao, W., Zhu, S., et al. (2003). The genetic legacy of the Mongols. *American Journal of Human Genetics, 72*, 717-721.

Zimmerman, C. (2000). The development of scientific reasoning skills. *Developmental Review, 20*, 99-149.

Zimmerman, C. (2005). *The development of scientific reasoning skills: What psychologists contribute to an understanding of elementary science learning* (Report to the National Research Council's Board of Science Education, Consensus Study on *Learning Science, Kindergarten through Eighth Grade*). http://www7 .nationalacademies.org/bose/Corinne_Zimmerman_Final_Paper.pdf

CHAPTER 2

KNOWLEDGE, ABILITIES, AND WILL

Phillip L. Ackerman

Dr. Geary presents an impressive framework for the evolutionary aspects of abilities and their implications for education. While there is much positive to take from this work, there are a few major concerns about the basis for both the underlying theoretical and empirical justification of the framework, and there are some concerns about whether this framework provides any new insights into the content and conduct of the educational enterprise.

OVERINTERPRETATION OF THE IMPORTANCE OF Gf

Much of Dr. Geary's discussion about the nature of intelligence and its role in education appears to substantially overestimate the role of fluid intelligence (Gf) in both educational contexts and the everyday world. It is convenient for his arguments that there is a presumed basis for the evolutionary context for Gf. Also, it is certainly true that Gf is a major component of general intelligence. However, there is a great deal more to the construct of intelligence than is captured by Gf (or even by both Gf and

Educating the Evolved Mind: Conceptual Foundations for an
Evolutionary Educational Psychology, pp. 101–108

crystallized intelligence [Gc]). As noted by both Cattell and Horn (e.g., see Horn, 1989; Horn & Cattell, 1966) and by Carroll (1993), there are many different (though correlated) higher order factors of intelligence, including, for example, short term acquisition and retrieval, tertiary storage and retrieval, general quantitative ability, general visualization, and general auditory ability. A reduction of intelligence to just Gf and Gc misses a significant portion of the variance in general intelligence, and limits the degree to which it is possible to predict real-world behaviors, such as academic performance.

In addition, although it is true that measures of general intelligence provide "the best single predictor of grades in school and years of schooling completed" (Geary, this volume, p. 15), a great deal of variance is still left unaccounted for, and the proportion of variance explained in school grades decreases with increasing levels of schooling (from elementary to secondary and postsecondary education—see, for example, Anastasi (1976). Less than half of the variance in elementary school success is attributable to general intelligence, and this level of correlation is only attained when omnibus one-on-one tests of intelligence are used (such as the Wechsler Intelligence Scale for Children or the Stanford-Binet—Anastasi, 1976). It has been well-known since the early 1900s that the best measures of intelligence, in the context of predicting school success, are *not* measures of Gf (e.g., such as Raven's Progressive Matrices) but rather are measures of verbal comprehension and fluency (e.g., see Krueger & Spearman, 1907). Ability scales that are more highly associated with Gf than Gc tend to be somewhat more highly correlated with course grades in math and sciences, but are less highly correlated with courses that involve a significant amount of verbal content (e.g., see Himelstein, 1966).

What should we make of these findings? First, it is critical to keep in mind Ferguson's (1954, 1956) thesis that abilities, as expressed in behavior, are more about learning and transfer than they are about performance in the absence of learning (except for very young infants). That is, individuals do not present themselves at school or in the psychology lab devoid of knowledge and skills. Rather, we often attempt to strip our tasks of as much context as possible, so as to make the knowledge and skills of the individual largely irrelevant. However, in day-to-day cognitive activities in school, work, or home, recall or transfer are much more important influences on behavior than is Gf. Solution of real-world problems benefits to some degree from higher levels of Gf, but in the absence of prior knowledge and skills, the highest levels of Gf cannot usually provide the basis for an adequate real-time solution. With increasing age into early adulthood and beyond, it appears that Gf becomes less important in day-to-day cognitive life, except when the individual confronts a highly novel problem—that is, one that cannot be solved by extension of prior knowledge or by analogy.

Abilities and Skills. The relationship between abilities and individual differences during skill acquisition provides an excellent example of a limitation of Geary's arguments. Geary (this volume, p. 57) argues that Ackerman's (1988) theory describes three stages of "learning"—cognitive, perceptual speed, and psychomotor. This much is correct, but Geary goes on to say that "these different abilities are related to individual differences in academic and job-related performance.... With enough practice, the eventual result is the automatic implicit processing of task features and automatic behavioral responses to these features." The problem with this line of reasoning is that Ackerman's (1988) theory pertains *only* to tasks where "goal attainment is importantly dependent on motor behavior" and that "[t]ypes of tasks that fall under this rubric include operating simple machinery, aspects of driving a car, technical aspects of playing musical instruments, and so on. Excluded from this domain are a variety of *nonmotor* learned behaviors, such as chess mastery, physics problem solving, and analogical reasoning" (Ackerman, 1988, p. 288). Moreover, the tasks subsumed by the theory are limited to those where nearly all individuals can perform the task successfully, albeit slowly. The theory does not apply when the task is so difficult so as a significant portion of the sample cannot perform it correctly.

Thus, although there is a range of tasks that fall within the parameters of Ackerman's theory, there is a wide range of tasks that do not do so. Tasks that do not importantly depend on motor behavior do not typically show the kind of shift from general (and broad content abilities) to perceptual speed to psychomotor ability involvement. In fact, relatively little content of elementary to postsecondary school curricula depends importantly on motor behaviors. In addition, there are many tasks that are not within the capabilities of most of the population, in which case there is typically a much higher involvement of intellectual abilities, simply because the lower-ability individuals never master the task.

There is an important distinction between "closed" and "open-ended" tasks (e.g., see Ackerman & Lohman, 1990). The kinds of tasks that the Ackerman (1988) theory pertains to are closed-ended tasks. That is, there is a fixed set of stimuli and corresponding responses that define the task. Once an individual has acquired knowledge of these correspondences (e.g., through declarative knowledge), the individual can develop a highly learned set of conditioned responses (typically involving proceduralized knowledge), and then increasingly improve the speed and accuracy of responding to the task stimuli. This kind of learning is relatively easily achieved in the laboratory context, where the experimenter controls the entire task situation. It is achieved with some local success in the real world (such as learning where the controls are in the car an individual owns, or how to operate one's current cell-phone). However, in life more frequently than in the laboratory, things change. When they change, there is an increased requirement for both transfer of training and processing of new information. Processing of new information may require broad content abilities and Gf, but it usually also involves prior knowledge and skills in the context of transfer.

In many domains of education, most tasks are essentially "open-ended" rather than closed tasks. In math, for example, elementary arithmetic is made up of closed subtasks (of addition, subtraction, multiplication and division). However, once the student achieves a level of competence in each of these successive skill domains, he/she is presented with a new skill to learn. Although transfer-of-training is usually involved to a substantial degree, new learning takes place that cannot be achieved automatically or with perceptual-speed and psychomotor abilities, at least until the consistent relations between stimuli and responses are learned. Eventually (and this occurs relatively early for some students who do not adequately acquire the fundamental skills), the new task domains become sufficiently complex that they are not within the "zone of tolerable problematicity (e.g., see Snow, 1989), and some individuals simply quit the learning progression.

UNDERWEIGHTING OF Gc
(INCLUDING INTERESTS, PERSONALITY, ETC.)

There is little doubt that operationally, factors derived from measures that are traditionally associated with Gf and Gc tend to be moderately correlated (in the neighborhood of .4 to .6). Such correlations are likely to be confounded by the fact that marker tests for each factor have components that are more highly determined by the other factor. That is, there is no such thing as a factor-pure test (e.g., see Humphreys, 1962). However, while the nature of Gf remains relatively constant from late childhood to adulthood, the nature of Gc is much different, especially when one considers the difference between what Cattell called "historical Gc" and "present Gc" (see Cattell, 1971). Most traditional tests of Gc given to adults are similar in content to those presented to adolescents, even though the knowledge and skill repertoire of adults is often very different from that of adolescents. Traditional tests of Gc do not give adults credit for a substantial portion of the occupational and avocational knowledge and skills that they have acquired over their lifetime (e.g., see Ackerman, 2000). Indeed, few traditional Gc-type tests adequately sample knowledge that is not *common* to a dominant culture. As a result, the associations between abilities, personality, and motivational variables are relatively small (e.g., see Ackerman & Heggestad, 1997). The hypothesis that affective and conative traits do not matter much in the direction and level of ultimate educational attainment is really only tenable when one focuses on a very narrow sample of Gf and historical Gc measures. What individuals do with their intellectual resources of the course of adult development appears to have far less to do with their level of Gf than it does with a variety of other influences, most notably their interests and "will to learn" (e.g., see Covington's, 1998, recommendations for education that are predicated on a motivational framework).

Hayes (1962), in his examination of "genes, drives, and intellect" proposed that "The hereditary basis of intelligence consists of drives, rather than abilities as such." (p. 302). That is, like Ferguson (1956) and others (e.g., Harlow, 1953), Hayes argued that the pattern of knowledge, skills, and abilities that individuals acquire is determined to a large degree by their "tendencies to engage in certain kinds of intrinsically-motivated activities" (p. 203). Individuals with similar levels of Gf, therefore, may choose quite different patterns of activities that lead, for example, in one case to a high vocabulary, but in another case, to high levels of physical skills (Hayes, 1962). In this framework, it is individuals' choice of where to invest their effort and time during childhood and adolescence that determines their respective intellectual standing at adulthood. To some degree, this approach is consistent with the data on individual and group differences (e.g., gender, race/ethnicity) on the patterns of strengths and weaknesses in ability profiles (e.g., see Lesser, Fifer, & Clark, 1965). Whether or not society or individual educators can change the outcome of ability profiles is an open question, and one that may go to the essence of gender differences in science and math occupational achievement (e.g., see Ackerman, 2006).

WHAT DOES IT MEAN FOR EDUCATION?

Trying to come up with a rational policy for universal education is fundamentally a task that calls for satisficing different social and educational goals, in the context of real differences between students, in terms of preparation for schooling, social support, interests, and abilities. Tracking of students was once an approach supported by educators and scientists (for a review, see Slavin, 1990). In the context of larger social forces, mainstreaming became more or less official public policy during the 1980s. However, in recent years that has been pressure applied from various sources for increased differentiation in curricula, especially at the secondary school level, in the form of gifted and talented programs (e.g., Honors, Advanced Placement, International Baccalaureate, etc.). These programs have met with substantial amount of enthusiasm in some quarters, and resentment in other quarters. The struggle to find the best balance between "equality of instruction" and "equality of opportunity" is one that inevitably will shift back and forth into an uneasy equilibrium.

However, if we follow Hayes (1962), we would take note of the fact that individuals differ in both abilities and in interests. Some courses of instruction are deemed critical for every citizen who has the "ability to benefit" from instruction. To maximize the utility of education, it would appear that optional courses of study are best determined by an appropriate weighting of ability, interest, and personality characteristics of the individual that result in the optimization of success and satisfaction. Whether these assignments are optimized by organizational decisions, by individual student and parent decisions, or some combination is a question that is best addressed by empirical study.

Ultimately, the question of "what should each student be taught?" is one that requires a real-time answer for real students. Should every high-school student learn calculus? Advanced algebra? Geometry? What about art, music, and drama? Even though many topics (like the scientific reasoning and "core concepts" described by Geary) sound reasonable to a scholarly audience, universal education is somewhat of a zero-sum game. Is teaching scientific reasoning more important than learning how to complete an employment application form? Also, what looks to be an important content domain to the current generation may not be so important to future generations. A look at the content of knowledge tests used by Learned and Wood (1928) might give one pause to consider the state of the knowledge repertoire of today's high school seniors.

CONCLUSIONS

In the final analysis, Geary's framework offers an interesting perspective and recommendations for education. However, it is not clear whether these recommendations are equally well justified on the basis of other perspectives that do not require an evolutionary framework.

AUTHOR NOTES

Correspondence concerning this article should be addressed to Phillip L. Ackerman, School of Psychology, Georgia Institute of Technology, 654 Cherry Street, Mail Code 0170, Atlanta, GA 30332-0170 or e-mail phillip.ackerman@psych.gatech.edu.

REFERENCES

Ackerman, P. L. (1988). Determinants of individual differences during skill acquisition: Cognitive abilities and information processing. *Journal of Experimental Psychology: General, 117*, 288-318.

Ackerman, P. L. (2000). Domain-specific knowledge as the "dark matter" of adult intelligence: gf/gc, personality and interest correlates. *Journal of Gerontology: Psychological Sciences, 55B (2)*, P69-P84.

Ackerman, P. L. (2006). Cognitive sex differences and mathematics and science achievement. *American Psychologist, 61*, 722-723.

Ackerman, P. L., & Heggestad, E. D. (1997). Intelligence, personality, and interests: Evidence for overlapping traits. *Psychological Bulletin, 121*, 219-245.

Ackerman, P. L., & Lohman, D. F. (1990). *An investigation of the effect of practice on the validity of spatial tests*. (Final report to the Navy Personnel Research & Development Center, Contract #N66001-88-C-0291). San Diego, CA: Author.

Anastasi, A. (1976). *Psychological testing*. New York: Macmillan.

Carroll, J. B. (1993). *Human cognitive abilities: A survey of factor-analytic studies*. New York: Cambridge University Press.

Cattell, R. B. (1971). *Abilities: Their structure, growth and action*. Amsterdam: North-Holland.

Covington, M. V. (1998). *The will to learn*. New York: Cambridge University Press.

Ferguson, G. A. (1954). On learning and human ability. *Canadian Journal of Psychology, 8*, 95-112.

Ferguson, G. A. (1956). On transfer and the abilities of man. *Canadian Journal of Psychology, 10*, 121-131.

Harlow, H. F. (1953). Mice, monkeys, men, and motives. *Psychological Review, 60*, 23-32.

Hayes, K. J. (1962). Genes, drives, and intellect. *Psychological Reports, 10*, 299-342.

Himelstein, P. (1966). Research with the Stanford-Binet, Form L-M: The first five years. *Psychological Bulletin, 65*, 156-164.

Horn, J. L. (1989). Cognitive diversity: A framework of learning. In P. L. Ackerman, R. J. Sternberg, & R. Glaser (Eds.). *Learning and individual differences. Advances in theory and research* (pp. 61-116). New York: W. H. Freeman.

Horn, J. L., & Cattell, R. B. (1966a). Refinement and test of the theory of fluid and crystallized general intelligences. *Journal of Educational Psychology, 57*, 253-270.

Humphreys, L. G. (1962). The organization of human abilities. *American Psychologist, 25*, 313-323.

Lesser, G. S., Fifer, G., & Clark, D. H. (1965). Mental abilities of children from different social-class and cultural groups. *Monographs of the Society for Research in Child Development, 30* (Whole No. 102).

Krueger, F. & Spearman, C. (1907). Die Korrelation zwischen verschiedenen geistigen Leistungsfähigkeiten [The correlation between different mental efficiencies]. *Zeitschrift für Psychologie (Leipzig), 44*, 50-114.

Learned, W. S., & Wood, B. D. (1938). *The student and his knowledge*. New York: The Carnegie Foundation for the Advancement of Teaching.

Slavin, R. E. (1990). Achievement effects of ability grouping in secondary schools: A best-evidence synthesis. *Review of Educational Research, 60*, 471-499.

Snow, R. E. (1989). Aptitude-treatment interaction as a framework for research on individual differences in learning. In P. L. Ackerman, R. J. Sternberg, & R. Glaser (Eds.), *Learning and individual differences: Advances in theory and research* (pp. 13-59). New York: Freeman.

CHAPTER 3

INSTRUCTING EVOLVED MINDS

Pedagogically Primary Strategies for Promoting Biologically Secondary Learning

Daniel B. Berch

"Whether you love it or hate it, the field of evolutionary psychology ... seems to have little difficulty arousing people's passions" (Brase, 2002, p. 147). Consistent with this assertion, David Geary's groundbreaking essay on laying the conceptual foundations for an evolutionary educational psychology is likely to arouse the passions of some of the commentators, not to mention a fair proportion of its readers. To say that the ideas he presents here are provocative will no doubt prove to be an understatement. Yet as Geary notes in the preface to his recent book, *The origin of mind: Evolution of brain, cognition, and general intelligence,* "I have on occasion, been accused of choosing topics that will provoke and irritate, and I have to say that I wish that this were true. I have chosen these topics not to irritate and offend, but rather because they represent a good set of problems to attempt to solve." Indeed, the current paper not only treats topics that represent a good set of problems to solve, but also provides a

Educating the Evolved Mind: Conceptual Foundations for an Evolutionary Educational Psychology, pp. 109–118
Copyright © 2007 by Information Age Publishing
109

scholarly, theoretically cogent, and empirically grounded perspective on the need for formal schooling.

Although Geary underscores that this perspective is "not ready for direct translation into school curricula," he is nevertheless unequivocal about recommending what I refer to here as a "pedagogically primary" approach to fostering the learning of biologically secondary skills. Specifically, throughout numerous sections of his essay, Geary contends that the efficient acquisition of such skills is likely to be significantly dependent on "teacher- and curriculum-driven selection of content," as well as a form of instruction that he variously characterizes as "direct," "explicit," "formal," and "solid." He states this view succinctly as follows: "most children will not be sufficiently motivated nor cognitively able to learn all of secondary knowledge needed for functioning in modern societies without well organized, explicit and direct teacher instruction." As the success of any given curriculum (i.e., a course of study, a set of materials, and knowledge to be transmitted) is tightly linked to the nature of the instructional practices used to implement it, Geary's stance on this matter deserves careful scrutiny. This is the goal of the present commentary, in which I examine the nature of explicit instruction, explore the degree to which this class of pedagogical approaches is incompatible with discovery-oriented, child-centered techniques, and analyze whether social interactive methods such as cooperative learning are inconsistent with an evolutionary perspective on the acquisition of biologically secondary knowledge.

DECONSTRUCTING DIRECT INSTRUCTION

What precisely constitutes direct or explicit instruction? The prototype for this class of pedagogical approaches is a model originally developed by Siegfried Englemann and Wesley Becker in the 1960s, which provides the foundation for a series of commercially available programs currently marketed by SRA/McGraw-Hill under the label of Direct Instruction (DI). Briefly, among other features, DI is comprised of explicit and systematic instructional formats based on scripted lesson plans, flexible skill grouping of students, brisk pacing of instruction, sequencing of skills, teaching to mastery, recurrent assessment, error correction, and the use of positive reinforcement. According to Huitt, Monetti, & Hummel (in press), devotees of DI programs take great pains to differentiate these from *teacher-made* lessons based on more generic models of direct instruction (di), mainly because the former have undergone rigorous standardization and field testing.

More importantly for purposes of the present analysis, Hempenstall (2001, cited in Huitt et al., in press) maintains that generic models possess many of the same features as DI itself. On the face of it then, the essential features of explicit instructional approaches appear to be completely consistent with Geary's educational perspective. Nevertheless, what remains unclear is the extent to which, if any, methods that do not fall under the rubric of explicit instruction could still be useful for promoting the acquisition of biologically secondary knowledge. As it turns out, Geary is quite candid about what he alleges to be the inappropriateness of certain kinds of pedagogical methods for teaching secondary skills that he variously refers to as "discovery," "child-centered," and "problem-based." Coupled with his previously published criticisms of social-interactive, cultural, contextual and situative approaches to mathematics education (Geary, 1994, 1995), Geary seems to be arguing that the effectiveness of this entire collection of methods for enhancing secondary skills is weak at best. A similar conclusion was recently arrived at in a review article by Kirschner, Sweller, and Clark (2006), which is evident from their title per se: "Why minimal guidance during instruction does not work: An analysis of the failure of constructivist, discovery, problem-based, experiential, and inquiry-based teaching."

Such a conclusion begs the following questions: Are the specific pedagogical practices associated with this class of instructional approaches truly inconsistent with the principles underlying the use of direct or explicit methods? Are generic models of explicit instruction expansive enough to encompass the use of methods that initially might appear to be incompatible with these models? Is the seemingly endless controversy about direct versus child-centered instructional approaches at least in some measure attributable to how these are operationalized? Closer examination of Geary's essay reveals that even he admits that part of the problem underlying this debate may be associated with how these practices are defined. For example, in pointing out how Zimmerman's (2005) analysis of the development of scientific reasoning led her to conclude that this dispute is at least partially due to definitional factors, Geary notes that "direct instruction often includes a 'hands-on' component, and discovery is often guided (e.g., by prompts, questions) by teachers or experimenters." Interestingly, Klahr and Li (2005) arrive at a similar conclusion. In discussing the precise nature of the explicit training methods used in the Klahr and Nigam (2004) study (described in Geary's essay), they note that "by some definitions, we could classify the learning via explicit instruction script as 'guided' or 'scaffolded' discovery" (p. 228). So apparently, the distinctions between these two classes of instructional procedures are not as hard and fast as their proponents frequently claim.

If one accepts that the boundary between these two pedagogical categories is fuzzier than might otherwise have been assumed, it seems reasonable to ask whether any specific elements of child-centered approaches can truly be encompassed by models of explicit instruction. Indeed, according to Huitt et al. (in press) the generic form of direct instruction is comparatively eclectic in that it can readily incorporate features of other approaches, such as *cooperative learning*. This would constitute a rather surprising assertion in some quarters, as cooperative or group learning techniques seem to be virtually antithetical to well-organized, teacher-directed forms of instruction. Moreover, from Geary's perspective, the use of cooperative learning procedures in classroom contexts should have potentially little likelihood of overcoming the kinds of biologically primary folk knowledge that frequently leads students to experience difficulties in learning scientific concepts about the natural world. However, this does not have to be the case. For example, Brown, Collins, and Duguid (1989) note that working in groups can provide an efficient means for drawing out, confronting, and discussing common misconceptions that students harbor about the physical world! But how can this occur, if as Geary claims, children do not have the built-in motivational mechanisms necessary for driving child-centered learning of secondary skills?

CO-OPTING COOPERATIVE LEARNING
FOR THE TEACHING OF SECONDARY SKILLS

Geary cites research demonstrating that children and adolescents are much happier when socializing with their friends than while doing their homework, listening to lectures, or doing mathematics. So then why can't teachers try to co-opt this interest in socializing with peers by having students engage in cooperative problem-solving exercises? Admittedly, just putting them together in unstructured groups with no guidance or controls and letting them discuss whatever they want will no doubt yield little more than teasing, gossiping, and other assorted behaviors that are inconsistent with secondary learning. Fortunately, however, that is not the only alternative. Anderson, Reder, and Simon (2000) suggest that the effectiveness of the cooperative learning approach depends on the degree to which it is structured or scripted: "Cooperative learning needs to be structured with incentives (for children at least) that motivate cooperation and a sharing of the goal structure" (p. 12). Consistent with this view, Ladyshewsky (2006) argues that simply assigning learners to work together under the supervision of an instructor or even independently does not guarantee the success of this kind of experience. He claims that what is required is putting specific reward structures in place, as these are crucial for creating the desired cooperative behaviors. Moreover, he suggests that such a structure can be achieved when learners recognize that "the only way to achieve their personal goal is to ensure that the group achieves its goal" (p. 5). Finally, he points out that it is the formation of a cooperative reward structure by the instructor that regulates students' motivation to learn.

However, even with a cooperative reward structure in place, there is no guarantee that cooperative learning will be superior—much less comparable—to individual learning. Indeed, numerous factors can thwart the potential effectiveness of this approach. For example, in their extensive critique of situated cognition, Anderson et al. (2000) cite a 1994 National Research Council report on cooperative learning, which concluded that "a number of detrimental effects arising from cooperative learning have been identified—the "free rider," the "sucker," the "status differential," and "ganging up" effects" (p. 11). Likewise, Meegan and Berg (2002) point out that the verbalizations of group members can interfere with the thought processes of other group members or impede them from elaborating upon their own ideas. In addition, the attitudes of the group members regarding collaboration can influence the effectiveness of their collaboration as well as their willingness to engage with others in a problem-solving situation.

Assuming these potentially dampening effects on cooperative learning can be effectively controlled, at least under experimental conditions, how can one rigorously test whether the performance of a group in fact exceeds that of individuals? Laughlin, Hatch, Silver and Boh (2006) attempted to answer this question using a letters-to-numbers coding problem, which combines facets of mathematical and logical reasoning as well as hypothesis testing. However, rather than simply comparing a group's outcome with that of the average individual, these investigators used a more stringent test in which they examined multiple groups (n) of a given size (m) and an equivalent number of individuals (nm) (e.g., 40 groups of size 4 compared with 160 individuals), with subjects randomly assigned to these conditions. This approach permitted a comparison of the mean of the consensus responses for each replication of a given-sized group with the mean of the best individuals' responses, second best, third best, and so on, drawn from each of the replications (e.g., the mean consensus response of the 40 groups of size $m = 4$ compared with the mean of the 40 best individuals' responses, 40 second best, etc.). Laughlin et al. found that while groups of three, four, and five undergraduates did not differ from each other, they all performed better than an equivalent number of the best individuals (and all were better than groups of two). Of particular interest with respect to the present analysis is the suggestion of these researchers that letters-to-number problems would be useful for studying "group-to-individual transfer;" that is, whether effective group problem solving subsequently enhances individual problem solving.

Research of this type with schoolchildren using the comparatively strin-gent design of the Laughlin et al. study would not only provide a more rigorous test of hypotheses regarding the presumed advantages of coop-erative problem solving, but also would allow an assessment of the extent to which individual members can benefit by exposure to a group learning environment. Concomitantly, Dansereau, Johnson, and Druckman (1994) point out that while it is not surprising that performance of a cooperative group frequently exceeds that of individuals, one of the foremost criteria for judging the effectiveness of cooperative learning is whether subse-quent *individual* achievement by group members is enhanced. "In this regard, there are far fewer studies that have successfully demonstrated advantages for cooperative versus individual learning" (p. 95). These authors also suggest that individual achievement in cooperative learning situations can be improved through the use of "direct" methods, such as explicit, teacher-supplied, interaction scripts for orchestrating the coop-erative activities, training of vital peer interaction skills, and guidance and monitoring of the interactions.

DECOMPOSING DISTRIBUTED COGNITION

Given that putting students together in cooperative groups at least has the potential of contributing to improvements in learning, how can one characterize the kind of thinking that can emerge from these interac-tions? In other words, is there any evidence that such collaborative efforts yield a group-level or distributed form of cognition, and if so, how if at all can this perspective be integrated with the classic symbolic view that treats cognition as something that only occurs inside the heads of individuals?

To begin with, Geary treats the cognitive system as being comprised of covert representations within individual minds and the internal computa-tional processes that operate on these representations. This so-called "tra-ditional cognitive science" account of scientific thinking can be contrasted with what Nersessian (2005) refers to as the "sociocultural" position, which includes the following perspectives: situated cognition, distributed cognition, embedded cognition, and cognition in context, among others. Although there are certainly important differences among these, there are also many similarities. And it is their commonalities that are of primary interest for the present analysis. Basically, these perspectives all share the idea that a complete account of cognition and learning requires examina-tion of the social/environmental contexts in which thinking and learning frequently occur. Furthermore, they all assume that collaborative cogni-tion yields a product over and above what each individual may provide on his or her own. For example, as Keil (2003) describes it, "In distributed cognition, a group of individuals shares a task in ways suggesting that the group as a whole be considered a cognitive organism" (p. 371).

Some of the most intriguing findings from the study of distributed cognition emanate from investigations of the reasoning of scientists while they are actively engaged in their work. As Dunbar has noted, "One of the most significant changes in the structure of science over the past century has been a switch from science as an individual process, where one scientist conducts all the steps in a scientific project, to science as a group enterprise, where the reasoning and knowledge are distributed over many scientists (Dunbar, 2000, p. 55). By studying "in vivo" distributed reasoning during scientific laboratory meetings of molecular biologists and immunologists, Dunbar (1997, 2000) discovered that more than 50% of the reasoning that occurs during such meetings is distributed in nature (operationally defined as instances of reasoning in which more than one individual is involved). He also reports that distributed reasoning is equally likely to take place whether scientists are discussing methods, results, or theory, with most of this reasoning directed toward future research activities. Despite the apparent benefits of distributed reasoning exemplified by this line of work, several types of factors can detract from its effectiveness, similar to what I previously illustrated from the cooperative learning literature. For example, Dunbar and his colleagues were able to identify two circumstances in which distributed reasoning is ineffective: (1) when the laboratory members all come from a very similar background; and (2) when they are extremely diverse and possess differing and competing goals.

Finally, it is certainly important to understand how distributed reasoning may relate to or impact the internal cognitive processing as well as subsequent achievements of the individuals who comprise such groups. Keil (2003) highlights this issue by pointing out that under distributed reasoning conditions, it may prove difficult to know "who knows what." Thus he argues that rather than eliminating the need for depicting cognition in the minds of the individual group members, phenomena associated with distributed cognition actually underscore this need: "The 'epidemiology of mental representations' in a community poses strong demands on characterizing the domain specific cognitions of individuals and how those cognitions are causally related to their more public products" (p. 371). Similarly, in examining the shortcomings of social constructivist theories of learning, Waschescio (1998) points out that while the constructivist perspective places great emphasis on social interaction, it rejects the idea that the shared meanings constructed from classroom interactions are internalized by the individual members of the group. Consequently, he argues that there is a missing link between social and internal processes, which can only be explained by means of a psychological theory of learning and development.

CONCLUSION

In this commentary, I have examined some of the ways in which forms of pedagogy other than direct instruction as narrowly defined can potentially enhance biologically secondary learning. In other words, it appears that a rapprochement between the putatively extreme positions of explicit instruction and child-centered/situative approaches may ultimately prove feasible. Attempting to achieve such a goal is reminiscent of Allen Newell's classic book chapter titled "You can't play 20 questions with nature and win" (Newell, 1973). Essentially, Newell indicated his distress with the propensity of experimental psychologists to formulate dichotomous questions (e.g., "Is processing serial vs. parallel?" Is learning continuous or all-or-none? Is search exhaustive or self-terminating?), in that this strategy was not generating cumulative progress toward the development of a unified theory of information processing. He concluded that this binary approach to posing questions is a poor model for doing science. Consistent with developing a more unified approach, Nersessian (2005) has recently attempted to achieve a rapprochement between the traditional cognitive science and sociocultural accounts of scientific reasoning by positing an integrative approach. She argues that even if one begins with the view that cognition is distributed within a system, it is also important to understand the individual person's contribution (i.e., internal representations and processes) in the system. At the same time, she asserts that these representations and processes need to be viewed as "inherently integrated with the 'external' environment" (p. 51).

Analogously, perhaps continuing to ask "Which is more effective, explicit instruction or child-centered/discovery learning?" will impede the development of a truly comprehensive model of instruction. For example, on the face of it, one might argue that the Klahr and Nigam (2004) experiment described by Geary demonstrated unequivocally the superiority of explicit instruction over discovery learning—at least with respect to the acquisition of the Control of Variables Strategy (CVS). However, even Klahr himself takes a less sanguine view of this accomplishment: "From the studies reported here, we can say that our particular specification of learning via explicit instruction worked better than an extreme form of learning via discovery for learning CVS. We certainly do not know if our CVS instruction is the 'best way' to teach CVS, or if Direct Instruction is the best way to teach *all* process skills" (Klahr & Li, 2005). In sum, rather than continuing to try to demonstrate the generic superiority of one of these methods over the other in an *experimentum crucis*, it may ultimately prove more beneficial to examine the conditions under which specific types of instructional methods are most effective in promoting the acquisition of particular facets of secondary knowledge by children of varying ages and abilities.

AUTHOR NOTE

The assertions and opinions expressed here are those of the author and should not be taken as representing official policies of the National Institute of Child Health and Human Development, the National Institutes of Health, or the U.S. Department of Health and Human Services.

REFERENCES

Anderson, J. R., Reder, L. M., & Simon, H. A. (2000, Summer). Applications and misapplications of cognitive psychology to mathematics education. *Texas Educational Review.*

Brase, G. L. (2002). Review of *Conceptual challenges in evolutionary psychology: Innovative research strategies*. *Human Nature Review, 2*, 147-152.

Brown, J. S., Collins, A., & Duguid, P. (1989). Situated cognition and the culture of learning. *Educational Researcher, 18*(1), 32-42.

Dansereau, D., Johnson, D. W., & Druckman, D. (1994). Cooperative learning (pp. 83-111). In D. Druckman & R. A. Bjork (Eds.), *Learning, remembering, believing: Enhancing human performance*. Washington, DC: National Academy Press.

Dunbar, K. (1997). How scientists think: Online creativity and conceptual change in science. In T. B. Ward, S. M. Smith, & S. Vaid (Eds.), *Conceptual structures and processes: Emergence, discovery and Change* (pp. 461-493). Washington, DC: APA Press.

Dunbar, K. (2000). How scientists think in the real world: Implications for science education. *Journal of Applied Developmental Psychology, 21*, 49-58.

Geary, D. C. (1994). *Children's mathematical development: Research and practical applications*. Washington, DC: American Psychological Association.

Geary, D. C. (1995). Reflections of evolution and culture in children's cognition: Implications for mathematical development and instruction. *American Psychologist, 50*, 24-37.

Geary, D. C. (2005). *The origin of mind: Evolution of brain, cognition, and general intelligence*. Washington, DC: American Psychological Association.

Hempenstall, K. (2001, December 12). What's the difference between "direct instruction" and Direct Instruction? Message posted to Direct Instruction listserve, owner-di@lists.oregon.edu

Huitt, W. G., Monetti, D. M., & Hummel, J. H. (in press). Designing Direct Instruction. In C. Reigeluth & A. Carr-Chellman (Eds.), *Instructional-design theories and models: Volume III. Building a common knowledge base.* Mahwah, NJ: Erlbaum.

Keil, F. (2003). Folkscience: Course interpretations of a complex reality. *Trends in Cognitive Sciences, 7,* 368-73.

Kirschner, P. A., Sweller, J., & Clark, R. E. (2006). Why minimal guidance during instruction does not work: An analysis of the failure of constructivist, discovery, problem-based, experiential, and inquiry-based teaching. *Educational Psychologist, 41,* 75-86.

Klahr, D., & Li, J. (2005). Cognitive research and elementary science instruction: From the laboratory, to the classroom, and back. *Journal of Science Education and Technology, 14,* 217-238.

Ladyshewsky, R. K. (2006). Building cooperation in peer coaching relationships: Understanding the relationships between reward structure, learner preparedness, coaching skill, and learner engagement. *Physiotherapy, 92,* 4-10.

Laughlin, P. R., Hatch, E. C., Silver, J. S., & Boh, L. (2006). Groups perform better than the best individuals on letters-to-numbers problems: Effects of group size. *Journal of Personality and Social Psychology, 90,* 644-651.

Meegan, S. P., & Berg, C. A. (2002). Contexts, functions, forms, and processes of collaborative everyday problem solving in older adulthood. *International Journal of Behavioral Development, 26,* 6-15.

Nersessian, N. J. (2005). Interpreting scientific and engineering practices: Integrating the cognitive, social, and cultural dimensions. In M. E. Gorman, R. D. Tweney, D. C. Gooding, & A. Kincannon (Eds.), *Scientific and technological thinking* (pp. 17-56). Mahwah, NJ: Erlbaum.

Newell, A. (1973). You can't play 20 questions with nature and win: Projective comments on the papers of this symposium. In W. G. Chase (Ed.), *Visual information processing* (pp. 283-308). New York: Academic Press.

Waschescio, U. (1998). The missing link: Social and cultural aspects in social constructivist theories. In F. Seeger, J. Voigt, & Y. Waschescio (Eds.), *The culture of the mathematics classroom* (pp. 221-241). New York: Cambridge University Press.

Zimmerman, C. (2005). *The development of scientific reasoning skills: What psychologists contribute to an understanding of elementary science learning* (Report to the National Research Council's Board of Science Education, Consensus Study on *Learning Science, Kindergarten through Eighth Grade*). http://www7.nationalacademies.org/bose/Corinne_Zimmerman_Final_Paper.pdf

CHAPTER 4

THE MOST EDUCABLE
OF ANIMALS

David F. Bjorklund

There are many features that make humans different from other animals, but perhaps our most distinctive one is our ability to learn. We are the most educable of animals, and have been, I imagine, since the first members of the *Homo* genus roamed Africa. Humans are not the only behaviorally and cognitively plastic animal, of course, but we are better at learning "new things" and passing this knowledge on to others than any other animal, the consequence of a cognitive system that allows the explicit (i.e., self-aware) representation of information, which may be unique to *Homo sapiens*.

Learning "new" things—facts, procedures, and theories—is an everyday occurrence for our children, and surely was for our forechildren. In traditional societies, and certainly for all but the briefest of our species' existence, this learning occurred via "hands on" experience in the contexts in which the skill, once acquired, would be used (Rogoff, 1998; Rogoff, Mistry, Göncü, & Mosier, 1993). Language often accompanies such informal instruction, but children learn by watching and by doing, often incorporating aspects of adult work in their play (e.g., Bock & Johnson, 2005; Lancy, 1996). Children in contemporary societies con-

Educating the Evolved Mind: Conceptual Foundations for an
Evolutionary Educational Psychology, pp. 119–129
Copyright © 2007 by Information Age Publishing
All rights of reproduction in any form reserved.

tinue to do this, but modern culture has become increasingly complex, making it impossible for children to master all the skills "in context" they need in order to succeed.

As Geary makes clear, the requirement of out-of-context, or context-independent, learning makes formal schooling an evolutionarily novel and "unnatural" experience (Bjorklund & Bering, 2002). Children did not evolve to sit quietly at desks in age-segregated classrooms being instructed by unrelated and unfamiliar adults. Yet such procedures, to varying degrees, are necessary. They are necessary because the demands of modern culture require that children master basic technological skills, the most important of which are reading, writing, and mathematics, as well as knowledge in a broad realm of domains, including history, government, music, art, and the physical, natural, and behavioral sciences, among others. Not all children will master all topics of course, and one can still be a "success" in a strictly Darwinian sense by achieving only a moderate degree of literacy and numeracy. However, "success" in developed countries includes more than becoming a parent and grandparent (i.e., inclusive fitness), but attaining an economic level that permits enhanced creature comforts and a longer and healthier life. As Geary points out, this is also true at the societal level. Countries that fail to educate their children for success in an information-age society risk losing jobs to other nations with a better-educated and prepared populace (see Friedman, 2005). Given what is at stake, educating our children has never been so important and, because of our escalating ability to generate knowledge, it may never have been so complicated.

FOUNDATIONS OF CHILDREN'S LEARNING

Geary's proposal is that we can best educate children if we have a solid understanding of the evolved nature of their cognition. Natural selection has provided people with intellectual and motivational systems that permit them to acquire the necessary skills and knowledge of their culture and to pass some of that knowledge on to subsequent generations. By understanding children's inherent dispositions and motivations and how evolved cognitive abilities develop, we can better create curricula and educational systems to foster learning. Moreover, and perhaps somewhat ironically, some of our evolved cognitive and motivational biases may actually interfere with formal schooling and the learning of context-independent information. Having an understanding of both how to take advantage of evolved abilities and how to circumvent other evolved biases that may make some types of modern learning more difficult, is the task of the new field of evolutionary educational psychology.

This goal is a worthy one, but one that will not be achieved easily. First, Geary argues that placing the field of education on a more scientific foundation will reduce the conflict among competing educational approaches, and that "evolutionary developmental psychology and accompanying insights into children's cognitive development and motivational biases will provide the first level of this foundation" (p. 76). I am in full agreement with this sentiment, but I believe that we may be years away before such a foundation is agreed upon. Evolutionary approaches to psychology have gained in acceptance over the past 2 decades, and this includes developmental psychology, thanks in no small part to Geary's own efforts (e.g., Bjorklund & Pellegrini, 2002; Bugental, 2000; Ellis & Bjorklund, 2005; Geary, 1995, 1998; Geary & Bjorklund, 2000; MacDonald & Hershberger, 2005). However, evolutionary developmental psychologists are a minority in their discipline, and there are some who are openly hostile to such an approach, arguing that an evolutionary analysis of ontogeny as advocated by Geary (and myself) is wrongheaded (e.g., Lickliter & Honeycutt, 2003). One task of evolutionarily-oriented psychologists is to convince our colleagues that evolutionary psychology, especially when applied to ontogeny, does not represent a philosophically extreme position, but rather one that can be incorporated easily with mainstream issues in developmental and educational psychology.

Second, assuming that developmental and educational psychologists can agree on the evolutionarily developmental foundations of cognition and learning, this will in itself not bring an end to conflict. Although perhaps seeming so to an outsider, evolutionary psychology is not monolithic. This is also true for developmental psychologists who have embraced evolutionary theory, and it will be true of educational psychologists who adopt such an approach. Although Darwin's ideas of evolution by natural selection and the continuity of form and function from a common ancestor may be shared by all evolutionarily minded scientists, there can be considerable debate about the specifics of evolution, both among biologists concerned mainly with evolution of structure (e.g., Gould, 2002) and biologists and psychologists concerned mainly with the evolution of cognition and behavior (e.g., Tooby & Cosmides, 2005; West-Eberhart, 2003). Moreover, even if psychologists and educators are in basic agreement about the evolved foundations for education, there will be different emphases and opinions on how to best apply this enlightened perspective, as well as differences in what constitutes educational success. For instance, in the last pages of the monograph, Geary makes a proposal for paying special attention to the education of intellectually gifted children—that the best and the brightest should not be hampered by focusing on educational practices that benefit the masses. I agree with Geary on this, but others will not, and I can imagine other issues related to the

societal "purpose" of education on which he and I may disagree. Nonetheless, should the field of developmental or educational psychology be
fortunate enough to share a common belief on the foundational issues,
disagreements and conflicts should be more easily resolved, hopefully
through the evaluation of empirical research testing hypotheses derived
from evolutionary developmental theory.

THE ADAPTIVE NATURE OF COGNITIVE IMMATURITY AND EDUCATING YOUNG CHILDREN

One perspective from evolutionary developmental psychology that is per-
tinent to educational psychology, I believe, is the idea that aspects of children's immature cognition are sometimes adaptive—well-suited to the
niche of childhood in which they find themselves, even if, initially, they
make learning culturally important information or skills more difficult
(Bjorklund, 1997; Bjorklund & Green, 1992; Bjorklund & Pellegrini,
2002). In other words, some aspects of developmental immaturity are not
simply the inevitable byproduct of an extended juvenile period that must
be overcome so that children can acquire the important technological
skills that will determine their success or failure in the adult world; rather,
from an evolutionary developmental perspective, they represent naturally
selected, age-related, intuitive biases that serve to "prepare" children for
making sense of species-typical experiences at different times in ontogeny. Some aspects of immaturity may influence how children evaluate or
process information, such as a bias for relating new information to oneself
(e.g., Piaget & Inhelder, 1969) or processing literal versus "gist" aspects of
stimuli (e.g., Brainerd & Reyna, 1990), or for overestimating one's intellectual abilities and task performance (e.g., Stipek, 1984). Others may
affect children's interests or the contexts in which they prefer to engage,
such as a preference for rough-and-tumble play, especially for boys (Pellegrini & Smith, 1998), interest in caring for babies, especially for girls
(Maestripieri & Rooney, 2006), or an orientation toward dominance relations (Hawley, 1999). These biases may involve evolved mechanisms that
serve to adapt children to specific times in ontogeny, referred to as *ontogenetic adaptations* (Oppenheim, 1973), or they may serve instead (or more
likely in addition) to prepare children for life as adults, referred to as
deferred adaptations (Hernández Blasi & Bjorklund, 2003). These evolved
biases change over time, and educators must keep such developmental
differences in mind when creating curricula.

The use of direct instruction in young children is a case in point. For
example, Geary notes emphatically that: "*The gist is that the cognitive and
motivational complexities of the processes involved in the generation of secondary*

knowledge and the ever widening gap between this knowledge and folk knowledge leads me to conclude that most children will not be sufficiently motivated nor cognitively able to learn all of secondary knowledge needed for functioning in modern societies without well organized, explicit and direct teacher instruction" (p. 43, italics in the original). This is a warning to educators who insist that true learning is only achieved via a process of *discovery*, and who hold, much as Piaget (1972) did, that "less is more" when it comes to teacher-directed instruction. ("It is despite adult authority, and not because of it, that the child learns. And also it is to the extent that the intelligent teacher has known to efface him or herself, to become an equal and not a superior, to discuss and to examine, rather than to agree and constrain morally, that the traditional school has been able to render service" [Piaget, 1977, cited in Rogoff, 1998, p. 38]). I am in basic agreement with Geary on this point, although I fear that some educators will read this as meaning that nearly all instruction for children of any age should be teacher directed, and this is not a position that I believe is consistent with what we know about children's developing cognitive systems from an evolutionary perspective.

Particularly in the United States, there have been efforts to introduce formal education to the crib, and even the uterus, based on the seemingly remarkable perceptual and cognitive abilities of infants (see Spelke & Newport, 1998; Stone, Smith, & Murphy, 1973). Research has shown that newborns can learn to recognize stories their mothers had read during the last months of pregnancy (e.g., DeCasper & Spence, 1986); newborns can match facial expressions of adult models (e.g., Meltzoff & Moore, 1977); and infants within the first 6 months of life appear to have some quantitative abilities, such as recognizing the addition and subtraction of small quantities of objects (e.g., Wynn, 1992) or understanding many of the physical properties of objects (e.g., solidarity, continuity; e.g., Spelke & Newport, 1998). These are biologically primary abilities in the realms of folk psychology and folk physics, and although such abilities may one day serve as the basis for biologically secondary abilities, this does not mean that formal "instruction" should begin in the playpen, to say nothing of in the womb. Although these abilities may prepare infants for dealing with their social and physical worlds, they are not necessarily well-suited to serve as a basis for more formal instruction, at least not at this time in their lives.

Yet, parents are quick to buy books and gadgets designed to provide intellectual stimulation to infants, and even fetuses, believing that earlier is better. For example, Logan (1991) developed *BabyPlus*, a "fetal enrichment technology" that fits around a pregnant mother's belly and plays sounds to her fetus. The rationale for this is that prenatal brain stimulation can prevent the usual pattern of brain-cell death that occurs before birth, increasing the number of neurons and synapses a baby has when it first sees the world, setting the stage for better learning and greater intelligence. Yet, selective cell death during the prenatal and postnatal months is the species-typical pattern, and preventing such cell loss (if that is what *BabyPlus* would actually do) may have unintended consequences. According to neuroscientist Peter Huttenlocher (2002, p. 214): "One has to consider the possibility that very ambitious early enrichment and teaching programs may lead to crowding effects and to an early decrease in the size and number of brain regions that are largely unspecified and that may be necessary for creativity in the adolescent and adult." Similar arguments can be made for overly ambitious postnatal instruction. In fact, research evidence from a variety of species indicates that perceptual and learning experiences provided to young animals that exceed the species-normal range can produce maladaptive outcomes, including disruption of auditory attachment behaviors when quails are given visual experience before hatching (e.g., Lickliter, 1990) to slower rates of learning when infant rats (e.g., Rudy, Vogt, & Hyson, 1984), monkeys (e.g., Harlow, 1959), or humans (e.g., Papousek, 1977) are given learning experiences earlier than is typical (see Bjorklund, 1997; Bjorklund & Green, 1992 for more in depth discussion).

This theme of "earlier is not necessarily better" can be extended into the preschool years. Most children in the United States and Europe spend some time during these years in daycare, with varying degrees of educational enrichment. Programs in the United States have often emphasized formal instruction, preparing children for kindergarten and first grade. The argument is straightforward and logical: if education is the key to success in modern society, then beginning formal education early should provide children with an advantage. However, an alternative perspective, consistent, I believe, with what we know about children's developing cognition from an evolutionary perspective, is that the thinking of preschool children is, in many (but not all) ways, qualitatively different from that of older children, is well-suited to understanding their surroundings, and that learning is best achieved in more "playful" and "natural" settings (Bjorklund, 1997; Bjorklund & Green, 1992).

Most educators, psychologists, and social policymakers today recognize the need for daycare for preschool children and acknowledge that "quality daycare" is not only not harmful for children but can be intellectually beneficial (e.g., Lamb & Ahnert, 2006). Quality daycare often involves an educationally relevant curriculum, designed to provide young students with intellectually stimulating activities. The question then arises, if one is going to educate preschoolers, how does one do it? Should 3- and 4-year olds receive formal instruction in the important technological skills of reading and arithmetic, much as is provided for early school-age children (referred to as *direct-instructional programs*)? Or should the curriculum be geared to children's "natural" propensities (referred to as *developmentally appropriate programs*)? I do not believe that there is an obvious answer to this based on Geary's proposals. For example, one could argue that adults should take advantage of children's inherent motivation to acquire basic knowledge in the realms of folk psychology, biology, and physics, which could best be done in developmentally appropriate programs. The argument could also be made that children's intuitive notions in these areas interfere with learning of important technological skills, and formal instruction is required so as not to make subsequent learning even more difficult.

Research examining the effects of developmentally appropriate versus direct-instructional preschools programs has produced mixed results. Some studies report superior number and prereading skills at the end of the school year for children in developmentally appropriate programs (e.g., Stipek, Feiler, Blyer, Ryan, Milburn, & Salmon, 1998); others find better performance on some academic measures for children in direct-instructional programs (e.g., Stipek, Feiler, Daniels, & Milburn, 1995); and still others find no appreciable differences (e.g., Hirsh-Pasek, Hyson, & Rescorla, 1990). More studies have found long-term (1 year or longer) benefits associated with developmentally appropriate programs relative to direct-instructions programs (e.g., Burts et al., 1993; Marcon, 1999). For example, Marcon (1999) followed children for 6 years who had attended either a developmentally appropriate or direct-instructional preschool and reported that although there was no difference in academic performance between the two groups of children by the end of third grade, by the end of fourth grade children who had the developmentally appropriate preschool curriculum had higher grades than those who had attended the direct-instructional programs.

The difference between developmentally appropriate and direct-instructional programs is clearer when motivational and psychosocial factors are considered. Most studies have found that children attending developmentally appropriate programs experience less stress, like school better, are more creative, and have less test anxiety than children attending direct-instructional programs (Burts et al., 1993; Hirsh-Pasek et al., 1990; Schweinhart & Weikert, 1988; Stipek et al., 1995, 1998). For example, in a study by Stipek and her colleagues (1995), preschool and kindergarten children from a range of households attended either developmentally appropriate or direct-instructional programs. Although children who attended direct-instructional programs demonstrated greater knowledge of letters and reading achievement than children attending developmentally appropriate programs, no differences were found on knowledge of numbers, and children in the developmentally appropriate programs rated themselves as having greater intellectual abilities, were less dependent on adults for permission and approval, expressed greater pride in accomplishment, had higher expectations for success on school-like tasks, chose more challenging math problems to perform, and said they worried less about school than children in the direct-instructional programs. In other words, any academic benefits gained from a teacher-directed program had its costs in terms of motivation.

My conclusion from reviewing this admittedly limited literature is that, overall, preschool children who attend developmentally appropriate programs fare better than children who attend direct-instructional programs. I interpret this as being consistent with an evolutionary developmental perspective that emphasizes taking advantage of the intuitive learning biases of young children when constructing educational curricula. This is not an argument against direct instruction, some of which surely takes place in even the most "developmentally appropriate" of programs. Direct instruction is a crucial mechanism for transmitting cultural knowledge, and it seems obvious that it should be a key instrument in all teachers' toolkits. It is only when direct instruction replaces more child-centered learning for young children that problems potentially arise.

David Geary's call for an evolutionary educational psychology is timely and one I hope will be heard and heeded by a wide audience. His proposal to base education on a more serious, scientific basis is not new, of course, but one that has been made by most generations of educational psychologists. The novelty of Geary's approach is to base educational practices not only on science that examines proximal causes of behavior, but also on science that explores its distal causes. An evolutionary perspective on development and education, particularly when combined with traditional psychological investigations and advances in neuroscience, can provide insights that may revolutionize how culturally important information is transmitted across generations.

REFERENCES

Bjorklund, D. F. (1997). The role of immaturity in human development. *Psychological Bulletin, 122,* 153–169.

Bjorklund, D. F., & Bering, J. M. (2002). The evolved child: Applying evolutionary developmental psychology to modern schooling. *Learning and Individual Differences, 12,* 1-27.

Bjorklund, D. F., & Green, B. L. (1992). The adaptive nature of cognitive immaturity. *American Psychologist, 47,* 46–54.

Bjorklund, D. F., & Pellegrini, A. D. (2002). *The origins of human nature: Evolutionary developmental psychology.* Washington, DC: American Psychological Association.

Bock, J., & Johnston, S. E. (2004). Play and subsistence ecology among the Oka-vango Delta Peoples of Botswana. *Human Nature, 15*, 63-81.

Brainerd, C. J., & Reyna, V. F. (1990). Gist is the grist: Fuzzy-trace theory and the new intuitionism. *Developmental Review, 10*, 3–47.

Bugenthal, D. B. (2000). Acquisition of the algorithms of social life: A domain-based approach. *Psychological Bulletin, 126*, 187–219.

Burts, D. C., Hart, C. H., Charlesworth, R., DeWolf, D. M., Ray, J., Manuel, K., et al. (1993). Developmental appropriateness of kindergarten programs and academic outcomes in first grade. *Journal of Research in Childhood Education, 8*, 23-31.

DeCasper, A. J., & Spence, M. J. (1986). Prenatal maternal speech influences new-borns' perception of speech sounds. *Infant Behavior & Development, 9*, 133-150.

Ellis, B. J., & Bjorklund, D. F. (Eds.). (2005). *Origins of the social mind: Evolutionary psychology and child development.* New York: Guilford.

Friedman, T. L. (2005). *The world is flat: A brief history of the twenty-first century.* New York: Farrar, Straus and Giroux.

Geary, D. C. (1995). Reflections of evolution and culture in children's cognition: Implications for mathematical development and instruction. *American Psychologist, 50*, 24-37.

Geary, D. C. (1998) *Male, female: The evolution of human sex differences.* Washington, DC: American Psychological Association.

Geary, D. C., & Bjorklund, D. F. (2000). Evolutionary developmental psychology. *Child Development, 71*, 57–65.

Gould, S. J. (2002). *The structure of evolutionary theory.* Cambridge, MA: Harvard University Press.

Harlow, H. F. (1959). The development of learning in the Rhesus monkey. *American Scientist*, 459-479.

Hawley, P. A. (1999). The ontogenesis of social dominance: A strategy-based evo-lutionary perspective. *Developmental Review, 19*, 97-132.

Hernández Blasi, C., & Bjorklund, D. F. (2003). Evolutionary developmental psy-chology: A new tool for better understanding human ontogeny. *Human Devel-opment, 46*, 259-281.

Hirsh-Pasek, K., Hyson, M. C. & Rescorla,, L. (1990). Academic environments in preschool: Challenge or pressure? *Early Education and Development, 1*, 401–423.

Huttenlocher, P. (2002). *Neural plasticity: The effects of environment on the development of the cerebral cortex.* Cambridge, MA: Harvard University Press.

Lamb, M. E., & Ahnert, L. (2006). Nonparental child care: Context, concepts, cor-relates, and consequences. In W. Damon & R. M. Lerner (Gen. Eds.), *Hand-book of Child Psychology* (6th ed.), K. A. Renninger & I. E. Sigel (Vol. Eds.), *Vol. 4, Child psychology in practice*, (pp. 950-1016). New York: Wiley.

Lancy, D. F. (1996). *Playing on the mother-ground: Cultural routines for children's devel-opment.* New York: Guilford Press.

Lickliter, R. (1990). Premature visual stimulation accelerates intersensory func-tioning in bobwhite quail neonates. *Developmental Psychobiology, 23*, 15-27.

Lickliter, R. & Honeycutt, H. (2003). Developmental dynamics: Towards a biologically plausible evolutionary psychology. *Psychological Bulletin, 129*, 819-835.

Logan B. (1991) Infant outcomes of a prenatal stimulation pilot study. *Pre and Perinatal Psychology Journal, 6*, 7-31.

MacDonald, K., & Hershberger, S. L. (2005). Theoretical issues in the study of evolution and development. In R. L. Burgess & K. MacDonald (Eds.) *Evolutionary perspectives on human development* (2nd ed., pp. 21-72). Thousand Oaks, CA: Sage.

Maestripieri, D., & Roney, J. R. (2006). Evolutionary developmental psychology: Contributions from comparative research with nonhuman primates. *Developmental Review, 26*, 120-137.

Marcon, R. A. (1999). Differential impact of preschool models on development and early learning of inner-city children: A three cohort study. *Developmental Psychology, 35*, 358-375.

Meltzoff, A. N., & Moore, M. K. (1977). Imitation of facial and manual gestures by human neonates. *Science, 198*, 75–78.

Oppenheim, R. W. (1981). Ontogenetic adaptations and retrogressive processes in the development of the nervous system and behavior. In K. J. Connolly & H. F. R. Prechtl (Eds.), *Maturation and development: Biological and psychological perspectives* (pp. 73-108). Philadelphia: International Medical Publications.

Papousek, H. (1977). Entwicklung der Lernfähigkeit im Säuglingsalter [The development of learning ability in infancy]. In G. Nissen (Ed.) *(Intelligenz, Lernen und Lernstörungen* [Intelligence, learning, and learning disabilities] (pp. 75-93). Berlin: Springer-Verlag.

Pellegrini, A. D., & Smith, P. K. (1998). Physical activity play: The nature and function of neglected aspect of play. *Child Development, 69*, 577-598.

Piaget, J. (1972) *Play and development* (M. W. Piers, Ed.). New York: Norton.

Piaget, J., & Inhelder, B.. (1969). *The psychology of the child.* New York: Basic.

Rogoff, B. (1998). Cognition as a collaborative process. In D. Kuhn & R. S. Siegler (Vol. Eds.), *Cognition language, and perceptual development* (Vol. 2, pp. 679-744.) In W. Damon (Gen. Ed), *Handbook of child psychology.* New York: Wiley.

Rogoff, B., Mistry, J. Göncü, A., & Mosier, C. (1993). Guided participation in cultural activity by toddlers and caregivers. *Monographs of the Society for Research in Child Development, 58* (Serial No. 236).

Rudy, J. W., Vogt, M. B., & Hyson, R. L. (1984). A developmental analysis of the rat's learned reactions to gustatory and auditory stimulation. In R. Kail & N. E. Spear (Eds.), *Memory development: Comparative perspectives* (pp. 181-208). Hillsdale, NJ: Erlbaum.

Schweinhart, L. J., & Weikart, D. P. (1988). Education for young children living in poverty: Child-initiated learning or teacher-directed instruction? *The Elementary School Journal, 89*, 212-225.

Spelke, E. S., & Newport, E. L. (1998). Nativism, empiricism, and the development of knowledge. In R. Learner (Vol. Ed.), *Theories of theoretical models of human development, Vol. 1* (pp. 275-340). In W. Damon (Gen. Ed.), *Handbook of child psychology* (5th ed.). New York: Wiley.

Stipek, D. (1984). Young children's performance expectations: Logical analysis or wishful thinking? In J. G. Nicholls (Ed.), *Advances in motivation and achieve-*

ment: Vol. 3. The development of achievement motivation (pp. 33-56). Greenwich, CT: JAI Press.

Stipek, D., Feiler, R., Daniels, D., & Milburn, S. (1995). Effects of different instructional approaches on young children's achievement and motivation. *Child Development, 66* 209-223.

Stipek, D., Feiler, R., Blyer, P., Ryan, R., Milburn, S., & Salmon, J. M. (1998). Good beginnings: What differences does the program make in preparing children for school. *Journal of Applied Developmental Psychology, 19*, 41-46.

Stone, L. J., Smith, H. T. & Murphy, L. B. (Eds.). (1973). *The competent infant: Research and commentary.* New York: Basic Books.

Tooby, J., & Cosmides, L. (2005). Conceptual foundations of evolutionary psychology. In D. M. Buss (Ed.), *The handbook of evolutionary psychology* (pp. 5-67). Hoboken, NJ: Wiley.

West-Eberhard, M. J. (2003). *Developmental plasticity and evolution.* New York: Oxford University Press.

Wynn, K. (1992). Addition and subtraction by human infants. *Nature, 358,* 749–750.

CHAPTER 5

EDUCATING THE EVOLVED
AND THE DEVELOPING MIND

Commentary on Geary's "Educating the Evolved Mind: Conceptual Foundations for an Evolutionary Educational Psychology"

Andreas Demetriou

Any kind of educational psychology must be evaluated at two distinct but related levels. The first is concerned with the general epistemological assumptions made about the nature of the human mind. The second is concerned with the implementation of the general assumptions and principles into applicable concepts, methods and practices. Any good educational system needs both of these notions right if it is to succeed. Epistemological assumptions are important because they guide the design of policies and general educational principles. If right, there is a possibility that a successful model of education may be crafted. If wrong, any attempt is doomed from the beginning, because it will be misdirected. Implementation concepts and tools are important because good theories are not directly applicable to real life qua theories. Describing and

Educating the Evolved Mind: Conceptual Foundations for an Evolutionary Educational Psychology, pp. 131–139
Copyright © 2007 by Information Age Publishing
All rights of reproduction in any form reserved.

explaining reality is not tantamount to affecting and changing it. Therefore, implementation concepts and tools connect the general epistemological level with actual educational life. I will discuss Geary's offer for an evolutionary educational psychology along these lines.

THE GENERAL MODEL OF THE HUMAN MIND

A satisfactory theory of the human mind must offer a satisfactory account of its *architecture*, its *development*, and *individual differences* in architecture and development. Let us specify each of these dimensions of a general theory of the developing mind and examine how Geary's model compares to it.

The architecture of the mind.   Any theory of the human mind must specify what mental functions and processes exist in the mind and how they are organized and inter-related. A model of the mental architecture is relevant to education because it enables it to direct its programs and interventions to the appropriate mental functions and processes. The more that education takes into account what we know about the organization of the human mind, the better it can organize curricula and interventions to touch the right mental organs and functions. It is like medicine. The better the doctor knows the human body, from basic organs down to the structure and organization of cells and genes, the more efficient, appropriate, and focused the doctor's healing operations can be.

The architecture advocated by Geary seems convincing and substantiated in some respects and questionable in others. Specifically, the analysis of the mind in two levels, one involving general purpose processing potentials (that is, speed of processing, control and inhibition, and working memory) and one involving specialized domains or modules (that is, folk psychology, folk biology, and folk psysics) seems to be on the right track. Scholars in the psychometric (Carroll, 1993; Gustafsson & Undheim, 1996), the cognitive (Anderson, 1992), and the developmental tradition (Demetriou, 2004) converge on the premise that the mind is indeed hierarchically organized, involving general purpose mechanisms and constraints, and specialized abilities and processes. Moreover, there is wide agreement as to what is involved in the level of the general purpose mechanisms: the processes proposed by Geary are certainly part of it.

It may be noted, however, that the role of self-awareness and self-regulation is underestimated in Geary's formulation as stated in the target monograph. This is important because of the very function of general intelligence as specified in his formulation: to conceive of "ideal" worlds and to design ways of reducing the distance between these worlds and reality. Creatures capable of creating ideal worlds and working for their realization are by definition self-aware and self-regulated in a specific way: They possess models of their own mind, other people's minds and also their own mental strengths and weaknesses as well as other people's mental strengths and weaknesses. It is through these models that they evaluate differences between ideal and real worlds, call pon their cognitive systems and processes to minimize differences, and activate or invite other people to assist, if considered necessary (Demetriou & Kazi, 2006). Geary needs to develop his model for an educationally relevant model in the directions discussed in his own recent book about the origins of mind (Geary, 2005).

Concerning domain-specific abilities, Geary espouses the partitioning proposed by evolutionary psychologists. That is, he accepts that the mind involves three general systems of specialized modules that are used to organize understanding and problem solving. They are the systems of folk psychology, folk biology, and folk physics. According to this conception, these modules evolved out of humans' interactions with each other, the biological, and the physical world, respectively. In the process of evolution the modules acquired automated inferential and conceptual schemes that are activated by stimuli within each of the respective reality realms and they still organize our current understanding and problem-solving tendencies, facilities, and proclivities. Even modern science and, by implication, education, are organized according to these modules. That is, humanities and social science correspond to folk psychology, biological science to folk biology, and natural science to folk physics. Thus, the argument goes, scientific knowledge is secondary to the primary knowledge associated with each of the modules. Therefore, teaching within these domains must start from these modules and respect their dynamics and constrains.

Some strong objections may be raised about this partitioning of the human mind. Conceptually, it is not obvious why this partition is preferable over alternative ones as there are no clear physical boundaries between the three domains. Humans, living organisms other than humans, and inanimate objects do share many common properties so that one cannot be sure how evolution would so clearly differentiate among them. In fact, the boundaries associated with the three domains are not clear at all in the mind of the developing child. Children's difficulties in establishing the animate-inanimate and the appearance-reality distinction (Flavell, Green, & Flavell, 1986) strongly attest to this. This mixing up of the three domains in the minds of young children suggests that these domains do not have the status of biological modules, such as, for instance, the perception of color, shape, or distance. Moreover, the arguments about these modules come from small-scale developmental studies of young children that do not test for the psychometric qualities of the presumed modules, even when they are carefully designed (Gelman,

2003). I suggest, however, that domains of thought must stand the psychometric test, if they are to be accepted. To my knowledge, there is not a single study that was designed to test the psychometric status of these modules. Therefore, their status is suspect on both conceptual and empirical grounds. Obviously, one cannot build an educational psychology on such a shaky ground.

Moreover, even if components of these systems do have the status of a biological-like module, such as, for instance, the perception of emotional signals in the system of folk psychology, we will need to investigate their relations with long and well established systems of thought and problem solving, such as spatial, quantitative, categorical, and causal though (Carroll, 1993; Demetriou, 2004; Demetriou, Efklides, & Platsidou, 1993). It might be the case that the mind evolved tools to represent and process specific relations in the environment, such as orientation tracking or mental rotation in spatial relations, counting and mental number line in quantitative relations, cause-effect interactions in causal relations, similarity-difference relations in class relations, etc. These specialized processing systems are naturalized, so to speak, in each of the broad domains proposed by Geary (folk psychology, biology, and physics) through personal development and cultural learning. Obviously, the question of how Geary's domains relate to these other well established domains revealed by psychometric and developmental research opens a whole new research program.

Development.   Any model of the mind must be able to specify what the understanding and problem-solving capabilities of the mind are at different phases of life, the causes of their change, and the mechanisms effecting the change. A precise model of the succession of capabilities in all of the dimensions presumably involved in the architecture of the mind as well as their dynamics of change are relevant and important for any theory of education, because from preschool to graduate school individuals undergo extensive changes in all aspects of their mind. Therefore, education needs a map of the developmental course of all mental abilities so that it can satisfactorily map the demands of skills and knowledge in the curriculum with the assimilatory capabilities of students. Bruner (1968) may have been right in arguing that any thing can be taught at any age in an honest way, but honesty can only be attained if the initial conceptual and understanding conditions of students will be seriously taken into account. Moreover, a model of the causes and mechanisms of change is important because teaching methods and practices can capitalize on them in order both to build stable and robust learning outcomes and develop learning to learn abilities and habits in the student.

Does Geary's model satisfy these conditions of a developmental model? Unfortunately, Geary's educational psychology may be evolutionary but it is nondevelopmental. Specifically, it does not involve any proposals concerning the development of the human mind, either in concern to successive levels of possibilities of understanding and problem solving or in concern to mechanisms that transform and enhance these possibilities with growth. The only developmental assumption offered is that there is primary knowledge emerging from the components within each of the three main modules mentioned above, that this knowledge comes early, and that secondary knowledge is built onto this primary knowledge. To extrapolate, the idea is, for instance, that numerical operations emerge somehow from subitization and the mental number line through the activation of the processes and functions involved in general intelligence, such as attention and working memory. However, there is no description of the mechanisms leading from primary to secondary knowledge or of any succession of levels in this process.

To be successful, any educational psychology must address the individual, not the species. In other words, we need a precise and detailed theory about the ontogenesis of mind. A phylogenetic theory might be useful as a frame for understanding ontogenesis but it is not useful for organizing educational and teaching policies and practices, even if right. These policies and practices require the detailed structuring of teaching materials, examples, concepts, skills, and methods on a year-to-year, month-to-month, week-to-week, and even day-to-day basis. Even Piaget's theory, which was very precise in its description of stages and transition mechanisms in the individual, failed to meet the needs of education, because both the stages and the mechanisms proposed were too general and too global.

Individual differences. Any model of the mind that aspires to be useful for education must specify where, why, how, and when individuals differ in mental organization and development. Education is the land of individual differences. Students differ in their learning efficiency, their learning preferences and dispositions, and their strength of motivation, and nature and direction of ambitions. Ideally, education must be able to meet the learning and assimilatory capabilities of each individual in every domain or subject of interest, so as to maximize the learning outcomes for each particular person at every particular moment in every particular subject or course, and enable individuals to develop their talents, dispositions, and ambitions to the extreme, if they so wish. Therefore, a good theory of individual differences is needed to enable education to individualize teaching and learning.

Geary's model is weak in relation to individual differences as well. It does not specify how and when individuals differ either in the various dimensions of the mental architecture or in their development. Admittedly, the conception of individual differences espoused by differential theories of intelligence may be imported into Geary's evolutionary educational psychology through the importation of differential constructs, such as fluid intelligence. Or, the conception of individual differences espoused by personality theories may be imported through the importation of constructs from the Big Five Factor theory (MacCrae & Costa, 1999), to explicate differences in motivation or general orientations to others or the styles of handling information. But these conceptions are already on the market and a new theory must convince us of its own additive value. In the present context, one would expect to see how individual differences in g are related to individual differences in the functioning and development of the three primary folk domains that may explain differences in the construction of secondary knowledge within the domains, if they exist at all. These products are not offered in Geary's package.

THE IMPLEMENTATION LEVEL

To be implemented in actual classrooms, any educational psychology needs to involve a system of mental diagnosis and a roadmap for educational interventions and teaching.

Mental diagnosis. Traditional tests of intelligence or personality are good examples of diagnostic systems that have both academic and practical value. From the practical point of view they can enable one to make predictions about learning ability in schools (intelligence tests) or about functioning in the work environment (personality tests). In Geary's model, a new conception of intelligence is offered that integrates traditional concepts from cognitive and differential psychology with concepts from modern evolutionary theory. Aggregating ready-made tests from different traditions is not enough. We need to have a full well-integrated measurement system that would implement the theory as a coherent system and would therefore be able to diagnose the condition of the various dimensions and processes presumably involved in the mind of an individual relative to both other individuals and relative to general ontogenetic patterns concerning each of the dimensions. Therefore, we would expect Geary to come up with such an integrated diagnostic system.

A roadmap for intervention and learning. In applied cognitive developmental research there are some good examples of intervention programs which are based on developmental theory and are intended as tools for the development of general reasoning skills and specialized thinking skills in domains such as mathematics, physics, and social understanding. The programs of Klauer (1989) for the development of inductive reasoning and the programs of Shayer and Adey (2002) for the development of thought in mathematics and science are very detailed in the concepts targeted, the steps to be followed and the materials to be used. Moreover, they present extensive empirical substantiation of their effectiveness. In fact, all of these programs proved to be very successful both in developing skills and abilities in their target domains and in demonstrating stable generalization to other domains and general school learning. Finally, the Feuerstein's (Feuerstein, Rand, Hoffman, & Miller, 1980) instrumental enrichment program is well known for its beneficial effects on underprivileged children. Unfortunately, these programs are not even referred to by Geary. Definitely, these programs fall short of the prescriptions that a modern comprehensive theory of the developing mind must satisfy. However, they do possess many useful elements that any theory must consider, evaluate, choose from, improve, and use, together with new elements emanating from its new constructs, to develop a new roadmap of intervention and learning, if it is going to be more successful than the old theories and intervention models. This roadmap must be well integrated with the diagnostic system to be used, because the diagnostic system must direct the educator in targeting and evaluating interventions.

CONCLUSIONS

This commentary revolves around a straightforward position. Educational psychology needs good and sound ontogenetic theories that at one and the same time account for the architecture and development of the human mind and individual differences in both. These theories have to satisfy a number of standards at both the general epistemological level guiding the formulation of general educational policies and the implementation level guiding the design of educational practices. We maintained that Geary's model is rather weak on both grounds.

Phylogenetic theories are too remote from the focus of education, which is the individual child rather than the species, to be of practical use. This is all the more so in cases, such as the Geary's model, where the evolutionary theory itself is too general and too unsubstantiated to be able to direct either general educational policies or day to day educational practice in the classroom. Very general theories lead to trivial predictions. For instance, we do not need an evolutionary theory to predict that children have or want to learn about the social, the biological, and the physical world. We knew this for ages. Moreover, having to learn about these three aspects of the world does not necessarily require the three respective modules of folk psychology, folk biology, and folk physics. Learning for or about these three aspects of the world may be attained through other more specialized "mental organs", such as the various mental operations related to the representation and processing of spatial, quantitative, causal, similarity relations, etc., which are coordinated to serve understanding and problem solving in the various complex aspects of the world (Demetriou, 2004; Demetriou & Raftopoulos, 1999; Demetriou, Raftopoulos, & Kargopoulos, 1999). It needs not be pointed out here that domains of this kind of mental operations are much more substantiated than Geary's domains (Carroll, 1993; Demetriou, 2004; Gustafsson & Undheim, 1996).

Moreover, a good educational theory would need a detailed roadmap of the development of each of these specialized mental organs, a detailed analysis of the demands posed on them by each of the many concepts and skills that need to be taught in each school subject at each school grade, a detailed description of how this teaching is to be done that would respect the mechanisms of developmental change assumed by the theory, and an accurate diagnostic system that would be able to inform us about initial conditions and the outcomes of our practice. These requirements are not met in Geary's model. Therefore, education, in my view, is not going to find the psychological framework it needs in Geary's offer. An alternative offer, which attempts to meet all of the requirements specified here, has recently been formulated by Adey, Csapo, Demetriou, Hautamaki, and Shayer (in press).

ACKNOWLEDGMENTS

Special thanks are due to David Geary and Antigoni Mouyi for their comments on an earlier version of this commentary

REFERENCES

Adey, P., Csapo, B., Demetriou, A., Hautamaki, J., & Shayer, M. (in press). Can we be intelligent about intelligence?: Why education needs the concept of general plastic ability. *Educational Research Review*.

Anderson, M. (1992). *Intelligence and development: A cognitive theory*. London: Blackwell.

Bruner, J. (1968). *Towards a theory of instruction*. New York: W.W. Norton.

Carroll, J. B. (1993). *Human cognitive abilities*. Cambridge, United Kingdom: Cambridge University Press.

Demetriou, A. (2004). Mind, intelligence, and development: A general cognitive, differential, and developmental theory of the mind. In A. Demetriou & A. Raftopoulos (Eds.), *Developmental Change: Theories, models and measurement* (pp. 21-73). Cambridge, United Kingdom: Cambridge University Press.

Demetriou, A., Efklides, A., & Platsidou, M. (1993) The architecture and dynamics of developing mind: Experiential structuralism as a frame for unifying cognitive developmental theories. *Monographs of the Society for Research in Child Development, 58* (5, Serial No. 234).

Demetriou, A., & Kazi, S. (2006). Self-awareness in g (with processing efficiency and reasoning). *Intelligence, 34,* 297-317.

Demetriou, A., & Raftopoulos, A. (1999). Modeling the developing mind: From structure to change. *Developmental Review, 19,* 319-368.

Demetriou, A., Raftopoulos, A., & Kargopoulos, P. (1999). Interactions, computations, and experience: Interleaved springboards of cognitive emergence, *Developmental Review, 19,* 389-414.

Feuerstein, R., Rand, Y., Hoffman, M., & Miller, M. (1980). *Instrumental enrichment: An intervention programme for cognitive modifiability.* Baltimore: University Park Press.

Flavell, J. H., Green, F. L., & Flavell, E. R. (1986). Development of knowledge about the appearance-reality distinction. *Monographs of the Society for Research in Child Development, 51* (1, Serial No. 212).

Geary, D. C. (2005). *The origin of the mind: Evolution of brain, cognition, and general intelligence.* Washington, DC: American Psychological Association.

Gelman, S. A. (2003). *The essential child.* Oxford, England: Oxford University Press.

Gustafsson, J. E., & Undheim, J. O. (1996). Individual differences in cognitive functions. In D. C. Berliner, & R. C. Calfee (Eds.), *Handbook of educational psychology* (pp.186-242). New York: Macmillan.

Klauer, K. J. (1989). Teaching for analogial transfer as a means of improving problem solving, thinking, and learning. *Instructional Science, 18,* 179-192.

MacCrae, R. R., & Costa, P. T. (1999). A five-factor theory of personality. In A. Pervin & O. P. John, (Eds.), *Handbook of personality* (pp. 139-153). New York: Guilford.

Shayer, M., & Adey, P. (Eds.). (2002). *Learning intelligence: Cognitive acceleration across the curriculum from 5 to 15 years.* Milton Keynes, England: Open University Press.

CHAPTER 6

WHAT IS THE MEANING OF EVOLUTIONARY PSYCHOLOGY FOR EDUCATION?

Earl Hunt

INTRODUCTION

Geary (this volume) has provided us with a plethora of data about the evolution of brain-cognition relations, approaching a précis of his excellent book on the topic (Geary, 2005) concluding that findings from evolutionary psychology should provide us with an informed evolutionary educational psychology.

The adjectives say it all. Evolutionary psychology makes no sense unless evolution makes sense, and evolutionary educational psychology makes no sense unless evolutionary psychology makes sense. I will try to unfold each of these ideas in turn. In order to do so, however, I will state what I believe are Geary's main ideas, for I must confess that there is so much detail in his writing that I have a bit of difficulty extracting the main themes.

Educating the Evolved Mind: Conceptual Foundations for an
Evolutionary Educational Psychology, pp. 141–154

EVOLUTION

The theory of evolution is one of the great achievements of the age of science. I am certainly not going to question it here. It is worth talking about why the theory of evolution is a sensible scientific theory.

The first criterion any scientific theory must meet is falsifiability; There must be some configuration of data that, if observed, would be contrary to an implication of the theory. Indeed, the strongest scientific argument against the theory of Intelligent Design, and other quasireligious theories of the origin of the species, is that they fail this test. The theory of evolution is falsifiable. All that is needed is evidence of the sudden appearance of a life form without predecessors, accompanied by a clear record of times, to show that there cannot be any "missing links." We know of no such evidence. We cannot say that such evidence will not be produced tomorrow, but that is true of any scientific theory. A good theory covers all known evidence and could, in principle, be falsified by yet-undiscovered evidence. Until such evidence is uncovered the theory remains tenable. The theory of evolution is certainly tenable today.

EVOLUTIONARY PSYCHOLOGY

Geary argues that humans have certain evolved mechanisms (e.g., expanded frontal lobes) that support a collection of information-processing functions (e.g. working memory). He identifies these, collectively, with the psychometric concept of fluid intelligence (Cattell, 1972; Horn & Noll, 1995). He then argues that these information-processing capacities interact with universal human experiences to produce certain types of *folk knowledge (folk physics, folk psychology, folk biology)* that he regards, collectively, as biological primary knowledge. In the absence of elaborate instruction (i.e., education) biological primary knowledge is used to represent and reason about the world. This provides the basis for evolutionary psychology. Therefore both the form of folk knowledge and the mechanisms that are used to manipulate it provide a starting point for formal education, which Geary refers to as the acquisition of biologically secondary knowledge. Before dealing with this idea, let us look at the theory of evolutionary psychology itself.

Evolutionary psychology rests on the idea that the behaviors that humans (and other animals) exhibit today are due to inheritance of a requirement to exhibit such behavior (e.g., the patellar reflex), or are the result of an interaction between experience and an inherited capacity to learn to exhibit those behaviors. But if you accept evolution, *any* behavior exhibited by extant humans would fit this explanation because, by definition, we are only capable of doing what we have evolved to be capable of doing. Evolutionary psychology cannot be falsified by analyses of contemporary behaviors.

Another way to investigate evolutionary theories is to look at the fossil records for evidence of paths from extinct to modern life forms. Evolutionary psychology is in trouble here, for behavior does not leave direct evidence. Once we get beyond the historical period the best we can offer is "it might have been that" because we do not really know what happened. We can develop models of how our predecessors, *Homo erectus*, early *Homo sapiens,* such as the Cro-Magnons, and our evolutionary cousins Neanderthals (*Homo neaderthalensis*) behaved, but we have precious little data to constrain these models.

It is sensible, in theory, to examine varieties of existing behavior in order to extract universal rules about how people deal with the natural and social worlds. However we must admit the possibility that in a species that has evolved powerful capacities for learning and reasoning, and has spread over many ecological niches, such universal rules do not exist. Or, if they do, they may be so general that biologically primary knowledge does not constrain the acquisition of biologically secondary knowledge. Absent the constraints of data, the existence or nonexistence of universal folk knowledge is an open question.

To develop this idea further it helps to look at a close analogy, language. Logically, language is a behavior, so the study of the origins of language could be thought of as a subset of studies in evolutionary psychology. As a historic matter, though, the study of the origin and nature of language predate psychology itself (Hunt, 2002). Therefore what has happened in that field is a useful case study for what may happen to the study of evolutionary psychology.

While we do not know everything about the neuroscience of language, we do know a good deal about the brain structures that support language. We do not know the evolutionary pathways that lead to these structures, but conceivably we may learn this some day. On the other hand, we may not. The relevant structures are part of the soft tissue of the brain, and therefore essentially unrecoverable from the fossil record by our current techniques. There is a good chance that information about the finer details of brain structure in extinct hominids may have been lost forever.

We also do not know, and are unlikely to find out, the nature of language in hominid species prior to or related to our own. For example, we know from physical evidence that some Neanderthal groups buried their dead, occasionally with grave goods (Pettit, 2002). We cannot imagine how such practices would have arisen without some powerful method of communication. But would we have recognized Neanderthal communication as language? Does this imply that some common ancestor of the

Neanderthals and modern *Homo sapiens* had a protolanguage or did the protolanguage emerge with the advent of modern man? Perhaps the Neanderthals were limited to a "Me Tarzan, you Jane" form of communication. Perhaps they could say the equivalent of *Good Morning, madam. I am Lord Greystoke, often referred to as Tarzan. I believe you are named Jane.* I doubt that we shall ever know.

We are even less likely to be able to trace the development of folk knowledge prior to the beginnings of the historic record, roughly 5,000 years before the present era (BP). This is in no small measure because our information about folk knowledge prior to our own time is gained largely by analysis of written records of early historic cultures, such as those in Mesopotamia, Egypt, and China. In Geary's terms this means that our understanding of early primary knowledge has to be strained through the sieve of a secondary knowledge technology, literacy. Furthermore, while 5,000 years is a long time in terms of our everyday experience, by 5,000 BP modern *Homo sapiens* was the only hominid left standing.[1]

When linguists attempt to understand the nature of language, they do not rely solely, or even primarily, on historical records. They analyze extant languages to derive general rules that appear to apply to all language, the "universal grammar." The universal grammar can be regarded as a set of constraints on language that are, presumably, due to the structure of the human brain and, therefore, are evolved. This assumption fits science's desire for simple explanations, but it is not necessary. The argument for its not being necessary is somewhat involved, so I have placed it in a footnote.[2]

The second reason for analyzing extant languages is to establish the historical development of languages. This tradition of scholarship has, for instance, led to our understanding that languages fall into major classes (e.g. Indo-European languages, Sinotic languages) and has even given us some ideas about the nature of the "mother languages," such as proto-Indo-European, from which modern languages derived. Two points about this effort are worth noting.

First, the results are highly debatable, for they depend on choosing a method of data analysis, and then applying that method to data on existing languages. Another method of data analysis may produce different results. Which is correct? We think we know what Middle English sounded like, but Chaucer and his contemporaries are no longer with us, and so we do not really know. When linguists disagree they are reduced to arguing about the accuracy of the data input to different analytic techniques, something that can be determined empirically, and about the reasonableness of the data analytic techniques themselves, which is a matter of opinion.[3]

In principle, one might trace language trees back, not just to proto-Indo-European and proto-Sinotic, but all the way back to the great, biologically determined Mother Language. However our theories of the form of extinct languages are very much influenced by cultural rather than biological evolution. To take one example, consider the shift in use of vowels that occurred in English from the fourteenth to the sixteenth century. No one that I am aware of has proposed that there was a shift in Englishmen's brains at that time. A somewhat similar vowel shift appears to be occurring in the American Great Lakes region today (MacNeil & Cran, 2005). No one has seriously proposed that Michigan brains have evolved in a way that separates them from Texas brains.

The principles illustrated by the linguistic analyses map onto attempts to define folk knowledge by analyzing the folk knowledge of extant cultures. In theory "true" folk knowledge could be determined by finding general principles that applied to the folk knowledges of all cultures. Differences in folk knowledge could be used to illuminate either changes associated with the historic record or changes due to differences in the natural world experienced by different cultures.

In practice we are very far from having such knowledge. Consider Geary's folk biology. A teleological explanation in biology is the idea that some feature of an animal has been created to fulfill a purpose, such as a giraffe having developed a long neck in order to eat leaves off a tree. Prior to instruction, teleological explanations are accepted by a fairly broad range of contemporary American children. Indeed, many adults also seem to accept them (Evans, 2001, Kelemen, 1999). This fact may be problematical for instruction in biology, but the fact that it is widespread in our society does not allow us to infer that it is an evolutionarily determined part of a universal folk biology. In order to do that we would have to know that young children from many cultures display teleological reasoning about biology. Until the necessary cross-cultural research has been done we have to admit the possibility that teleological ideas are the result of experiences that are specific either to American and perhaps other post-industrial societies.[4]

Geary and others have made out a reasonable case for the proposition that certain aspects of preinstructed human knowledge are due to evolutionary pressures. However the case is very far from proven, simply because the necessary data to constrain such theorizing has not yet been collected. It is reasonable to pursue a research agenda that might result in data that would constrain theorizing in evolutionary psychology, just as comparative linguistics constrains theorizing about the development of language. What strikes me as more risky, though, is using the conclusions of currently underconstrained theorizing in evolutionary psychology as the basis for further theorizing about the acquisition of secondary knowledge(i.e., about education). This brings us to Geary's ideas about evolutionary educational psychology.

EVOLUTIONARY EDUCATIONAL PSYCHOLOGY

Geary's evolutionary educational psychology is based on two principles that he derives from evolutionary psychology. The first is that children are evolutionarily set to acquire folk knowledge. The form of this biologically primary knowledge will interact with attempts to develop biologically secondary knowledge; the sorts of things that we expect people to learn when we educate them. The second principle is although virtually all people are formidable general problem solvers compared to nonhuman animals, there are substantial individual differences between people with respect to our ability to deal with novel problems, which Geary (and others) consider the essence of fluid intelligence (Gf) or, on occasion, general intelligence (g). Rather than enter into a debate over terms, I will use the Gf notation. Let us explore these notions in more detail.

According to Geary, humans are driven toward acquiring folk knowledge by an inherited motivation to control the environment, including the social environment. This strikes me as the weakest part of his argument. It is also somewhat contrary to reasoning based on evolution. The argument that an ability to acquire folk knowledge evolved in order to satisfy a motivation to control is uncomfortably analogous to the argument that the giraffe's long neck evolved in order to let the animal reach the leafier branches. I think it would be more in line with evolutionary reasoning to show that the acquisition of folk knowledge facilitates survival of the genotype, and let it go at that.

Fortunately we do not have to resolve this argument in order to analyze the case for evolutionary educational psychology. That case depends on understanding the implications of folk knowledge.

Humans, both as individuals and as societies, benefit greatly (compared to other animals) by complicated social structures and superior understanding of the physical and biological world. Until very recently, when we began to make things like airplanes and vaccines, our understanding had to be sufficient to guide useful action, but did not have to be correct in any scientific sense. Take folk physics as an example. A theory that assumes that force is required to keep something moving will direct a person to take appropriate actions in our friction-filled world. In one of the most brilliant analyses in human history, Isaac Newton pointed out that our world is a special case, and that in general the application of force changes velocity rather than maintaining it. The point remains that the folk physics notion of using force to maintain motion tells us what to do in the world we live in. And for the vast majority of humans who have ever lived that is all that is important.

I could offer similar examples from folk biology and folk psychology, but in the interest of space I will not. I hope that the point is clear.

A hominid society, with all its advantages, will have much higher survivability if all individuals in that society master folk knowledge quickly. In the case of *Homo sapiens,* the evolutionarily most successful hominid, the mechanisms of evolution, random variability and selection, have produced brain mechanisms and processes that strongly bias humans toward acquiring folk knowledge without explicit instruction, simply through interaction with the natural world and with conspecifics.

Let us assume that this has happened. We know enough of the genetics of intelligence to know that cognitive power depends on multiple genes. In a situation where fitness (in the evolutionary sense) depends on possession of enough genetic intelligence to master folk knowledge there will be a tendency for the genetics of variability and selection to overshoot. Virtually all humans will have enough intelligence to master folk knowledge. Many of them will have more then enough, but how much more will be highly variable because, for most of the roughly 250,000 years that *Homo sapiens* has been on Earth there was no marked survival advantage to being able to solve problems that were not being posed.

This happy situation began to go downhill at the dawn of civilization, say 5,000 years BP. Things have been getting worse ever since. We have even reached a point at which we have graduate education and postdoctoral training! As we have developed societies that depend upon secondary knowledge we have placed higher and higher demands on the spare capacity, if you will, that people have left over from the cognitive capacity required to master folk knowledge. And there is great variability in the extent to which people possess spare capacity. Virtually everyone can grasp the folk physics of force and motion. Less than half of our high school students take and understand introductory physics. *String theory for dummies* will never make the best seller lists.

This is the point at which Geary parts company with many modern educational theorists. The influential National Academy of Science report, *How People Learn* (Bransford, Brown, & Cocking, 1999), and many other books and articles in the 1980s and 1990s emphasized what came to be called discovery learning, in which students are supposed to acquire knowledge by exploring problems that are of interest to them. The argument for this is that such exploration is natural. This contrasts to what I was told in high school in the 1940s. Quoting a Latin master, whom I have never been able to forget (though I would like to):

> You are here to learn. And what do I mean by learn? Memorize, retain, and be able to recite.

He actually said this. I think he believed it.

Geary's argument is that my long-remembered, little-beloved teacher had a point. According to Geary, learning by exploration is indeed the natural way that we learn primary (folk) knowledge. However when we set out to acquire secondary knowledge, which we have not evolved to receive, learning by exploration imposes a cognitive load that many people simply cannot handle. Therefore effective learning is best achieved by presenting what Geary refers to as *direct instruction*. I do not think that he means by this that educators should go back to the troglodyte methods of instruction by rote memorization prevalent in my high school in the 1940s. It does mean that educators should concentrate on presenting the desired knowledge directly to students, with appropriate assessments to ensure that the students are receiving that knowledge, and without letting the students go into side explorations. Taken to the extreme, Geary has tried to justify by evolutionary theory an educational program that throws down the gauntlet to educators who are advocates of discovery learning throughout the educational establishment.

AN EVALUATION OF EVOLUTIONARY EDUCATIONAL PSYCHOLOGY

Modern educational theory has been very much influenced by what is called the "constructionist" approach, in which children are supposed to learn by active and relatively free-form exploration of projects that they see as meaningful. On its face, this appears to be the form of education that Geary rejects, on evolutionary grounds. However, we do not want to overstate the contrast between Geary's approach and the constructionist approach.

Insofar as I can see, Geary is not calling for a return to rote learning, except for a few instances (e.g., the multiplication table) where the goal of education is to produce automatic rather than controlled recall (Schneider & Schiffrin, 1977). He is calling for an educational system in which the instructor exerts a strong guiding hand in choosing, and where necessary explaining, the learning situations that the student encounters. Similarly, constructionism, as it is actually practiced, seldom if ever involves free exploration of intrinsically interesting problems. It has been well established that such an extreme constructivist approach simply does not work (Mayer, 2002). In practice virtually all instruction is a mixture of student-initiated and instructor-initiated activities that vary from fairly free student exploration to classic lectures.

Geary takes issue with modern educational practice at another point. He believes that more intelligent students can acquire secondary knowledge from instruction, but that less intelligent ones require direct instruction. This idea, if widely adopted, would naturally lead to streaming of students by talent, into classes that were taught by different methods.

This is not a new idea. A number of years ago Cronbach and Snow (1977; Snow, 1982) argued that high-ability students can benefit by being offered challenging problems to explore, while low-ability students require a structured learning environment. The problem with such aptitude-by-interaction approaches (including Geary's) is that the cross-over point from low ability to high ability is not defined. Presumably this varies with the material to be learned and the degree of student preparation, not just with a biologically determined characteristic of the student. As a result, aptitude by treatment effects have been hard to replicate and therefore did not provide a useful basis for generalizing from laboratory studies to educational practice.

Geary's approach emphasizes individual differences in Gf, fluid intelligence, or the ability to deal with novelty. This is a reasonable argument to present when dealing with the education of very young children. It is less reasonable as the educational system advances, for knowledge builds upon knowledge. In psychometric terms, Gc, culturally acquired knowledge and problem solving skills, become important.

In practice, though, it is well known that both Gf and Gc have shown marked increases in the industrialized world in the past century. This will be referred to as the *cohort effect*. The early results on this topic are discussed in various articles in Neisser (1998). Later results (e.g. Colom, Lluis-Font, & Andres-Puyo, 2005; Teasdale & Owen, 2000) indicate that the gains are primarily among low-scoring individuals.

The cohort effect has profound implications for Geary's evolutionary argument. While the causes of the cohort effect are not clear, the fact that the cohort effect has occurred within a century (the blink of an evolutionary eye) shows that intelligence is much more malleable than Geary's approach would lead you to believe. He is certainly correct that there are biological limits on any one person's intelligence. They may be quite broad, and cultural influences may be far more important within the normal range of mental capacity. This should not be taken to mean that at this moment anyone can be taught anything. What it means is that at any time the concept of "high" and "low" intelligence has to be considered with respect to the cultural context. This has clearly been reflected in educational settings. Calculus used to be considered a rather advanced topic for university students. It is now taught widely in high schools.

Another idea inherent in Geary's approach is that when we attempt to instruct people in secondary knowledge we ought to consider the nature of folk knowledge in the same field, for that is what the student is biased toward thinking. That is the idea behind techniques that rely on obtaining a careful organization of the knowledge to be acquired, assessing the student's current state of knowledge, and then offering instruction tailored to the student. For instance, suppose that the task was to teach techniques for multiplying multidigit numbers. This skill depends on several subskills; knowing the multiplication table for single digit numbers, understanding addition, understanding the concept of carrying, and understand how to line up numbers to reflect the appropriate power of ten being used. An educational program that evaluates the extent to which each student has each of these skills, and then tailors instruction to actual student accomplishment, strikes me as being more useful than considering students to be of high or low ability, and then tailoring instructional methods to that distinction. This idea traces back at least to Gagné (1965). Programs that use this technique of individualizing instruction have variously been called *dynamic assessment* (Carlson & Weidl, 2000), *the development of knowledge spaces* (Falmagne, Koope, Villano, & Doignant, & Johannesen, 1990) or *evidence centered design* (Mislevy, Steinberg, Almond, & Lukas, 2006). They are more expensive than regular instruction, but appear to be quit effective.

A slightly different interpretation of Geary's ideas about folk knowledge would be to take ideas about folk knowledge as a given, and consider how to build on folk knowledge to establish the desired secondary knowledge. This idea has also been tried in education, notably in Minstrell's (2000) program of *facet-based instruction*. In facet-based instruction an attempt is made to understand what a student's ideas about a topic are, prior to instruction. This is a somewhat finer distinction than determining what parts of desirable knowledge a student has. To take an example from physics, if you were teaching the topic of force and motion from a dynamic assessment point of view you would want to determine whether or not a student understood the concept of force as an interaction between objects, but you would not be terribly interested in what misconceptions a student has. From a facet-based instruction viewpoint you would be quite interested in knowing whether or not a student believed that a force is an inherent property of an object or perhaps of motion.

If facet-based instruction is looked at from Geary's point of view an educational program that attempted to assess students' ideas prior to instruction should discover the relevant bit of folk knowledge. This is an interesting idea. For instance, prior to instruction students do often believe that force is inherent in large, rapidly moving objects, and thus reject the idea that if a large football player collides with a small cheerleader, then there is an equal and opposite force exerted by the player on the cheerleader and the cheerleader on the player. Similar ideas can be applied to biology where, as I have already noted, teleological thinking appears to be widespread prior to instruction.

The upshot of all of these observations is that Geary's proposal for an educational psychology informed by evolution leads to conclusions that are essentially redundant to conclusions that many educators and educational psychologists have already reached, quite without any reference to evolution. Of course, this does not make Geary's ideas wrong. Also, one can argue that the educational community has been slow to adopt either the idea of conditionalizing instructional methods upon ability or upon prior knowledge. Perhaps if people were convinced that such methods were compatible with evolution educators would change their methods because "Darwin made me do it."

But I doubt it. I believe that resistance to the widespread adoption of the individualization of instruction comes from three rather different sources: (1) an absolute bar on the adoption of flexible methods of teaching due to the cost of such methods, both in terms of time and teacher preparation; (2) a legitimate concern over the cost effectiveness of these methods compared to one-size-fits-all techniques of instruction; and (3) in the case of aptitude-treatment interactions, a philosophical disinclination to offer one method of instruction for the quick and another for the slow.

SUMMARY

So where are we? Geary's statement that our behavioral and cognitive capacities are the result of evolved brain structures acting on the human environment is certainly true, but it is something of a tautology. Evolutionary psychology begins to have teeth when concrete claims are made about folk knowledge. Geary has made such claims, and they may be true, but given the present state of cross-cultural research on folk physics, biology, and psychology, we have a long way to go before they can be accepted as reasonably well established. Indeed, we may never know the extent to which the features of folk biology, psychology, and physics are due to necessary constraints because of brain structures or happenstance restrictions due to historic developments. I say this because we do not understand this aspect of language, and far more research has been done on cross-cultural comparisons of language than on cross-cultural comparisons of folk knowledge.

What about evolutionary educational psychology? The idea has led Geary to some interesting conclusions about how education ought to proceed. I, for one, would like to see a movement toward them. But the same ideas have already been put forward by many people, without an accompanying evolutionary argument. The evolutionary argument certainly does no harm, and if it can be developed this will be an important step in reducing psychology to biology. Such an effort is extremely important for the unification of knowledge. The fact that the same conclusions about education can be reached without resorting to evolutionary arguments should not detract from this effort.

NOTES

1.   There is good evidence for coexistence between Neanderthals and modern man as late as 25,000 years BP in the Middle East, and (currently) highly controversial evidence for the possible existence of a small population of non-*Homo sapiens* hominids on an isolated island in Indonesia as late as 18,000 years before the present era (Falk et al., 2005).

2.   Suppose that the brain structures supporting human language contain a capacity to support several different universal grammars, and that which one is supported depends on environmental circumstances. Suppose further that several groups of hominids, speaking languages that conformed to several different grammars, existed at some point in time, but that only one of these groups survived. In that case an analysis of extant languages could uncover the features of the surviving grammar, which would be universal with respect to all existing languages but that grammar itself would be partly due to environmental circumstances at the point of its origin. This argument assumes that the hominid brain evolved a capacity for acquiring several different very complex patterns of behavior and cognition, while only one of these patterns was strictly necessary. Is it reasonable to think that evolution would have produced such an overcapacity? We have an excellent case where it has. Experimentation has shown that the nonhuman great apes, and even more surprisingly, the bottle-nosed dolphin (*tursiops truncates*) are capable of learning complex signaling systems that allow them to communicate with humans. There is even some evidence that once these systems are learned, apes will use them to communicate with each other. Insofar as we can detect, none of these animals uses anything like these communication systems in the wild. Evolution seems to have produced brains with a capacity that is totally unused in the animals' normal ecological niches.

3.   I point out that this is normal science. A model for data (e.g.. a hypothetical family tree for languages) is proposed. Other models may also fit. The debate is carried on by extending the range of the data to be fit or by presenting various criteria for models, such as minimization of the numbers of parameters. Such criteria are essentially criteria by which the culture of science judges the beauty, if you will, of an explanation. Different criteria can lead to preferences for different models.

4.   It is fair to ask what explanation, other than evolution, one might offer to explain a belief in teleology. There is one. Children in postindustrial society have a great deal of experience with designed objects, ranging from hammers to automobiles. Teleology does apply to the features of a designed object; a hammer has the features it has in order to accomplish

goals. Children might simply be overgeneralizing the concept from designed to biological objects.

REFERENCES

Bransford, J. D., Brown, A. L., & Cocking, R. R. (Eds.). (1999) *How people learn: Brain, mind, experience and school.* Washington DC: National Academy Press.

Carlson, J. S., & Wiedl, K. H. (2000). The validity of dynamic assessment. In C. Lidz & J. Elliott (Eds.), *Dynamic assessment* (pp. 681-712). New York: Elsevier.

Cattell, R. B. (1971). *Abilities: Their structure, growth, and action.* Boston: Houghton Mifflin.

Colom, R., Lluis-Font, J. M., & Andres-Pueyo, A. (2005). The generational intelligence gains are caused by decreasing variance in the lower half of the distribution: Supporting evidence for the generational hypothesis. *Intelligence, 33*, 83-91.

Cronbach, L. J., & Snow, R. E. (1977). *Aptitudes and instructional methods: A handbook for research on interactions.* New York: Irvington.

Evans, E. M. (2001). Cognitive and contextual factors in the emergence of diverse belief systems: Creation versus evolution. *Cognitive Psychology, 42*, 217-266.

Falk, D., Hildebold, C., Smith, K., Morwood, M. J., Suitkna, T., Brown, P., et al. (2005). The brain of LB1, *homo floresiensis. Science, 308*(5719), 242-245.

Falmagne, J. -C., Koope, M., Villano, M. & Doignant, J. P., & Johannesen, L. (1990). Introduction to knowledge spaces: How to build, test, and search them. *Psychological Review, 97*, 201-224.

Gagné, R. M. (1965). *The conditions of learning.* New York: Holt, Rineheart, & Winston.

Geary, D. C. (2005). *The origin of mind: Evolution of brain, cognition, and general intelligence.* Washington, DC: American Psychological Association.

Horn J. L., & Noll, J. (1994.) A system for understanding cognitive capabilities: A theory and the evidence on which it is based. In D. Detterman (Ed.), *Current topics in human intelligence: Vol. 4. Theories of intelligence* (pp. 151-204). Norwood, NJ: Ablex.

Hunt, E. (2002). *Thoughts on thought: A discussion of formal models of cognition.* Mahwah, NJ: Erlbaum.

Kelemen, D. (1999). The scope of teleological thinking in preschool children. *Cognition, 70* , 241–272.

MacNeil, R., & Cran, W. (2005). *Do you speak American?: A companion to the PBS television series.* New York: Talese/Doubleday.

Mayer, R. E. (2002) Should there be a three-strikes rules against pure discovery learning?: The case for guided methods of instruction. *American Psychologist, 59*, 14-19.

Minstrell, J. (2001). The role of the teacher in making sense of classroom experience and effecting better learning. In S.M. Carver & D. Klahr (Eds.), *Cognition and instruction: 25 years of progress* (pp. 121-150). Mahwah, NJ: Erlbaum.

Mislevy, R. J., Steinberg, L. S., Almond, R. G., & Lukas, J. F. (2006). Concepts, terminology, and basic models of evidence-centered design. In D. M. Williamson, R. J. Mislevy & I. I. Bejar (Eds), *Automated scoring of complex tasks in computer-based testing* (pp. 15-47). Mahwah, NJ: Erlbaum

Neisser, U. (Ed.). (1998) *The rising curve. Long term gains in IQ and related measures.* Washington DC: American Psychological Association.

Pettit, P. B. (2002). The Neanderthal dead: Exploring mortuary variability in middle Paleolithic Eurasia. *Before Farming, 1* [online journal]. Available: www.waspjournals.com/beforefarming/

Schneider, W., & Shiffrin, R. M. (1977). Controlled and automatic processing: I. Detection, search, and attention. *Psychological Review, 84,* 1-66.

Snow, R. E. (1982). Education and intelligence. In R. J. Sternberg (Ed.), *Handbook of human intelligence* (pp. 493–585). New York: Cambridge University Press.

Teasdale, T. W., & Owen, D. R. (2000) Forty-year secular trends in cognitive abilities. *Intelligence, 28,* 115-120.

CHAPTER 7

EVOLUTION OF SCIENTIFIC THINKING

Comments on Geary's "Educating the Evolved Mind"

David Klahr

When the editors of this volume invited me to write a commentary on David Geary's paper on evolutionary educational psychology, I was surprised, because I do not view evolutionary psychology as an intellectual niche in which my own scientific contributions have any roots. Moreover, one thing that I have gleaned from evolutionary theory is that it is dangerous for an organism to stray very far from its adapted niche. However, upon reading the paper, I discovered that Geary's ideas about the educational implications of human evolutionary history are directly relevant to an area with which I am quite familiar: the development of scientific reasoning skills. Indeed, I believe that some of his ideas can be used to expand and enrich my own perspective on the development and instruction of scientific reasoning processes.

I first offer a summary of the points and principles of evolutionary educational psychology in Geary's Table 1.1, by compressing them into

Educating the Evolved Mind: Conceptual Foundations for an
Evolutionary Educational Psychology, pp. 155–164
Copyright © 2007 by Information Age Publishing

my own list of seven "Geary-isms," with an emphasis on the implications for science education:

1.   "Mind" is an evolved entity emerging in a biological organism, not an artifact created by humans, and it comprises two quite distinct types of entities: *biologically primary* and *biologically secondary* domains (or knowledge, or systems, or competencies—Geary uses these terms interchangeably).

2.   Understanding the consequences of Mind's evolution may provide insights that will enable us to teach more effectively.

3.   Doing so requires that we look carefully at the "fit" (or lack of it) between the biologically primary forms of knowledge and motivation, on the one hand, and the structure and content of instructional objectives and the motivations and behaviors necessary to achieve those objectives, on the other.

4.   The processes that constitute scientific reasoning are far distant and, in many cases in conflict with, many of the biologically primary forms of cognition and motivation.

5.   The survival of human societies requires that some, but not necessarily all, people acquire the cognitive processes and motivations that advance science and technology.

6.   Therefore, societies in which a nontrivial proportion of adults are expected to acquire scientific and technical knowledge, skills, and attitudes must provide formal schooling based on carefully crafted instructional design.

7.   Instructional designers who do not recognize and adapt to the inherent misalignment—in Geary's words the "ever growing gap" between primary and secondary scientific knowledge—are unlikely to be successful.

My commentary will focus on points 4 and 5 above. To anticipate: I do not agree with point 4, and I would have liked to see more discussion of the implications of point 5.

SCIENTIFIC REASONING PROCESSES: BIOLOGICALLY PRIMARY OR SECONDARY?

Geary is quite correct in his depiction of the large gap between "everyday reasoning" and scientific reasoning, and the necessity for formal instruction to fill that gap. He notes that:

Without solid instruction, children do not: (a) learn many basic scientific concepts, ... (b) effectively separate and integrate the hypothesis and experiment spaces; (c) effectively generate experiments that include all manipulations needed to fully test and especially to disconfirm hypotheses; and (d) learn all of the rules of evidence for evaluating experimental results as these relate to hypothesis testing. (Geary, this volume, p. 68)

It is clear that in order to become a practicing scientist, or even a scientifically literate citizen, one must acquire an enormous amount of highly specific conceptual and procedural knowledge—all of it biologically secondary. However—and here is the main point of this commentary—I believe that the most creative scientific advances are highly dependent on the fundamental, biologically primary, broadly applicable, problem-solving heuristics—"search processes," as Newell and Simon (1972) called them, such as generate-and-test, hill-climbing, and means-ends analysis. As Simon and his colleagues put it:

It is understandable, if ironic, that "normal" science fits pretty well the description of expert problem solving, while "revolutionary" science fits the description of problem solving by novices. It is understandable because scientific activity, particularly at the revolutionary end of the continuum, is concerned with the discovery of new truths, not with the application of truths that are already well known.... It is basically a journey into unmapped terrain. Consequently, it is mainly characterized, as is novice problem solving, by trial-and-error search. The search may be highly selective—the selectivity depending on how much is already known about the domain—but it reaches its goal only after many halts, turning, and backtrackings. (Simon, Langley, & Bradshaw, 1981, p. 5)

This perspective—that the really creative leaps in science utilize some very fundamental (biologically primary) processes—is held not only by cognitive psychologists who study the nature of extraordinary mental accomplishments (Klahr & Simon, 1999), but also by many of the world's greatest nonpsychologist scientists. Their speculations and introspections on the mental processes that led to their own scientific advances imply that the real "action" in scientific discovery rests on the bedrock of biologically primary problem-solving processes.

The whole of science is nothing more than a refinement of every day thinking. It is for this reason that the critical thinking of the physicist cannot possibly be restricted to the examination of concepts of his own specific field. He cannot proceed without considering critically a much more difficult problem, the problem of analyzing the nature of everyday thinking. (Einstein, 1936, p. 59)

The scientific way of forming concepts differs from that which we use in our daily life, not basically, but merely in the more precise definition of concepts and conclusions; more painstaking and systematic choice of experimental material, and greater logical economy. ("The Common Language of Science," 1941, reprinted in Einstein, 1950, p. 98)

I think what needs to be emphasized about the discovery of the double helix is that the path to it was, scientifically speaking, fairly commonplace. What was important was *not the way it was discovered*, but the object discovered—the structure of DNA itself. (Crick, 1988, p. 67; emphasis added)

The weak methods involved in problem solving—of all kinds—are available to children quite early. While there are many studies demonstrating that very young children can execute a variety of problem solving methods (e.g., Chen & Siegler, 2000; Sodian, Zaitchik, & Carey, 1991; Welsh, 1991; Willatts, 1990), I will illustrate the point with just an anecdote from my own experience. Several (many, actually) years ago, I had the following exchange with my daughter, who was 5 or 6 years old at the time.

Scene: Child & father in back yard. Child's playmate appears riding a bike.

Child: *Daddy, would you unlock basement door?*
Father: Why?
Child: *I want to ride my bike.*
Father: Your bike is in the garage.
Child: *But my socks are in the dryer.*

At the time, it was quite clear to me what my daughter wanted, and why she wanted it, and thus I found the conversation quite unremarkable. But later that week, as I was preparing a lecture on problem solving, I realized that a tremendous amount of thinking had occurred in the few seconds that led her to formulate the request. My armchair analysis is illustrated in Table 7.1. As is evident from the amount of subgoaling, retrieval, and inferencing, this little episode required a substantial amount of problem solving, and yet it is hard to imagine that any formal instruction was necessary to get a child of this age to accomplish this kind of thinking. More formal studies have demonstrated quite convincingly that by the time they enter preschool, children are quite capable of generating two or three subgoals in their problem-solving behavior, even in contexts that are quite unfamiliar and arbitrary (Klahr, 1978; Klahr & Robinson, 1981), and even infants have been shown to demonstrate simple means-ends analysis.

Many years later I found myself reflecting on another piece of effortless problem solving in another mundane circumstance. The problem I faced was getting from my office at Carnegie Mellon to a conference room

Table 7.1.   Hypothetical Sequence of Problem-Solving Steps

Goal: Ride bike (with friend)
  Memory retrieval: family rule—must have shoes on for biking
  Fact: feet are bare
  Subgoal 1: Get shoes
    Observation: Shoes in yard
    Memory retrieval: Shoes hurt on bare feet
    Subgoal 2: Protect feet (get socks)
      Memory retrieval: Sock drawer empty this morning
      Inference: socks still in dryer
      Subgoal 3: Get to dryer
        Memory retrieval: dryer in basement
        Subgoal 4: Enter basement
          Memory retrieval: short route through yard door to basement
          Memory retrieval: yard door always locked
          Subgoal 5: Unlock yard door to basement
            Memory retrieval: Dad has keys
            Subgoal 6: Ask Dad to unlock door

in Colorado. The "difference" between my initial state and my goal state was one of distance, and among the set of distance-reduction operators were: flying, walking, biking, and so forth. Flying was the operator of choice, but I could not fly directly from my office to Breckenridge, Colorado. This presented the subproblem of creating conditions for flying (e.g., getting to an airport, getting on a plane, etc.). Getting to the airport could best be done via taxi, but there was no taxi at Carnegie Mellon. The sub-subproblem involved making a phone call to the cab company. But all the university phones were out of order for the day during a transition to a new system; only the pay phones worked. An even deeper subproblem: how to make a call on a pay phone (remember them?) when I had no change?. However, a Coke machine was handy, and it accepted dollar bills and gave change. So I bought a Coke in order to get on the solution path to transport myself to Colorado.

My claims here are that the processes I used in this example are the same as those used by my 6-year-old daughter, that these general problem solving methods are biologically primary, that they change very little over the life span, and that they need no formal instruction. Of course, all of these weak methods, these problem-solving heuristics, these processes that guide search in the space of hypotheses and the space of experiments (Klahr, 2000), must be augmented by the specific knowledge and methods that are relevant to each scientific domain, and this domain-specific knowledge is unlikely to be acquired without formal instruction. In contrast, biologically primary weak methods remain, at their core, pretty much the same throughout the life span. There is scant evidence that any of the techniques aimed at improving these fundamental problem solving processes are effective (Sweller, 1990).

This is not to say that the so called "scientist in the crib" (Gopnik, Meltzoff, & Kuhl, 1999) is prepared to make the discoveries of a Crick, or a Darwin, or an Einstein. Clearly, formal education, and quite a lot of it, is necessary to provide the context and the massive knowledge accumulation that characterizes expertise in any area. In fact, I wish that Geary had been even more specific about exactly the type of instruction that he deems necessary to help students acquire all of this knowledge. In an earlier paper (Geary, 1995), he is quite direct in this regard in discussing the implications of his evolutionary perspective for instruction in mathematics, but the argument is equally valid for the biologically secondary aspects of scientific reasoning.

> "many constructivist researchers reject outright the use of drill-and-practice for acquiring mathematical skills. Indeed, formal drill-and-practice does not appear to be necessary for the acquisition and maintenance of many biologically primary cognitive abilities.... The evolved natural activities of humans, however, do not include embedded practice of the abilities that are associated with biologically secondary domains.... The acquisition and maintenance of biologically secondary abilities over the long-term almost certainly require some amount of sustained practice.... Cultural values that support student involvement in this practice are essential ... because evolution has not provided children with a natural enjoyment of the activities, such as drill-and-practice, that appear to be needed in order to master the abilities that are associated with complex secondary domains.... Although drill-and-practice is the bane of many contemporary educational researchers, it is probably the only way to ensure the long-term retention of basic, biologically secondary procedures. (pp. 32-33)

ADVANCING THEORY IN THE CRUCIBLE OF PRACTICE: PASTEUR'S QUADRANT IN SCIENCE EDUCATION

At the outset, Geary warns that his theory "is not a perspective that is ready for direct translation into school curricula." I agree, and I believe that one important way to advance that theory is to move from the "science" of analyzing different aspects of scientific thinking, to the "engineering" of specific instructional objectives. We can view this effort as occurring in Pasteur's Quadrant (Stokes, 1997), where the attempt to solve applied problems leads to advances in basic theory.

There is a venerable history of this type of bi-directional boundary crossing between basic research in the psychology laboratory and applied research on instructional development, richly described in Lagemann's (2000) account of how—during any particular period—the dominant theories in psychology have tended to frame efforts at "instructional engineering." Thus, for a period during the last century, they were heavily influenced by the behaviorist tradition. The Sixties produced several new efforts based on the excitement and promise of the "cognitive revolution" (e.g., Atkinson, 1968; Gagne, 1968; Glaser & Resnick, 1972; Suppes & Groen, 1967). More recent efforts, based on emerging perspectives on cognition and cognitive development, are exemplified by the work of Case (1992), who pioneered research that sought both basic understanding of child development and effective instruction for children. Brown and colleagues (Brown, 1992; Brown & Campione, 1994; Palincsar & Brown, 1984) led a successful research program that took "reciprocal teaching" from the laboratory to the classroom across many school topics. Rittle-Johnson, Siegler, and Alibali (2001) showed how an examination of good learners could guide improved instruction in decimal fractions. My colleagues and I have followed this path in our work on the acquisition of experimental design skills in middle school children (Klahr & Li, 2005). Anderson and colleagues (Anderson, Corbett, Koedinger, & Pelletier, 1995) developed an effective intelligent tutoring system for learning algebra—now used in thousands of schools nationwide—from a basic research program in computational modeling of cognition. These educational engineering efforts have led to important advances in fundamental theoretical issues such as the effects of feedback, practice, and metacognition on learning (Mathan & Koedinger, 2005).

The point of all this, with respect to Geary's evolutionary educational psychology, is that the theory probably can't be advanced much beyond where it now stands until educators begin to attempt to fashion science instruction that is sensitive to the many distinctions that Geary delineates between different forms of biologically primary scientific knowledge, and the secondary forms of scientific knowledge that are required in different domains. One important outcome of such efforts will be the discovery of just what can and cannot be taught and how much is already there, ready to be harnessed as children first enter the science classroom.

VARIATION AND SELECTION IN EDUCATING SCIENTISTS

At the outset of this commentary, I acknowledged the dangers of venturing beyond my own areas of scientific expertise. However, I can't resist the temptation—speaking more as a citizen speculating on the values of a society than as a scientist—to respond to another fundamental theme in Geary's paper: the fact that evolution produces distributions of important attributes in a population. Intelligence and motivation are two such distributed attributes, and Geary suggests that this evolved variability has clear implications for society's educational goals and practices. More specifically, Geary argues that the evolution of mind has produced substantial variation in children's starting points for learning science. " ... *most children will not be sufficiently motivated nor cognitively able to learn all of secondary knowledge needed for functioning in modern societies without well organized, explicit and direct teacher instruction* (p. 43, emphasis in original). This implies that it is folly to construct a one-size-fits-all approach to science education, with respect to both starting points and desired end states. As Geary puts it: "attempts to achieve within-culture 'equity' may come at a long-term cost in terms of the ability to compete with other cultures" (p. 75). This position has important political implications, and I wish that Geary had been clearer in elucidating the policy recommendations that he thinks might flow from his position.

In contemporary society, in the United States at least, the idea of an educational system that acknowledges and adapts to the existence of intellectual elites is pretty unpopular—often among those very elites. Nevertheless, Geary appears to argue for the inevitability, indeed the necessity, for educational planners to recognize this variability as a biological fact, no different from the much more widely accepted idea of elites in sports or the arts. I was frustrated by his reluctance to state this more boldly, and to address the kind of likely response it would generate once readers figured out the implications of his account of intelligence. But perhaps that must await Geary's next thoughtful and provocative paper.

ACKNOWLEDGMENTS

Preparation of this commentary was supported in part by a grant from the National Science Foundation, 0132315, "Fundamentals of Experimental Science in Early Science Education." I thank my colleagues, Sharon Carver and Robert Siegler for their comments and suggestions on an earlier version of this commentary.

REFERENCES

Anderson, J. R., Corbett, A. T., Koedinger, K. R., & Pelletier, R. (1995). Cognitive tutors: Lessons learned. *Journal of the Learning Sciences, 4*, 167–207.
Atkinson, R. (1968). Computerized instruction and the learning process. *American Psychologist, 23*, 225–239.

Brown, A. L. (1992). Design experiments: Theoretical and methodological challenges in creating complex interventions in classroom settings. *Journal of the Learning Sciences, 2*, 141–178.

Brown, A. L., Campione, J. C. (1994). Guided discovery in a community of learners. In K. McGilly (Ed.), *Classroom lessons: Integrating cognitive theory and classroom practice* (pp. 229-272). Cambridge, MA: MIT Press.

Case, R. (1992). *The mind's staircase: Exploring the conceptual underpinnings of children's thought and knowledge.* Hillsdale, NJ: Erlbaum.

Chen, Z,, & Siegler, R. S. (2000). Across the great divide: Bridging the gap between understanding of toddlers and older children's thinking. *Monographs of the Society for Research in Child Development, 65*(2, Serial No. 261).

Crick, F. (1988). *What mad pursuit: A personal view of scientific discovery.* New York: Basic Books.

Einstein, A. (1936). *Physics & reality.* New York: Philosophical Library.

Einstein, A. (1950). *Out of my later years.* New York: Philosophical Library.

Gagne, R. (1968). Contributions of learning to human development. *Psychological Review, 75,* 177–191.

Geary, D. C. (1995). Reflections of evolution and culture in children's cognition: Implications for mathematical development and instruction. *American Psychologist, 50,* 24-37.

Glaser, R., & Resnick, L. (1972). Instructional psychology. *Annual Review of Psychology 23,* 207–276.

Gopnik, A., Meltzoff, A. N., & Kuhl, P. K. (1999). *The scientist in the crib: What early learning tells us about the Mind.* New York: Harper Collins.

Klahr, D. (1978). Goal formation, planning, and learning by pre-school problem solvers, or: 'My socks are in the dryer'. In R. S. Siegler (Ed.), *Children's thinking: What develops?* (pp. 181-212). Hillsdale, NJ: Erlbaum.

Klahr, D. (2000). *Exploring science: The cognition and development of discovery processes.* Cambridge, MA: MIT Press.

Klahr, D. & Li, J. (2005) Cognitive research and elementary science instruction: From the laboratory, to the classroom, and back. *Journal of Science Education and Technology, 4*(2), 217-238.

Klahr, D., & Robinson, M. (1981). Formal assessment of problem solving and planning processes in preschool children. *Cognitive Psychology, 13,* 113-148.

Klahr, D., & Simon, H. A. (1999). Studies of scientific discovery: Complementary approaches and convergent findings. *Psychological Bulletin, 125,* 524-543.

Lagemann, E. C. (2000). *An elusive science: The troubling history of educational research.* Chicago: University of Chicago Press.

Mathan, S. A., & Koedinger, K. R. (2005) Fostering the intelligent novice: Learning from errors with metacognitive tutoring. *Educational Psychologist, 40,* 257-265.

Newell, A., & Simon, H. A. (1972). *Human problem solving.* Englewood Cliffs, NJ: Prentice-Hall

Palincsar, A., & Brown, A. (1984). Reciprocal teaching of comprehension-fostering and comprehension monitoring activities. *Cognition and Instruction, 1,* 117–175.

Rittle-Johnson, B., Siegler, R. S., & Alibali, M. (2001). Developing conceptual understanding and procedural skill in mathematics: An iterative process. *Journal of Educational Psychology, 93*, 346-362

Simon, H. A., Langley, P., & Bradshaw, G. L. (1981). Scientific discovery as problem solving. *Synthese, 47*, 1-27.

Sodian, B., Zaitchik, D., & Carey, S. (1991). Young children's differentiation of hypothetical beliefs from evidence. *Child Development, 62*, 753-766.

Stevenson, H. W., & Stigler, J. W. (1992). *The learning gap: Why our schools are failing and what we can learn from Japanese and Chinese education*. New York: Summit Books.

Stokes, D. E. (1997). *Pasteur's quadrant: Basic science and technological innovation.* Washington, DC: Brookings Institution Press,

Suppes, P., & Groen, G. (1967). Some counting models for first grade performance data on simple addition facts. In J. Scandura (Ed.), *Research In mathematics education* (pp. 35-43). Washington, DC: National Council of Teachers of Mathematics,

Sweller, J. (1990). On the limited evidence for the effectiveness of teaching general problem-solving Strategies . *Journal for Research in Mathematics Education, 21*, 411-415.

Welsh, M.C. (1991). Rule-guided behavior and self-monitoring on the Tower of Hanoi disk-transfer task. *Cognitive Development, 4*, 59-76.

Willatts, P. (1990). Development of problem solving strategies in infancy. In D. F. Bjorklund (Ed.), *Children's strategies* (pp. 23-66). Hillsdale, NJ: Erlbaum.

Zimmerman, C. (2005). *The development of scientific reasoning skills: What psychologists contribute to an understanding of elementary science learning*. (Report to the National Research Council's Board of Science Education, Consensus study on learning Science, kindergarten through eighth grade). Available: http://www7.nationalacademies.org/bose/Corinne_Zimmerman_Final_Paper.pdf

CHAPTER 8

EVOLUTIONARY BIOLOGY AND EDUCATIONAL PSYCHOLOGY

John Sweller

In his ambitious monograph "Educating the Evolved Mind: Conceptual Foundations for an Evolutionary Educational Psychology," David Geary successfully provides educational psychology with a new intellectual base. The work is encyclopaedic, novel, and timely.

Whether or not educational psychologists explicitly use evolution by natural selection in their theories, most are likely to agree that human cognition must have evolved according to the same Darwinian principles as all other biological structures and functions. If human cognition evolved according to Darwinian principles, that evolutionary process has implications for both the nature of human cognition and the manner in which we should present information to learners. Geary's work, concerned with those implications, demonstrates that by explicitly using biological evolution as a base for educational psychology, the discipline can take on an entirely different character with regard to many long-standing controversies. In this commentary, I will attempt to analyze further the use of evolutionary principles in educational psychology by

Educating the Evolved Mind: Conceptual Foundations for an
Evolutionary Educational Psychology, pp. 165–175
Copyright © 2007 by Information Age Publishing
All rights of reproduction in any form reserved.

both building on Geary's theoretical formulation and by indicating some of the specific instructional consequences that flow from the use of biological evolution as a foundation for educational psychology.

There are two related ways in which we can use biological evolution in psychology. The first, used by Geary, is to consider how and why particular human cognitive characteristics evolved. For example, we are able to assimilate the large amount of information required for a first language relatively easily but have much more difficulty assimilating mathematical principles because language has evolved as part of our social relations while mathematics is a relatively new invention. In his paper Geary considers a variety of human skills from an evolutionary perspective and in doing so, provides his base for educational psychology. This approach will be referred to as the instrumental application of evolutionary theory.

There is a second way in which evolution by natural selection may be relevant to psychology and education. Both biological evolution and human cognition provide examples of natural information processing systems. I will argue that the same principles underlie both biological evolution and cognition. Because the two systems have a common base, we not only can instrumentally apply evolutionary principles to determine how and why we have specific cognitive characteristics in the manner indicated by Geary, but we can use the very processes of evolution by natural selection to guide us in finding and understanding the cognitive processes that have evolved. Once that base is established, we can use it to assist in determining effective instructional processes. This approach will be referred to as the analogical application of evolutionary theory.

In summary, the instrumental approach considers the evolutionary reasons for particular cognitive characteristics in order: (a) to obtain a better understanding of those characteristics; and (b) to use that understanding to determine instructional procedures. This approach is used by Geary. At a more basic level, the analogical approach analyzes evolutionary processes and maps them onto cognitive processes. Both the instrumental and analogical uses of evolution by natural selection are, as might be expected, related. More importantly for present purposes, both uses provide a firm foundation for psychology and its implications for education. To clarify the analogical approach, I will begin by outlining the characteristics of natural information-processing systems, followed by a discussion of the instrumental approach in which I will consider the importance of natural information-processing characteristics for the issues raised by Geary. I will conclude by indicating some of the specific instructional consequences that flow from this formulation.

THE ANALOGICAL APPROACH:
NATURAL INFORMATION-PROCESSING SYSTEMS

Nature processes information. All living beings process information as does the system that creates living beings, evolution by natural selection. Irrespective of the use to which it is put, the basic logic of natural information-processing systems is invariant. There are many ways of specifying that logic (e.g., see Sweller, 2003) but in this commentary it will be described using five basic principles.

"Information store" principle.   Natural information-processing systems function in complex environments with the bulk of their activity determined by very large stores of information. A genome provides that store in the case of biological evolution while long-term memory provides a similar function in the case of human cognition. Initial evidence for the central importance of long-term memory in most human cognitive activity including problem solving came from de Groot's (1965) and Chase and Simon's (1973) ground-breaking work in which they found that the skill of chess grand-masters derived from memory of large numbers of board configurations along with the associated best moves for each configuration.

"Borrowing and reorganizing" principle.   Because of the great size of natural information stores, efficient techniques for building the stores must be available. Almost all information in a natural information store is borrowed from another store. While reorganization tends to be an associated characteristic of the procedure, the basic process is borrowing. Sexual reproduction provides a good example of the *borrowing and reorganizing* principle. As a consequence of sexual reproduction, an individual's entire genome is borrowed from his or her ancestors, apart from mutations. Nevertheless, no individual is a copy of his or her ancestors with the process structured to necessarily involve reorganization. That reorganization occurs in order to ensure diversity.

Similarly, almost all knowledge held in a person's long-term memory is borrowed from the memories of other individuals. We imitate others, listen to what they say and read what they write. While we borrow information, we rarely, if ever, obtain an exact copy. The borrowed information is schematic. New information is combined with old information in long-term memory to form schemas (Bartlett, 1932).

"Randomness as genesis" principle.   The *borrowing and reorganizing* principle does not create new information. At best, it reorganizes old information. Since human thought and creativity frequently create new information, mechanisms for creating novel information are required.

Random mutation is the engine of novelty in biological evolution. All variation between species and between individuals within species can be sourced back to random mutation. Each mutation is tested for effectiveness with effective mutations retained and ineffective mutations jettisoned. In human cognition, novelty is generated during problem solving. When deciding on a problem-solving move, we use (a) knowledge; (b) random generation followed by tests for effectiveness; or (c) most commonly, a combination of knowledge and random generate and test. No other basic mechanisms have been identified, just as biological evolution uses no other mechanisms to generate novelty.

"Narrow limits of change" principle.   The *narrow limits of change* principle is concerned with information flowing from the environment to the information store. The epigenetic system acts as a mediator between the environment and the DNA-based genome (Jablonka & Lamb, 2005). For example, the epigenetic system can determine mutation rates and locations (Jablonka & Lamb, 2005) and in this sense, the epigenetic system effects the information that is stored in DNA.

Working memory has the same role in cognition as the epigenetic system has in evolution by natural selection. Information from the environment to be stored in long-term memory is processed by working memory. At any given time, only very small amounts of new, environmental information can be processed because that information is generated via the previously mentioned *randomness as genesis* principle and the probability of a large amount of novel information being effective is slight. Most novel information will either be ineffective or worse, may damage information already stored in long-term memory. For this reason, alterations to the information store due to novel environmental information occur slowly over long periods of time. Specifically, effective mutation rates are always slow during biological evolution and in human cognition, working memory has severe capacity limitations when dealing with novel information (Cowan, 2001).

"Environmental organizing and linking" principle.   The ultimate purpose of all of the preceding principles is to enable information-processing systems to function in complex, natural environments. The *environmental organizing and linking* principle provides the necessary vehicle. Unlike the narrow limits of change principle that deals with information flowing from the environment to the information store, the *environmental organizing and linking* principle deals with information flowing from the information store.

Because it is organized, information from the information store has no processing limits, in contrast to the unorganized information from the environment that must have processing limits precisely because it is unorganized. Huge amounts of information in DNA can be and indeed, must be used for its ultimate function, the synthesis of protein to express particular phenotypes. Just as the epigenetic system mediated the flow of information from the environment to the information stored in DNA, that system also mediates the flow of information in the opposite direction from the information store to the environment. For example, it is the epigenetic system that determines whether a gene is activated or silenced. The variety of cells in the human body all contain identical DNA in their nucleus despite being disparate in their structure and function. It is the epigenetic system that determines which information will be used to determine cell structure and function.

Working memory has a similar function in human cognition. The characteristics of working memory are vastly different depending on whether we are dealing with novel information from the environment or organized information from long-term memory. Unlike the severely limited amount of unorganized information from the environment that can be handled by working memory, there are no known limits to the amount of organized information from long-term memory that working memory can process (Ericsson & Kintsch, 1995). We store organized information in long-term memory in order to permit us to transfer it to working memory and use it to govern our activities.

THE INSTRUMENTAL APPROACH: EVOLUTION OF HUMAN COGNITIVE CHARACTERISTICS

As indicated above, evolution by natural selection not only provides a template or analogy for human cognition via natural information processing systems, but we also can use evolution to analyze and explain particular human cognitive characteristics. That instrumental approach is used by Geary. One of Geary's major points is his distinction between primary and secondary knowledge. Primary knowledge is knowledge we have evolved to acquire. We do not have to be taught and do not consciously (i.e., through working memory) learn to listen to the immensely complex sounds that constitute our native language. We have evolved to acquire the auditory component of our native language. It is a primary skill. In contrast, while we have evolved to process spoken language, we have not evolved the ability to decode visual, or written language. That is secondary knowledge only relatively recently acquired—indeed, consciously invented, by humans and so it must be explicitly taught. Educational systems and organizations have been developed so that we can acquire secondary knowledge. We do not need educational institutions for the primary knowledge that we have evolved to acquire without explicit instruction. Primary knowledge is automatically acquired in any normal human environment.

The natural information-processing system discussed above, when applied to human cognition, deals entirely with secondary knowledge. It may appear paradoxical that a system based on evolutionary principles applies only to human knowledge that we have not evolved to specifically acquire and does not apply to knowledge we have evolved to acquire. The paradox is readily resolved. Evolution by natural selection is a system that deals with any category of information that impinges on an evolving species. It is designed to deal with any information, not with particular classes of information. In contrast, primary knowledge consists of particular classes of information with which we have evolved to deal. We have specific cognitive and brain structures (e.g., a visual cortex), and in some cases perceptual structures (e.g., eyes), to deal with those classes of information in particular ways and so do not need the more general, natural information-processing principles to deal with that type of information. We do need a system to deal with all other information that we have not specifically evolved to process. That system, I suggest, is the natural information-processing system discussed in the previous section. It is the same system that permits evolution by natural selection to deal with any type of information.

While secondary knowledge is acquired using the principles of natural information-processing systems, those principles rely on primary knowledge to function. We do not have to be explicitly taught to construct and accumulate knowledge in long-term memory. We have evolved to do so automatically and thus knowledge construction and accumulation is a primary skill. Similarly, as discussed under the *borrowing and reorganizing* principle, we acquire most of our knowledge by imitating other people, listening to what they say or reading what they write. Knowing how to imitate other people or knowing how to understand their speech or indeed, even knowing that imitating and listening are important activities, constitute primary knowledge. (Reading is primary to the extent that it relies on language and secondary in the sense that writing is an artificially devised activity rather than an evolved activity.) Furthermore, in the mirror neuron system, we now have physiological evidence for our biologically evolved predisposition to imitate. Mirror neurons fire when we engage in a particular motor action, when we think of engaging in that action, when we listen to sentences describing the action or when we observe someone else engage in that action (Grafton, Arbib, Fadiga, & Rizzolatti, 1996; Iacoboni, Woods, Brass, Bekkering, Mazziotta & Rizzolatti, 1999; Tettamanti et al., 2005). We do not have to teach people to imitate or listen to speech because we are physiologically structured to do so and in that sense, the *borrowing and reorganizing* principle is driven by primary knowledge. Similarly, we do not need to teach children to engage in random generate and test because the *randomness as genesis* principle ensures that we engage in this procedure without instruction and, of course, the function of working memory as a conduit between long-term memory and the environment, via the narrow limits of change and the environmental organizing and linking principles, are not learned functions.

In effect, evolution by natural selection has driven the evolution of human cognition to mimic the functions of evolution itself (Sweller, 2003, 2004). That process required the evolution of a considerable number of primary activities. In turn, those evolved primary activities can be used to permit secondary activities to function as part of a natural information processing system.

Thinking and general problem solving are primary activities that do not require instructional procedures. The principles of natural information-processing systems indicate the relevant mechanisms. Most problems are solved by using the *borrowing and reorganizing* principle. If problem solutions from long-term memory are available, then they will be used. If unavailable in long-term memory, they may be borrowed from others. If solutions also are unavailable from others, then a random generate and test process using the *randomness as genesis* principle will be used. Thus, problem solving is a combination of previous knowledge borrowed from one's own or someone else's long-term memory and random generate and test where knowledge is unavailable concerning which of two or more possible moves should be made.

None of the processes described here to explain thinking and general problem solving requires secondary knowledge. Rather, the primary knowledge used to drive the processes is used to acquire and deal with secondary knowledge. The processes, as opposed to most of the information used, are all based on primary knowledge. We know how to solve problems using these processes because we have evolved to solve problems, not because we have learned to solve them during deliberate, teaching/learning episodes. As a consequence of problem solving, we may acquire secondary knowledge that may be used to solve subsequent problems but our knowledge of general problem solving strategies remains primary knowledge that cannot be taught.

Thought, decision making, and planning are all variants of problem solving and so the processes involved also can be categorized as primary knowledge. If these processes require primary rather than secondary knowledge, there are implications for instructional procedures.

INSTRUCTIONAL IMPLICATIONS: COGNITIVE LOAD THEORY

Cognitive load theory is an instructional theory that has used variations of the cognitive architecture described above to generate specific instructional procedures (e.g. Sweller, 2003, 2004). It has not used Geary's distinction between primary and secondary knowledge but I believe the theory, like all instructional theories, will unavoidably have to take this distinction into account in future. Cognitive load theory is well placed to do so. The theory is entirely concerned with the instructional consequences of a limited working memory on building knowledge in long-term memory. As it happens and as might be expected of an instructional theory, that knowledge has in all cases been secondary. Furthermore, since its inception in the mid-1980s, the theory has been used to suggest that primary knowledge such as general problem solving strategies is unteachable and unlearnable (e.g., Sweller & Cooper, 1985) in an educational environment because learners already have the required knowledge. Teaching general problem-solving strategies is futile because we acquire such knowledge easily and quickly in any normal human environment. Accordingly, as might be expected, there is no body of literature demonstrating the advantages of teaching general problem-solving strategies (Kirschner, Sweller, & Clark, 2006).

Not only is there no body of literature demonstrating the advantages of teaching general problem-solving strategies; there is no body of literature demonstrating the advantages of using any constructivist teaching technique despite decades of advocacy (Kirschner, Sweller, & Clark, 2006). Constructing knowledge is a primary skill. We construct knowledge automatically via the *borrowing and organizing* and *randomness as genesis* principles. It follows that attempting to teach people how to construct knowledge is likely to be a pointless. Learning how to construct knowledge in long-term memory is a primary skill that we evolved to acquire.

As Geary indicates, in contrast to primary knowledge, the secondary knowledge characteristically emphasized in education is not easily and automatically assimilated by learners. It needs to be carefully organized and presented using direct instructional guidance. For the secondary knowledge dealt with in education, an emphasis needs to be placed on the *borrowing and organizing* principle, not the *randomness as genesis* principle. That means information needs to be presented to learners rather than have them generate it themselves using a random generate and test procedure. It is difficult to see what is gained by having learners engage in a random generate and test procedure when organized knowledge can be readily presented to them. We do not need to be taught how to engage in random generate and test because it is primary knowledge and generate and test is a poor technique for acquiring secondary knowledge.

Once these assumptions of cognitive load theory are made, there are many specific instructional techniques to facilitate learning that flow from the cognitive architecture discussed in this commentary (see Sweller, 2003, 2004). All are based on effects generated by randomized, controlled experiments. Only a few of these will be discussed here.

The worked example effect (e.g., Paas & van Gog, 2006; Reisslein, Atkinson, Seeling, & Reisslein, 2006; Sweller, 2006; Van Gog, Paas, & Van Merrienboer, 2006) is probably the best known cognitive load effect and the most relevant to current concerns. It occurs when learners presented worked examples to study perform better on a subsequent test than learners required to solve the equivalent problems. The effect has been replicated on many occasions and provides the strongest evidence for the importance of direct instruction when dealing with the secondary knowledge characteristically presented in educational contexts. Direct instruction maximizes use of the *borrowing and reorganizing* principle and minimizes use of the *randomness as genesis* principle.

The critical importance of Geary's distinction between primary and secondary knowledge is obvious when considering the worked example effect. Direct instruction is not required when dealing with primary knowledge because we have evolved to assimilate such information without instructional interventions. As Geary emphasizes, detailed, organized, direct instruction is critical when dealing with secondary knowledge.

There are several conditions under which the worked example effect does not occur. If a worked example or any form of instruction requires learners to split their attention between multiple sources of information that must be mentally integrated because they refer to each other (e.g., geometry statements referring to geometry diagrams), learning is inhibited compared to identical instruction in which the multiple sources of information are physically integrated (e.g., geometry statements physically integrated into a diagram). This split-attention effect (Ayres & Sweller, 2005) is caused by learners having to use working memory resources to mentally integrate information, resulting in a worked example being no better than solving a problem. When physically integrated, the instructions directly indicate which aspects of the information are related. In split-attention format, learners must use a form of random generate and test to work out relationships, reducing the influence of the *borrowing and reorganizing* principle.

The advantage of worked examples over solving equivalent problems only applies to novices. As expertise increases, differences first decrease and then reverse, with problems being superior to worked examples, providing an example of the expertise reversal effect (Kalyuga, Ayres, Chandler, & Sweller, 2003; Kalyuga, Chandler, Tuovinen, & Sweller, 2001). More expert learners in a particular area no longer need to search for solutions using random generate and test, rather, they need to practice solving problems. Studying worked examples is redundant for more expert learners, resulting in the redundancy effect that occurs when learners are presented information that they do not need (Sweller, 2005). Redundant information imposes an extraneous cognitive load.

Lastly, asking learners to imagine procedures or concepts can facilitate learning compared to simply studying the same material, resulting in the imagination effect (Leahy & Sweller, 2005). This effect indicates the importance of establishing new information in long-term memory.

There are many other specific cognitive load effects. All of them assume the cognitive architecture outlined in this commentary. Geary's distinction between primary and secondary knowledge has substantially (and to this researcher unexpectedly) widened the cognitive base that can be used to explain the current cognitive load effects and hopefully, generate additional findings. I believe Geary's theory will be influential for generations.

REFERENCES

Ayres, P., & Sweller, J. (2005). The split-attention principle. In R. E. Mayer (Ed.), *Cambridge handbook of multimedia learning* (pp. 135-146). New York: Cambridge University Press.

Bartlett, F. C. (1932). *Remembering: A study in experimental and social psychology:* Oxford, England: Macmillan.

Chase, W. G., & Simon, H. A. (1973). Perception in chess. *Cognitive Psychology, 4,* 55-81.

Cowan, N. (2001). The magical number 4 in short-term memory: A reconsideration of mental storage capacity. *Behavioral and Brain Sciences, 24,* 87-114.

De Groot, A. D. (1965). *Thought and choice in chess.* The Hague, Netherlands: Mouton. (Original work published 1946)

Ericsson, K. A., & Kintsch, W. (1995). Long-term working memory. *Psychological Review, 102,* 211-245.

Grafton, S., Arbib, M., Fadiga, L., & Rizzolatti, G. (1996). Localization of grasp representations in humans by positron emission tomography: 2. Observation compared with imagination. *Experimental Brain Research, 112,* 103-111.

Iacoboni, M., Woods, R., Brass, M., Bekkering, H., Mazziotta, J., & Rizzolatti, G. (1999). Cortical mechanisms of human imitation. *Science, 286,* 2526-2528.

Jablonka, E., & Lamb, M. J. (2005). *Evolution in four dimensions: Genetic, epigenetic, behavioral, and symbolic variation in the history of life.* Cambridge, MA: MIT Press.

Kalyuga, S., Ayres, P., Chandler, P., & Sweller, J. (2003). The expertise reversal effect. *Educational Psychologist, 38,* 23-31.

Kalyuga, S., Chandler, P., Tuovinen, J., & Sweller, J. (2001). When problem solving is superior to studying worked examples. *Journal of Educational Psychology, 93,* 579-588.

Kirschner, P., Sweller, J., & Clark, R. (2006). Why minimal guidance during instruction does not work: An analysis of the failure of constructivist, discovery, problem-based, experiential and inquiry-based teaching. *Educational Psychologist, 41,* 75-86.

Leahy, W., & Sweller, J. (2005). Interactions among the imagination, expertise reversal, and element interactivity effects. *Journal of Experimental Psychology: Applied, 11*, 266-276.

Paas, F., & van Gog, T. (2006). Optimising worked example instruction: Different ways to increase germane cognitive load. *Learning & Instruction, 16*, 87-91.

Reisslein, J., Atkinson, R., Seeling, P., & Reisslein, M. (2006). Encountering the expertise reversal effect with a computer-based environment on electrical circuit anaysis. *Learning and Instruction, 16*, 92-103.

Sweller, J. (2003). Evolution of human cognitive architecture. In B. Ross (Ed.), *The psychology of learning and motivation* (Vol. 43, pp. 215-266). San Diego, CA: Academic Press.

Sweller, J. (2004). Instructional design consequences of an analogy between evolution by natural selection and human cognitive architecture. *Instructional Science, 32*, 9-31.

Sweller, J. (2005). The redundancy principle. In R. E. Mayer (Ed.), *Cambridge handbook of multimedia learning* (pp. 159-167). New York: Cambridge University Press.

Sweller, J. (2006). The worked example effect and human cognition. *Learning and Instruction, 16*, 165-169.

Sweller, J., & Cooper, G. (1985). The use of worked examples as a substitute for problem solving in learning algebra. *Cognition & Instruction, 2*, 59-89.

Tettamanti, M., Buccino, G., Saccuman, M., Gallese, V., Dana, M., Scifo, P., et al. (2005). Listening to action-related sentences activates fronto-parietal motor circuits. *Journal of Cognitive Neuroscience, 17*, 273-281.

Van Gog, T., Paas, F., & Van Merrienboer, J. (2006). Effects of process-oriented worked examples on troubleshooting transfer performance. *Learning and Instruction, 16*, 154-164.

CHAPTER 9

EDUCATING THE EVOLVED MIND

Reflections and Refinements

David C. Geary

I thank the editors for the opportunity to write "Educating the Evolved Mind," and the commentators for providing many thoughtful and insightful remarks on the monograph. I am in agreement with nearly all of the issues raised by the commentators, including many of the criticisms of my model. I see the model only as a starting point for conceptualizing the how and why of education in modern society and for better defining the problem space, so to speak, of what is needed to translate theory into effective educational practice. As I stated, an evolutionary approach to education is not ready for the classroom but it can provide a useful perspective on issues that have confronted educators since and before the time of Rousseau's (1979) 1762 publication of *Emile*. In the following sections, I focus on issues raised by several or all of the commentators, as these seem to represent the most pressing questions for an evolutionary educational psychology. Several of the commentators are unsure as to whether an evolutionary approach has the potential to add value to what

Educating the Evolved Mind: Conceptual Foundations for an
Evolutionary Educational Psychology, pp. 177–203
Copyright © 2007 by Information Age Publishing

is already known about children's learning. In the first section I address this question and the more general question regarding the usefulness of evolutionary theory in the behavioral sciences. In the second and third, sections, respectively, I grapple with questions regarding whether more primary forms of learning (e.g., social collaboration) can be used to facilitate the acquisition of secondary knowledge, and on the role of traits other than general fluid intelligence (Gf) in this learning. In the final section, I focus on the implications of evolutionary theory for understanding individual differences in secondary learning.

DOES AN EVOLUTIONARY PERSPECTIVE PROVIDE ADDED VALUE?

Hunt questioned whether psychologists could generate falsifiable hypotheses based on evolutionary theory and thus make defensible inferences about our evolutionary past. Even if we could, he questioned whether any such inferences added value to our understanding of children's learning. Ackerman and Demetriou shared this latter concern. I first address the more general question of whether hypotheses generated through evolutionary theory are falsifiable, and then discuss the issue of added value.

Whither Evolutionary Psychology?

The re-emergence of evolutionary approaches to human behavior and psychology in the latter decades of the twentieth century, first as sociobiology and then as evolutionary psychology, created more than its share of social controversy and scientific debate (Segerstrale, 2000), and continues to do so today. Hunt is correct in stating that evolutionary scenarios can be generated for many current human behaviors, and thus considerable care must be taken in evaluating the scientific validity of any such scenarios. However, I believe that he has prematurely abandoned hope of creating scientifically falsifiable hypotheses based on evolutionary theory. In fact, evolutionary psychology is a highly empirical discipline, as evidenced by any volume of the journals *Evolution and Human Behavior* and *Human Nature*, and has resulted in a substantial and theoretically rich knowledge base in many areas that are of interest to psychologists and other behavioral scientists (Buss, 2005). Within the field of evolutionary biology, there are many empirical approaches that are routinely used to generate falsifiable hypotheses on the basis of evolutionary theory – see any issue of *American Naturalist* or *Proceedings of the Royal Society: Biological Sciences*, among others.

Darwin's (1871) theory of sexual selection provides an example of how evolutionary theory can lead to testable hypotheses and to a much richer understanding of the phenomena being studied. Darwin proposed that the evolution of many sex differences is related to intrasexual competition for mates and intersexual choice of mating partners. Among other things and as just one example, intense physical male-male competition for access to mates is predicted to result in larger and physically more aggressive males than females. The evolutionary aspect of this prediction can be tested by evaluating whether physical size and behavioral aggressiveness is related to reproductive outcomes and whether these differences are influenced by the proximate mechanisms involved in the expression of evolved sex differences, such as exposure to sex hormones; for instance, are sex hormones related to sex differences in growth trajectories and behavioral changes (e.g., increase in aggression) just prior to reproductive competition? Evolutionary theory has been successfully used to frame these empirical questions and they have been tested and largely confirmed across hundreds of species (see Andersson, 1994). These types of predictions are not limited to physical traits or behaviors. If finding mates requires a larger home range for males than females, then intrasexual competition will favor males with larger ranges. In these species, males are predicted to have better spatial-navigational abilities than females and these ability differences are predicted to be linked to exposure to male hormones. In a series of elegant field and experimental studies, Gaulin and his colleagues tested and confirmed these predictions across several species of vole (*Microtus*; Gaulin, 1992; Gaulin & Fitzgerald, 1986).

For humans, the range of potential evolutionary explanations for behaviors or cognitions can be substantially reduced with the triangulation of research results from the comparative literature, cross-cultural research, and of course psychological studies. Across species, physically larger males than females are associated with male-male competition for access to mates and polygyny, in keeping with Darwin's (1871) sexual selection. This pattern is found in humans and leads to a prediction of an evolutionary history of physical male-male competition, polygyny, and behavioral, cognitive, and developmental adaptations that facilitate and prepare men for this competition. Examination of the fossil record for species that are most likely to be our ancestors indicates that the pattern of larger males than females extends back at least four million years (e.g., Leakey, Feibel, McDougall, Ward, & Walker, 1998). In about 6 out of 7 traditional cultures there are no formal laws against polygynous marriage, and in these cultures dominant men tend to have several wives, to their reproductive advantage (Chagnon, 1979; Flinn & Low, 1986; Murdock, 1981).

One-on-one and coalitional male-male competition is common in these societies, and manifests as frequent raids on other villages and groups (Keeley, 1996). Across these cultures, Keeley found that 25% of males, on average, die as a direct result of male-male competition; for an example see Chagnon's (1988) studies of the Yanomamö. More recently, population genetic studies of Y-chromosome genes suggest a repeating pattern of one population of men replacing another population of men in Africa, Europe, and Asia (Underhill et al., 2001; J. Wilson, Weiss, Richards, Thomas, Bradman, & Goldstein, 2001), although the extent of replacement can vary from one region to the next (Capelli et al., 2003). There are also patterns of behavioral, psychological, and developmental sex differences that are found in all cultures in which they have been studied and that are consistent with predictions derived from Darwin's (1871) sexual selection (e.g., Geary, 1998; Geary, Byrd-Craven, Hoard, Vigil, & Numtee, 2003). At the same time, it is also clear that cultural factors, such as laws that suppress physical aggression, can have a substantial influence on how and whether evolved biases are expressed (Daly & Wilson, 1988)—there are core sex differences that are found in all cultures and that are consistent with cross-species patterns and Darwin's evolutionary theory of sexual selection, and there is cultural and historical variation in how these differences are expressed (Geary, 1998).

As with sex differences, the specifics can vary from one culture to the next, but beneath this surface structure there are many other human universals (Brown, 1981), including several mentioned by Hunt. A complex grammatical language is one of these universals, although as Hunt noted tracing the evolutionary origin is difficult and vigorously debated (Hauser, Chomsky, & Fitch, 2002; Pinker & Jackendoff, 2005). But, this does not mean that any potential evolutionary scenario is as feasible as all other scenarios. Core cross-cultural similarities as well as thoughtful simulations of the likelihood of alternative evolutionary pathways to these similarities can and have been used to narrow the range of feasible evolutionary paths (MacNeilage, 1998; MacNeilage & Davis, 2000; Nowak, Komarova, & Niyogi, 2001). These analyses can be complemented with studies of endocasts of the inner surface of fossil skulls; these allow for brain volume estimates and a partial recreation of the structure of the outer surface of the neocortex (Holloway, Broadfield, & Yuan, 2004). As just one example, endocast patterns suggest that with the emergence of *Homo habilis* about 2.5 million years ago there were modest evolutionary expansions in the volume of the frontal and parietal lobes and extensive remodeling of these brain areas (Falk, 1983; Tobias, 1987). One area of the frontal lobe that supports human speech and gesture, specifically, Broca's area, appears to have expanded with the emergence of *H. habilis* and may have had an architecture similar to that of modern humans. We may never know if *H. habilis* had the beginnings of a human-like protolanguage, but we can nonetheless use these types of data and variety of other empirical methods to test alternative evolutionary models and to eliminate many potential evolutionary paths.

Hunt also used folk biology as an example of potential difficulties in recreating models of human cognitive evolution. As with language, multi-perspective analyses have been used in attempts to understand people's naïve knowledge and biases related to biology, including the potential evolution of these biases (Atran, 1998; Caramazza & Shelton, 1998; Medin & Atran, 1999). As with language, cognitive biases that support the development folk biological knowledge is a human universal; humans throughout the world are able to categorize the flora and fauna in their local ecologies (Atran, 1998; Berlin, Breedlove, & Raven, 1966; Carey & Spelke, 1994). In fact, humans living in natural environments develop very elaborate and complex classification systems of the flora and fauna in the local ecology and develop mental models of the behavior (e.g., growth patterns) of these plants and animals (see Medin & Atran, 1999). Through ethnobiological studies, "it has become apparent that, while individual societies may differ considerably in their conceptualization of plants and animals, there are a number of strikingly regular structural principles of folk biological classification which are quite general" (Berlin, Breedlove, & Raven, 1973, p. 214). Peoples' classification of plants and animals in traditional societies is similar to the scientific classification of these same organisms (Atran, 1994; Diamond, 1966), although the degree to which particular aspects of the classification system are more or less elaborated is contingent on the social and biological significance of the plants or animals to people in the culture (Atran, 1998; Malt, 1995). Again, this research indicates that the combination of evolutionary theory and cross-disciplinary research provides a very powerful tool for generating and testing hypotheses regarding human universals, and cultural variation in how these are expressed.

Value Added by an Evolutionary Perspective

As I noted, Ackerman, Demetriou, and Hunt are not convinced that an evolutionary perspective adds much to our understanding of education and educational practices that cannot be achieved through other approaches. For many aspects of education, this is true. My proposal is that by framing educational goals and research on educational practices within an evolutionary perspective, we can narrow the problem space associated with determining the most effective ways to instruct children, better understand their interest and motivational biases, and more effectively grapple with the issue of individual differences. I address many of these questions in the following sections, and thus will not elaborate here.

An analogy from medicine addresses the more basic question of whether other approaches will give us the same answers, whether or not the questions are cast in an evolutionary frame. The discovery and development of antibiotics is of course a landmark contribution of modern biology and medicine to human society and occurred without consideration of evolutionary issues. Fifteen years ago, Neu (1992) published a very sobering review of widespread and growing bacterial resistance to antibiotics. Among many examples, he noted the resistance of the common bacteria, *Streptococcus pneunoniae*. "In 1941, 10,000 units of penicillin administered four times a day for 4 days cured patients of pneumococcal pneumonia. Today, a patient could receive 24 million units of penicillin a day and die of pneumococcal meningitis" (Neu, 1992, p. 1065). He detailed many examples of other species of bacteria that have developed resistance to many forms of antibiotic throughout the world.

From an evolutionary perspective, the relation between bacteria and antibiotics is an extension of host-parasite coevolution. The coevolution is between the immune system of the host (us in this example) and the immune-evasion mechanisms of the parasite (e.g., *Streptococcus pneunoniae*), creating a never ending "arms race" (Dawkins & Krebs, 1979). It does not lead to any particular end point, such as permanent immunity, but rather to a never-ending pattern of resistance and susceptibility to parasites (Ridley, 1993). As a result of host-parasite coevolution, the immune-evasion mechanisms of the parasite—and the corresponding immune system of the host (Nei & Hughes, 1991)—have evolved such that they are highly prone to mutations. The result is high levels of within species variation in the mechanisms that have evolved to evade immunological responses (e.g., Bjedov et al., 2003). The variation creates the potential for rapid evolutionary change in the parasite, as we have seen with the evolution of bacteria in response to exposure to antibiotics. Antibiotics, in effect, become an adjunct to humans' natural immune response and become just one more selection pressure for the bacteria.

The arms race with bacteria will never end and thus the need for new antibiotics will never end. But, measures can be taken to reduce the unnecessary use of antibiotics and thus slow the evolution of the bacteria they are designed to kill. If physicians had had a better understanding of host-parasite coevolution, then these measures could have been implemented decades before Neu's (1992) review and the rate of bacterial resistance would not now be approaching a potential crisis situation.

Of course, children's education is not a life or death issue, as is bacterial resistance, but I believe there is a lesson to be learned: An understanding of evolution as related to children's developmental, cognitive, and interest biases can lead to sounder theory about educational practices and lead to more focused hypotheses about what is most likely to be effective in promoting learning in school; Berch, Bjorklund, Klahr, and Sweller appear to be in agreement. If an evolutionary educational psychology provides even a small advantage in addressing these issues, then we will have that much more of an advantage in the worldwide educational-technological arms race in which we are now competing (Freidman, 2005).

THE WHEN AND WHERE OF
PRIMARY AND SECONDARY FORMS OF LEARNING

Berch, Bjorklund, Demetriou, Hunt, and Sweller all raise questions regarding the relation between children's more primary forms of learning (e.g., social play) and some of the secondary models of instruction, especially direct instruction, that I state will be necessary for mastery of many secondary domains. Berch and Klahr provide important examples as to how more primary forms of learning, such as group discussion of an academic problem or means-ends problem solving, can contribute to secondary learning, and Sweller provides useful discussion on potential proximate cognitive mechanisms involved in secondary learning and features of this learning that are analogous to the mechanisms of natural selection (see also Geary, 2006; Siegler, 1996; Sweller & Sweller, 2006). Bjorklund correctly, in my opinion, argues that more primary forms of learning are integrally linked to the evolution of children's ability to learn about culture and in novel contexts. These commentaries revolve around two core issues: specifically, instructional methods and the melding of primary forms of learning with mastery of secondary domains.

Instructional Methods

Many of the commentators suggest that my proposals regarding the need for teacher-driven, explicit and direct instruction might be too strong. I found myself in agreement with the vast majority of these comments and admit that many of my statements regarding the need for direct instruction or the insufficiency of more primary forms of learning would have been better stated as hypotheses. In fact, we do not fully understand when (e.g., grade, age), for whom, and for what topics methods such as direct, explicit instruction or discovery learning will be the most successful in terms of promoting student achievement. As Berch deftly illustrates, the issues are much more subtle and complex than is implied in the various and often polarized "reading and math wars" (e.g., Loveless, 2001), and as Klahr and Bjorklund note, the advantages of primary versus secondary modes of problem solving and learning may vary across age and level of expertise. With respect to age, Bjorklund makes an excellent point with the suggestion that ontogenetic adaptations may be particularly important for framing young children's reliance on more primary forms of learning (e.g., discovery learning in context; see also Bjorklund, 2006) and that direct instruction can be overdone, especially in the preschool years. Again, this is a testable hypothesis, but I am in agreement with Bjorklund to a large degree.

Melding Primary and Secondary Learning

I believe that a complete evolutionary educational psychology will eventually be built from a foundation of developmental knowledge in the areas of folk psychology, biology, and physics (S. Gelman, 2003; Leslie, 1987; Wellman & Gelman, 1992). With a more complete understanding of children's knowledge development in these domains and the primary mechanisms for adapting these systems to local conditions, we should be in a better position to study which combination of instructional methods will be most effective in modifying primary forms of knowledge (e.g., language acquisition) for the learning of culturally important secondary skills (e.g., recognition of letter names and sounds). In other words, during the preschool years and likely to some extent in later grades, the boundary between primary folk knowledge and secondary knowledge will at times be fuzzy. For young children without an extensive base of secondary knowledge, capitalizing on primary forms of learning might be particularly useful in the beginning stages of learning a secondary domain.

The building of secondary mathematics from primary mathematical knowledge provides an example of this fuzzy boundary and how more primary forms of learning might be useful in building a foundation of secondary knowledge. Although I did not emphasize it in my focal chapter, there is good evidence for an evolved system of primary mathematical knowledge in humans and many other species (Geary, 1995); on the basis of brain imaging studies, these primary mathematical competencies appear to be dependent on brain regions that overlap with regions that support folk physics (e.g., Dehaene, Spelke, Pinel, Stanescu, & Tsivkin, 1999; Rivera, Reiss, Eckert, & Menon, 2005; Zorzi, Priftis, & Umiltá, 2002). Many species of animal are able to discriminate smaller from larger amounts and some are able to make finer discriminations (e.g., 2 items vs. 3 items). Still other species have a rudimentary ability to count and to engage in simple addition and subtraction (Beran & Beran, 2004;

Boysen & Berntson, 1989; Brannon & Terrace, 1998; Hauser, Carey, & Hauser, 2000; Lyon, 2003; Nieder, Diester, & Tudusciuc, 2006; Pepperberg, 1987).

For humans in most traditional cultures, number words are found for "one," "two," sometimes "three," and for estimates of relatively larger amounts (e.g., "more than two"; Chagnon, 1997; Gordon, 2004; Pica, Lemer, Izard, & Dehaene, 2006). More sophisticated enumeration systems are found in some traditional cultures, but these appear to be less common and still limited to quantities less than 30 (De Cruz, 2006; Saxe, 1981). These and related studies, as well as studies of human infants and preschool children, are consistent with the evolution of a core system of primary mathematical abilities in many species. My hypothesized set of primary mathematical abilities in humans is shown in Table 9.1.

The extent to which children's primary forms of learning are needed to flesh out these primary mathematical abilities is not fully understood. Some features of primary mathematics—such as a sensitivity to differences in the quantity of small sets (e.g., 2 vs. 3)—are evident during infancy (Antell & Keating, 1983), and do not show developmental change (Mandler & Shebo, 1982). Other features of primary mathematics—such as understanding cardinal value (i.e., that the last number word stated represents the number of items in a counted set)—emerge slowly during the preschool years and only after other features of primary mathematics are in place (Bermejo, 1996; R. Gelman & Gallistel, 1978). These slowly developing competencies likely emerge epigenetically, as suggested by Bjorklund: Foundational abilities are defined by attentional and perceptual biases that orient infants to quantitative features of their environment and provide the skeletal structure for slower maturing abilities (R. Gelman, 1990). The fleshing out of the skeletal structure likely occurs as attentional and activity biases (e.g., counting) create experiences that feedback onto the developing cognitive systems to create more mature procedural skills (e.g., counting behavior), conceptual knowledge (e.g., cardinality), and declarative facts (e.g., number words) organized around the areas shown in Table 9.1.

The more slowly developing aspects of primary mathematical abilities may be open to early parental and instructional influences and may provide a means to begin to develop secondary mathematical abilities. For example, the fundamentals of the numerosity and estimation systems shown in Table 9.1 emerge with or without parental fostering of quantitative competencies (Dehaene, Izard, Pica, & Spelke, 2006; Pica et al., 2004), but the coordination of these systems with the culture's number words appears to require activities that involve counting sets of objects (e.g., candy) using these number words. The learning of specific quantities beyond three or four and associating number words with correspond-

Table 9.1.   Hypothesized Primary Mathematical Abilities

Numerosity: The ability to accurately determine the quantity of sets of up to three to four items, or events, without counting (Starkey & Cooper, 1980: Strauss & Curtis, 1984; Wynn, Bloom, & Chiang, 2002).

Ordinality: An implicit understanding of more than and less than for comparison of sets of three to four items (R. Cooper, 1984; Strauss & Curtis, 1984).

Counting: A nonverbal system for enumeration of small sets of items (Gallistel & Gelman, 1992; Starkey, 1992), and implicit knowledge of counting principles (e.g., one to one correspondence; R. Gelman & Gallistel, 1978).

Simple arithmetic: Sensitivity to increases (addition) and decreases (subtraction) in the quantity of small sets of items (Kobayashi, Hiraki, Mugitani, & Hasegawa, 2004; Wynn, 1992).

Estimation: Inexact estimation of relative quantity, magnitude, or size (Dehaene et al., 1999; Feigenson, Dehaene, & Spelke, 2004; Pica et al., 2004).

Geometry: Implicit understanding of shape and spatial relations (Dehaene et al., 2006; Geary, 1995).

---

ing amounts (e.g., "five" =) appears to involve mapping these words onto the primary estimation system. The latter represents general amounts, not specific quantities (Gallistel & Gelman, 1992), and thus children's conception of the quantities represented by larger number words is dependent to an important degree on their learning of the standard counting sequence (i.e., "one," "two," "three" ...), properties of this sequence (i.e., successive number words represent an increase of exactly "one"), and integrating them with the primary estimation system. The extent to which integration of the counting and estimation systems will emerge naturally from children's self-initiated activities or from informal parental or preschool instruction is not known (Saxe, Guberman, & Gearhart, 1987). In any case, these relations provide an example of the fuzzy boundary between primary and secondary abilities and areas in which more primary forms of learning—perhaps with subtle guidance or scaffolding from parents or teachers—may be particularly effective.

I described another example in the focal chapter, but it is worth repeating here: specifically on the relation between primary systems and learning of the base-10 system. A conceptual understanding of this system is essential for modern mathematics and learning of this system may be facilitated by an understanding of the mathematical number line and an ability to decompose the number line into sets of ten and then to organize these sets into clusters (e.g., 10, 20, 30, ...). Infants and young children implicitly organize collections of objects into sets and this may provide an early conceptual foundation for understanding sets at a more abstract level, but the creation of sets around 10 and the superordinate organization of these sets do not emerge naturally from this primary knowledge. The explicit organization of the number system around 10 must also be systematically mapped onto the number word system (McCloskey, Sokol, & Goodman, 1986), and integrated with school-taught procedures for solving complex arithmetic problems (Fuson & Kwon, 1992; Geary, 1994). The development of base-10 knowledge thus requires the extension of primary number knowledge to very large numbers; the organization of these number representations in ways that differ conceptually from primary knowledge; and, the learning of procedural rules for applying this new knowledge to the secondary domain of mathematical arithmetic (e.g., to solve 234 + 697). With this example, the secondary mathematics is "remote" from the supporting primary abilities, and is dependent on prior secondary learning (e.g., knowing number words). In these situations, I predict that direct instruction on concepts and procedures and extensive practice of procedures will be needed for many children to fully understand these concepts and to attain automaticity in use of the procedures; supportive evidence is provided in some of Sweller's earlier work (e.g., G. Cooper & Sweller, 1987; Sweller, Mawer, & Ward, 1983).

An evolutionary approach to education will require analogous knowledge bases in the folk domains of psychology, biology, and physics and a thorough understanding of children's ontogenetic adaptations and primary forms of learning as related to the fleshing out and adapting of this folk knowledge to local conditions. This fundamental knowledge base can then be used to begin to bridge the fuzzy boundaries between this primary knowledge and related secondary knowledge children will need to learn in school. This does not mean that more primary forms of learning, as in discovery learning or group projects, cannot be effective in the learning of more "remote" forms of secondary knowledge, as Klahr and Berch emphasized. In fact, if humans have evolved to create culture—shared knowledge that is passed across time and generations through stories, apprenticeships, and so forth (Baumeister, 2005)—then more primary forms of learning are likely to be useful throughout the life span and for many types of secondary domains.

Nonetheless, we are in an historical period in which there is rapid creation of secondary knowledge and an increasing remoteness between this knowledge and folk knowledge. The existing and widening gap leads me to hypothesize that a combination of explicit, detailed, and well organized curricula and direct instruction will be necessary, though perhaps not sufficient in all cases, for attaining a culturally sufficient level of competency, much less mastery, of many school-based secondary domains. I also predict that this need will only increase in coming decades.

MOVING BEYOND Gf

Ackerman, Demetriou, and Hunt argue that I overemphasized the importance of fluid intelligence (Gf) for understanding individual differences in academic development, or at least did not emphasize other traits enough. I agree that there is much more to academic development than Gf and address some of these concerns in the following sections.

Crystallized Intelligence

Ackerman and Hunt argue that I underestimate the importance of crystallized intelligence (Gc). I agree that crystallized intelligence and abilities in specific domains, such as numerical facility (i.e., basic computational arithmetic), are a very important component of schooling and life in modern society. In fact the whole point of school-based secondary learning is to increase the store of culturally-important crystallized knowledge. My proposal is that Gf is needed to modify folk systems in the creation of secondary, crystallized knowledge; Gf is not, however, needed to learn folk knowledge, as Hunt suggests, as I hypothesize that much of folk knowledge is built into evolved brain and cognitive systems. Once the school-based knowledge and other competencies are crystallized, Gf become less important for the specific domain.

I also want to mention that Ackerman suggests that my focus on his theory of skill acquisition (Ackerman, 1988) is not appropriate, because his focus is on tasks in which achieving the goal is based on motor behavior. I cannot argue with him on this point, but suggest that his model may be more useful, conceptually, than he suggests in his commentary. My point is that Gf is needed to cope with novel situations, and that solutions to these situations can be learned and eventually become automatically executed, if the situation is encountered many times. The automatic execution could be of a mental strategy (e.g., for dealing with a particular individual or social context) or a motor behavior. This does not mean that heuristics or other responses can be learned for all potential situations. As Ackerman states, much of life and some academic domains are more open-ended in their demands and thus automaticity can never be fully achieved. This is an excellent point, and in fact is the gist of my evolutionary model of Gf—that social complexity selected for the evolution of brain and cognitive systems (that is, Gf) for coping with dynamic change (Geary, 2005); Gf does not represent the only systems that evolved to cope with novelty and change, but is important part of them.

Secular Trends

Hunt correctly notes that mean levels of performance on measures of *g*, including Gf and Gc, increased significantly during the twentieth century and suggests that this clearly environmental effect is inconsistent with an evolutionary model of *g*. I do not see this as inconsistent at all (Geary, 2005). During the twentieth century, average life spans also increased dramatically, due to lower infant and child mortality and more recently to lower mortality risks for people over 60. The most substantive changes in infant and child mortality occurred for the segment of society that experienced the highest mortality rates, that is, the least privileged (e.g., Hed, 1987; Reid, 1997). This was the result of massive cultural and environment interventions—better sanitation, antibiotics, vaccines, and so forth—but does not mean that there are not evolved limits on the length of the human life span or that the life span has not been subject to evolutionary selection—it has (Allman & Hasenstaub, 1998; Bogin, 1999; Dean et al., 2001). In fact, even with these dramatic changes, people still age and eventually pass away. What has happened, in my opinion, is that these cultural and medical advances have allowed more individuals to approach the maximum life span of our species.

I believe a similar pattern has occurred with *g*. Crystallized knowledge related to schooling will necessarily increase as the proportion of the population that attends school increases, and as the mean length of schooling increases, both of which occurred during the twentieth century in modern societies. There is also evidence for secular increases in Gf (Flynn, 1987). If these increases are related to improvements in general health and perhaps levels of stimulation early in life (see Neisser, 1998), then the effects should be larger in the least advantaged segments of the population, as with changes in mortality rate.

Several studies by Teasdale and Owen (1989, 2000) are consistent with this hypothesis. In these studies, a measure of Gf, *Raven's Progressive Matrices* (Raven, Court, & Raven, 1993), was administered to 90% to 95% of all 18-year-old men born in eastern Denmark. These men were conscripted into the military and represented about 40% of the Danish men born between 1939 and 1980. During this 4 decade span, there was a modest improvement in mean raw IQ scores, but there was no change in raw scores for individuals at the 90th percentile and a substantial improvement in raw scores for individuals at the 10th percentile. The pattern suggests that during this time span there was little or no change in the general intelligence of the mentally gifted, whereas the intellectual abilities of individuals with IQ scores that are significantly below average increased substantially. Teasdale and Owen's findings are in keeping with the analyses of the relation between SES and environmental influences on individual differences in g within a specific generation (e.g., Turkheimer, Haley, Waldron, D'Onofrio, & Gottesman, 2003). More precisely, all of these findings are consistent with Scarr's (1992) prediction that growing up in difficult environments does not allow for the full expression of intellectual potential, especially for children with the highest intellectual potential (Duyme, Dumaret, & Tomkiewicz, 1999).

The cross-generational pattern suggests that the environments of the lower strata of human populations in industrial societies improved substantially during the twentieth century, consistent with change in risk of premature death. Of course, all segments of society have improved. What is important here is the achievement of the minimal levels of physical health and social and environmental stimulation to reach one's intellectual potential. The higher strata of human populations have probably had this level of health and stimulation for quite some time and only recently has it been achieved for a wider segment of society. In other words, the social and cultural changes that improved life span during the twentieth century also appear to have allowed for the more nearly complete expression of intellectual potential for larger segments of these populations, although not the entire population (Turkheimer et al., 2003).

Interests and "Will"

Ackerman argues that the profile of one's academic and cognitive skill (e.g., Gc) in adulthood will be influenced by where one invests time and effort during development and that these patterns of investment are related to intrinsic motivation. On the one hand, I agree that interests must be taken into account when attempting to understand academic development and later occupational choices and functioning. This is the reason I included a section on evolved interests and occupational niches. As outlined in the focal chapter, I believe that underlying the patterns of occupational interest that have been empirically identified in modern societies (Campbell & Holland, 1972; Holland, 1996; Strong, 1943) are at least two more fundamental and evolved interest dimensions: specifically, along a folk psychology (people) to folk physics/biology (things) dimension and along an abstract to concrete dimension.

On the other hand, engagement in the types of activities associated with these fundament interests, such as social discourse or ecological exploration, will not be sufficient for occupational functioning in modern societies. An inherent interest in folk biology might orientate an individual toward the natural world and may motivate self-initiated engagement in exploration of this world and reading about the associated work of other people with these same interests, as with Darwin. But, advances in biological science since the time of Darwin have made formal and extensive training necessary for professional work in biology, and much of this training will likely require learning that is outside of these folk biological interests (e.g., taking calculus, preparing cultures). In other words, there is still a link between evolved interests and motivations and academic and occupational choices in modern societies. However, as secondary knowledge builds across generations, the activities these inherent interests drive become increasingly remote from the activities needed to master the accumulating store of secondary knowledge.

Finally, Ackerman argues that children's "will to learn" is important and not addressed in my focal chapter. As I stated above and as argued by Berch, Bjorklund, and Klahr, children and adults will use natural means of learning and problem solving in modern settings, and will often do so effectively. Indeed, if humans are a species that evolved to create complex social communities and cultures, as we almost certainly have (Baumeister, 2005), then there is an inherent interest in and ability to learn novel and culturally important knowledge. My point is that the wealth of secondary knowledge available in modern societies and the increasing level of knowledge needed to function in these societies make reliance on any will to learn risky. Children do not understand what is needed to function in these societies and even if they did it is not likely that they could organize and sequence their learning to master these domains. Moreover, if we assume that the will to learn is normally distributed and that all children in modern societies need some amount of formal education, then there will be a substantial number of children with an insufficient will to learn in school.

Self-Awareness

Demetriou argues for the importance of self-awareness and self-regulation in human learning. Again, I agree that this is an important aspect of learning. Although I do not focus on self-awareness in the focal chapter, I do provide extensive discussion elsewhere (Geary, 2005). With respect to academic learning, self-awareness and the self schema represented in Figure 1.2 of the focal chapter are predicted to be the primary forms of cognition that support self efficacy and other forms of social-motivational cognitions that have been shown to be related to learning in school (Bandura, 1993; Eccles, Wigfield, Harold, & Blumenfeld, 1993; Grant & Dweck, 2003). These forms of self-knowledge are consistent with the broader theory of mind presented in my recent book, *Origin of Mind* (Geary, 2005). Nonetheless, I agree with Demetriou that the relation between these aspects of folk knowledge (i.e., self-awareness and self-schema) as related to achievement in modern cultures are in need of further study, as he is currently doing (see also Demetriou & Kazi, 2006), and in need of theoretical elaboration if we are going to understand education from an evolutionary perspective.

INDIVIDUAL DIFFERENCES

Demetriou, Hunt, and Klahr raise the question of how an evolutionary perspective relates to our understanding of individual differences in secondary learning. Approaching individual differences in any trait from an evolutionary perspective requires consideration of developmental experiences and cost-benefit trade-offs of the trait. These can be much nuanced relationships and are considered in detail in the area of evolutionary developmental biology (West-Eberhard, 2003). I can only touch on the basics of these relationships. I then place them in the context of secondary learning in modern society.

Evolution, Development, and Phenotypic Variation

It is often assumed that natural or sexual selection will result in the elimination of variance in the trait under selection, and this is sometimes the case. However, individual differences are found in many of the traits that under direct selection pressures. The variance in these traits is commonly related to a mix of heritable, developmental, and experiential (e.g., food availability) factors. Mousseau and Roff (1987) conducted a comprehensive review of the heritable variability of the morphological, behavioral, physiological, and life history (e.g., age of reproductive maturation) traits associated with survival and reproductive outcomes in wild animal populations. The analysis included 1,120 heritability estimates across 75 species. Although there was considerable variation—across species, contexts, and traits—in the magnitude of the heritability estimate, their analysis indicated that "significant genetic variance is maintained within most natural populations, even for traits closely affiliated with fitness" (Mousseau & Roff, 1987, p. 188). The median heritability estimates were .26 for life history traits, .27 for physiological traits, .32 for behavioral traits, and .53 for morphological traits, values that are similar to those found in human populations (Plomin, DeFries, McClearn, & McGuffin, 2001).

Heritable variation can be maintained in such traits because the associated genes or aspects of the phenotype itself have multiple effects, some of which are beneficial and some of which likely come at a cost (Williams,

1957). As an example, testosterone contributes to the development of men's cardiac morphology and capacity, muscularity, skeleton strength, and many other traits (Stauffer & Leinwand, 2004; Tanner, 1990; Weeden & Sabini, 2005). Muscularity, cardiac capacity, and so forth develop rapidly during puberty and peak during early adulthood in men (Fletcher, Balady, Froelicher, Hartley, Haskell, & Pollock, 1995; Tanner, 1990), and influence women's ratings of men's attractiveness (Weeden & Sabini, 2005). It is not a coincidence that this is the same point in the lifespan when physical male-male competition for social dominance, resource control, and attracting mates is at its peak (Geary, 1998; M. Wilson & Daly 1985).

However, the same hormonal influences that contribute to the development of these physical traits in young adulthood come at a cost of higher health risks later in life, including increased risk for hypertension and renal disease (Reckelhoff, Fortepiani, Yanes, & Cucchiarelli, 2004), certain forms of heart disease (Stauffer & Leinwand, 2004), and a significantly increased risk of premature death due to these conditions (e.g., Adams et al., 1999). Damon, Harpending, and Kannel, (1969) found that chest depth—a trait that young women find attractive in young men—was positively correlated with risk of heart disease in middle age. The patterns are consistent with Williams' (1957) prediction of life history trade-offs such that traits that confer advantage in reproductive competition early in life come at a cost of increased risk of later morbidity and early mortality. The result is that individuals who may be disadvantaged at one point in the life span may have advantage at another point, and vice versa. It is these types of trade-offs that contribute to the maintenance of heritable variation in naturally and sexually selected traits.

Moreover, variation and evolution cannot be fully understood without consideration of developmental experience; "the secret to understanding evolution is to first understand phenotypes, including their development and their responsiveness to the environment" (West-Eberhard, 2003, p. 28). In other words, an important source of the variation on which evolution operates is results from the sensitivity of the developing phenotype to the environment.

Sex differences again illustrate the point. Sex hormones influence: (a) whether the embryo develops as a male or a female (Tanner, 1990); (b) patterns of gene expression and thus later functional competencies in the developing and mature brain (Arnold, Xu, Grisham, Chen, Kin, & Itoh, 2004; Good et al., 2003); and (c) postnatal biases in social behavior (Cohen-Bendahan, van de Beek, & Berenbaum, 2005). At the same time, the individuals' internal (e.g., exposure to viruses) and external (e.g., social competitors, food availability) environment can substantively influence the expression of sex and other hormones and through this gene expression and thus the developing phenotype and later social behaviors (Goldizen, 2003; Stearns & Koella, 1986). By adulthood, these multi-factorial influences result in heritable and environmentally induced variation in reproductive behaviors, as I described earlier, which then results in variation in reproductive outcomes and the evolvability of associated phenotypes. A full understanding of all naturally occurring variation requires identification of important phenotypes and the multiple genetic, hormonal, ecological, and social factors and their interactions that effect phenotypic expression and development.

There are several crucial points: First, an evolutionary perspective on individual differences is *not* genetic determinism. Evolutionary developmental biologists assume phenotypic variation in evolved and evolving traits emerges from a mix of heritable influences, developmental experience, current context, and their interactions (West-Eberhard, 2003). As Bjorklund notes, the influence of developmental experiences and contexts is more important for understanding human cognition and variation in these traits than it is for any other species (see also Bjorklund, 2006). Second, when approached from an evolutionary perspective, most beneficial traits, especially those in which some genetic variance is maintained, come at a cost (Williams, 1957). Being higher or lower on the trait may not matter in some contexts or may be detrimental in others. Conversely, traits that may be detrimental in some contexts may confer other benefits or be beneficial in other contexts. In other words, there are no "free lunches" and an advantage on one trait or in one context does not imply advantage on all traits or in all contexts; "superiority" is trait specific and context dependent. Finally, to the extent culture and experience influence phenotypic variation, they can influence the course of evolution—as long as these traits also have some genetic variance.

Individual Differences in Secondary Learning

Heritable variation and variation in developmental experiences and current circumstances will result in individual differences in evolutionarily and culturally significant traits. As noted, the cost-benefit trade-offs associated with these traits will maintain this variation, even when the trait is under evolutionary selection. To the extent that culturally significant traits, such as the interest and ability to learn in school, are influenced by primary motivational and cognitive systems, they will also show individual variation, some of which will be heritable. This does not, however, imply that schooling is not beneficial to all children. As evidenced by international studies, a sound educational system can significantly influence the mean level of competency developed by children in the society (e.g.,

Mullis, Martin, Gonzalez, & Chrostowski, 2004), but individual differences remain. From an evolutionary/cultural perspective, the goal is to provide to all children the education necessary for social and occupational success in the society.

At the same time and for a variety of reasons, including ability, motivation, and opportunity, some children will learn more rapidly in school, will go farther in their education, and as adults will excel in their chosen occupations. This is an empirical fact (e.g., Lubinski, Webb, Morelock, & Benbow, 2001; Wai, Lubinski, & Benbow, 2005) and a pattern that will not change, even if mean levels of school-related outcomes are improved. From a philosophical perspective, this might seem like an unfair and inequitable outcome, but neither evolution nor life is about fair, and never have been. In my opinion, it is the responsibility of modern societies to provide equality of opportunity and to ensure that all children are provided with the education needed to be successful in the society, but social engineering will not eliminate individual variation in educational outcomes or social success and would not be a sound policy even if it could; attempts to eliminate this variation, as with several communist societies in the twentieth century, resulted in economic and social hardship for a large segment of the associated populations.

For all modern societies, future scientists, engineers, judges, and entrepreneurs will disproportionately come from the pool of individuals who excel in educational and occupational settings. And, it is individuals from this educated pool of citizens who will disproportionately make the innovations that increase economic productivity and the discoveries that reduce risk of disease (e.g., discovery of new forms of antibiotic). These types of contributions keep the society competitive and provide benefits to many of its citizens. While we must continue to study, better understand, and better facilitate the learning of children who struggle in school—I conduct some of this research (e.g., Geary, 2004)—we must also more seriously consider ways to foster the education of our most motivated and able students. This might be seen as elitist, but is in fact a way for societies to "take advantage" of these individuals. Technological, entrepreneurial, and scientific innovations do not typically occur within a 40-hour work week and over the course of an academic year, but rather emerge from years of preparation and long hours of work focused on a particular problem (e.g., Ericsson, Krampe, & Tesch-Römer, 1993; Howe, 1999). These individuals pay a price in terms of lost opportunities to pursue leisure interests and to socialize with friends and family. It is in any society's long-term interest to develop policies that prepare and reward these individuals for their contributions to the society and make pursuit of these contributions worth the personal cost.

FINAL WORDS

There are many other issues that were broached by individual commentators that will need to be eventually addressed if an evolutionary educational psychology is to emerge as a useful discipline; such as the issue of psychometric measurement of folk abilities (Demetriou). My focal chapter, the commentaries, and this reply are only the beginning stages in the development of the discipline and much remains to be accomplished. The development of evolutionary educational psychology will necessarily be a multidisciplinary undertaking, requiring knowledge derived from research in biology (e.g., developmental influences on phenotype expression; e.g., West-Eberhard, 2003), anthropology (e.g., identifying human cognitive universals and studying these across cultures; e.g., Pica et al., 2004), psychology (e.g., study of children's folk knowledge and its development; e.g., S. Gelman, 2003), and of course education.

The last of these will not only require studies of the effectiveness of instructional methods, but also a change in the culture of educational scholarship. In my opinion, much of the debate in education regarding instructional practices derives from a reliance on folk-psychological intuitions and biases. These intuitions are used to devise and make arguments for one educational practice or another. Modern education, however, is a recent cultural phenomenon and thus from the evolutionary perspective proposed in my focal chapter, folk intuitions are unlikely to be sufficient for the full development of effective instructional methods. These folk intuitions are at best starting points for the development of methods whose effectiveness can only be evaluated scientifically. In other words, reliance on biologically primary folk intuitions about children's learning, interests, and motivations is predicted to lead to poor outcomes when it comes to the instruction of biologically secondary knowledge.

REFERENCES

Ackerman, P. L. (1988). Determinants of individual differences during skill acquisition: Cognitive abilities and information processing. *Journal of Experimental Psychology: General, 117,* 288-318.

Adams, K. F., Sueta, C. A., Gheorghiade, M., Schwartz, T. A., Koch, G. G., Uretsky, B., et al. (1999). Gender differences in survival in advanced heart failure: Insights from FIRST study. *Circulation, 99,* 1816-1821.

Allman, J., & Hasenstaub, A. (1998). Brains, maturation times, and parenting. *Neurobiology of Aging, 20,* 447-454.

Andersson, M. (1994). *Sexual selection.* Princeton, NJ: Princeton University Press.

Antell, S. E., & Keating, D. P. (1983). Perception of numerical invariance in neonates. *Child Development, 54,* 695-701.

Arnold, A. P., Xu, J., Grisham, W., Chen, X., Kin, Y. -H., & Itoh, Y. (2004). Sex chromosomes and brain sexual differentiation. *Endocrinology, 145*, 1057-1062.

Atran, S. (1994). Core domains versus scientific theories: Evidence from systematics and Itza-Maya folkbiology. In L. A. Hirschfeld & S. A. Gelman (Eds.), *Mapping the mind: Domain specificity in cognition and culture* (pp. 316-340). New York: Cambridge University Press.

Atran, S. (1998). Folk biology and the anthropology of science: Cognitive universals and cultural particulars. *Behavioral and Brain Sciences, 21*, 547-609.

Bandura, A. (1993). Perceived self-efficacy in cognitive development and functioning. *Educational Psychologist, 28*, 117-148.

Baumeister, R. F. (2005). *The cultural animal: Human nature, meaning, and social life.* New York: Oxford University Press.

Beran, M. J., & Beran, M. M. (2004). Chimpanzees remember the results of one-by-one addition of food items to sets over extended time periods. *Psychological Science, 15*, 94-99.

Berlin, B., Breedlove, D. E., & Raven, P. H. (1966, October 14). Folk taxonomies and biological classification. *Science, 154*, 273-275.

Berlin, B., Breedlove, D. E., & Raven, P. H. (1973). General principles of classification and nomenclature in folk biology. *American Anthropologist, 75*, 214-242.

Bermejo, V. (1996). Cardinality development and counting. *Developmental Psychology, 32*, 263-268.

Bjedov, I., Tenaillon, O., Gérard, B., Souza, V., Denamur, E., Radman, M., et al. (2003, May 30). Stress-induced mutagenesis in bacteria. *Science, 300*, 1404-1409.

Bjorklund, D. F. (2006). Mother knows best: Epigenetic inheritance, maternal effects, and the evolution of human intelligence. *Developmental Review, 26*, 213-242.

Bogin, B. (1999). Evolutionary perspective on human growth. *Annual Review of Anthropology, 28*, 109-153.

Boysen, S. T., & Berntson, G. G. (1989). Numerical competence in a chimpanzee (*Pan troglodytes*). *Journal of Comparative Psychology, 103*, 23-31.

Brannon, E. M., & Terrace, H. S. (1998, October 23). Ordering of the numerosities 1 to 9 by monkeys. *Science, 282*, 746-749.

Brown, D. E. (1991). *Human universals.* Philadelphia: Temple University Press.

Buss, D. M. (Ed.). (2005), *The evolutionary psychology handbook.* Hoboken, NJ: John Wiley & Sons.

Campbell, D. P., & Holland, J. L. (1972). A merger in vocational interest research: Applying Holland's theory to Strong's data. *Journal of Vocational Behavior, 2*, 353-376.

Capelli, C., Redhead, N., Abernethy, J. K., Gratrix, F., Wilson, J. F., Moen, T., et al. (2003). A Y chromosome census of the British isles. *Current Biology, 13*, 979-984.

Caramazza, A., & Shelton, J. R. (1998). Domain-specific knowledge systems in the brain: The animate-inanimate distinction. *Journal of Cognitive Neuroscience, 10*, 1-34.

Carey, S., & Spelke, E. (1994). Domain-specific knowledge and conceptual change. In L. A. Hirschfeld & S. A. Gelman (Eds.), *Mapping the mind: Domain specificity in cognition and culture* (pp. 169-200). New York: Cambridge University Press.

Chagnon, N. A. (1979). Is reproductive success equal in egalitarian societies? In N. A. Chagnon & W. Irons (Eds.), *Evolutionary biology and human social behavior: An anthropological perspective* (pp. 374-401). North Scituate, MA: Duxbury Press.

Chagnon, N. A. (1997). *Yanomamö* (Fifth ed.). Fort Worth, TX: Harcourt.

Chagnon, N. A. (1988, February 26). Life histories, blood revenge, and warfare in a tribal population. *Science, 239,* 985-992.

Cohen-Bendahan, C. C. C., van de Beek, C., & Berenbaum, S. A. (2005). Prenatal sex hormone effects on child and adult sex-typed behavior: Methods and findings. *Neuroscience and Biobehavioral Reviews, 29,* 353-384.

Cooper, G., & Sweller, J. (1987). Effects of schema acquisition and rule automation on mathematical problem-solving transfer. *Journal of Educational Psychology, 79,* 347-362.

Cooper, R. G., Jr. (1984). Early number development: Discovering number space with addition and subtraction. In C. Sophian (Ed.), *Origins of cognitive skills: The eighteenth annual Carnegie symposium on cognition* (pp. 157-192). Hillsdale, NJ: Erlbaum.

Daly, M., & Wilson, M. (1988). *Homicide.* New York: Aldine de Gruyter.

Damon, A., Damon, S. T., Harpending, H. C., & Kannel, W. B. (1969). Predicting coronary heart disease from body measurements of Framingham males. *Journal of Chronic Disease, 21,* 781-802.

Darwin, C. (1871). *The descent of man, and selection in relation to sex.* London: John Murray.

Dawkins, R., & Krebs, J. R. (1979). Arms races between and within species. *Proceedings of the Royal Society of London B, 205,* 489-511.

Dean, C., Leakey, M. G., Reid, D., Schrenk, F., Schwartz, G. T., Stringer, C., et al. (2001, December 6). Growth processes in teeth distinguish modern humans from Homo erectus and earlier hominins. *Nature, 414,* 628-631.

De Cruz, H. (2006). Why are some numerical concepts more successful than others? An evolutionary perspective on the history of number concepts. *Evolution and Human Behavior, 27,* 306-323.

Dehaene, S., Izard, V., Pica, P., & Spelke, E. (2006, January 20). Core knowledge of geometry in an Amazonian indigene group. *Science, 311,* 381-384.

Dehaene, S., Spelke, E., Pinel, P., Stanescu, R., & Tsivkin, S. (1999, May 7). Sources of mathematical thinking: Behavioral and brain-imaging evidence. *Science, 284,* 970-974.

Demetriou, A., & Kazi, S. (2006). Self-awareness in *g* (with processing efficiency and reasoning). *Intelligence, 34,* 297-317.

Diamond, J. M. (1966, March 4). Zoological classification system of a primitive people. *Science, 151,* 1102-1104.

Duyme, M., Dumaret, A. -C., & Tomkiewicz, S. (1999). How can we boost IQ's of "dull children?": A late adoption study. *Proceedings of the National Academy of Sciences USA, 96,* 8790-8794.

Eccles, J., Wigfield, A., Harold, R. D., & Blumenfeld, P. (1993). Age and gender differences in children's self- and task perceptions during elementary school. *Child Development, 64*, 830-847.

Ericsson, K. A., Krampe, R. T., & Tesch-Römer, C. (1993). The role of deliberate practice in the acquisition of expert performance. *Psychological Review, 100*, 363-406.

Falk, D. (1983, September 9). Cerebral cortices by East African early hominids. *Science, 221*, 1072-1074.

Feigenson, L., Dehaene, S., & Spelke, E. (2004). Core systems of number. *Trends in Cognitive Sciences, 8*, 307-314.

Fletcher, G. F., Balady, G., Froelicher, V. F., Hartley, L. H., Haskell, W. L., & Pollock, M. L. (1995). Exercise standards. *Circulation, 91*, 580-615.

Flinn, M. V., & Low, B. S. (1986). Resource distribution, social competition, and mating patterns in human societies. In D. I Rubenstein & R. W. Wrangham (Eds.), *Ecological aspects of social evolution: Birds and mammals* (pp. 217-243). Princeton, NJ: Princeton University Press.

Flynn, J. R. (1987). Massive IQ gains in 14 nations: What IQ tests really measure. *Psychological Bulletin, 101*, 171-191.

Freidman, T. L. (2005). *The world is flat: A brief history of the twenty-first century.* New York: Farrar, Straus, Reese, and Giroux.

Fuson, K. C., & Kwon, Y. (1992). Korean children's understanding of multidigit addition and subtraction. *Child Development, 63*, 491-506.

Gallistel, C. R., & Gelman, R. (1992). Preverbal and verbal counting and computation. *Cognition, 44*, 43-74.

Gaulin, S. J. C. (1992). Evolution of sex differences in spatial ability. *Yearbook of Physical Anthropology, 35*, 125-151.

Gaulin, S. J. C., & Fitzgerald, R. W. (1986). Sex differences in spatial ability: An evolutionary hypothesis and test. *American Naturalist, 127*, 74-88.

Geary, D. C. (1994). *Children's mathematical development: Research and practical applications.* Washington, DC: American Psychological Association.

Geary, D. C. (1995). Reflections of evolution and culture in children's cognition: Implications for mathematical development and instruction. *American Psychologist, 50*, 24-37.

Geary, D. C. (1998). *Male, female: The evolution of human sex differences.* Washington, DC: American Psychological Association.

Geary, D. C. (2004). Mathematics and learning disabilities. *Journal of Learning Disabilities, 37*, 4-15.

Geary, D. C. (2005). *The origin of mind: Evolution of brain, cognition, and general intelligence.* Washington, DC: American Psychological Association.

Geary, D. C. (2006). Development of mathematical understanding. In D. Kuhl & R. S. Siegler (Vol. Eds.), *Cognition, perception, and language, Vol 2* (pp. 777-810). W. Damon (Gen. Ed.), *Handbook of child psychology* (6th Ed.). New York: John Wiley & Sons.

Geary, D. C., Byrd-Craven, J., Hoard, M. K., Vigil, J., & Numtee, C. (2003). Evolution and development of boys' social behavior. *Developmental Review, 23*, 444-470.

Gelman, R. (1990). First principles organize attention to and learning about relevant data: Number and animate-inanimate distinction as examples. *Cognitive Science, 14*, 79-106.

Gelman, R., & Gallistel, C. R. (1978). *The child's understanding of number.* Cambridge, MA: Harvard University Press.

Gelman, S. A. (2003). *The essential child: Origins of essentialism in everyday thought.* New York: Oxford University Press.

Goldizen, A. W. (2003). Social monogamy and its variations in callitrichids: Do these relate to the costs of infant care? In U. H. Reichard & C. Boesch (Eds.), *Monogamy: Mating strategies in birds, humans and other mammals* (pp. 232-247). Cambridge, UK: Cambridge University Press.

Good, C. D., Lawrence, K., Thomas, N. S., Price, C. J., Ashburner, J., Friston, K. J., et al. (2003). Dosage-sensitive X-linked locus influences the development of amygdala and orbitofrontal cortex, and fear recognition in humans. *Brian, 126*, 2431-2446.

Gordon, P. (2004, October 15). Numerical cognition without words: Evidence from Amazonia. *Science, 306*, 496-499.

Grant, H., & Dweck, C. S. (2003). Clarifying achievement goals and their impact. *Journal of Personality and Social Psychology, 85*, 541-553.

Hauser, M. D., Carey, S., & Hauser, L. B. (2000). Spontaneous number representation in semi-free-ranging rhesus monkeys. *Proceedings of the Royal Society B, 267*, 829-833.

Hauser, M. D., Chomsky, N., & Fitch, W. T. (2002, November 22). The faculty of language: What is it, who has it, and how did it evolve? *Science, 298*, 1569-1579.

Hed, H. M. E. (1987). Trends in opportunity for natural selection in the Swedish population during the period 1650-1980. *Human Biology, 59*, 785-797.

Holland, J. L. (1996). Exploring careers with typology: What we have learned and some new directions. *American Psychologist, 51*, 397-406.

Holloway, R. L., Broadfield, D. C., & Yuan, M. S. (2004). *Brian endocasts: The paleoneurological evidence.* In J. H. Schwartz & I. Tattersall (Series Eds.), *The human fossil record* (Vol. 3). Hoboken, NJ: John Wiley & Sons.

Howe, M. J. A. (1999). *Genius explained.* New York: Cambridge University Press.

Keeley, L. H. (1996). *War before civilization: The myth of the peaceful savage.* New York: Oxford University Press.

Kobayashi, T., Hiraki, K., Mugitani, R., & Hasegawa, T. (2004). Baby arithmetic: One object plus one tone. *Cognition, 91*, B23-B34.

Leakey, M. G., Feibel, C. S., McDougall, I., Ward, C., & Walker, A. (1998). New specimens and confirmation of an early age for Australopithecus anamensis. *Nature, 393*, 62-66.

Leslie, A. M. (1987). Pretense and representation: The origins of "theory of mind." *Psychological Review, 94*, 412-426.

Lyon, B. E. (2003, April 3). Egg recognition and counting reduce costs of avian conspecific brood parasitism. *Nature, 422*, 495-499.

Loveless, T. (Ed.). (2001). *The great curriculum debate: How should we teach reading and math?* Washington, DC: Brookings Institute.

Lubinski, D., Webb, R. M., Morelock, M. J., & Benbow, C. P. (2001). Top 1 in 10,000: A 10-year follow up of the profoundly gifted. *Journal of Applied Psychology, 86*, 718-729.

MacNeilage, P. F. (1998). The frame/content theory of evolution of speech. *Behavioral & Brain Sciences, 21*, 499-546.

MacNeilage, P. F., & Davis, B. L. (2000, April 21). On the origin of internal structure of word forms. *Science, 288*, 527-531.

Malt, B. C. (1995). Category coherence in cross-cultural perspective. *Cognitive Psychology, 29*, 85-148.

Mandler, G., & Shebo, B. J. (1982). Subitizing: An analysis of its component processes. *Journal of Experimental Psychology: General,111*, 1-22.

McCloskey, M., Sokol, S. M., & Goodman, R. A. (1986). Cognitive processes in verbal-number production: Inferences from the performance of brain-damaged subjects. *Journal of Experimental Psychology: General, 115*, 307-330.

Medin, D. L., & Atran, S. (Eds.). (1999). *Folkbiology.* Cambridge, MA: MIT Press/Bradford Book.

Mousseau, T. A., & Roff, D. A. (1987). Natural selection and the heritability of fitness components. *Heredity, 59*, 181-197.

Mullis, I. V. S., Martin, M. O., Gonzalez, E. J., & Chrostowski, S. J. (2004). *TIMSS 2003 international mathematics report: Findings from IEA's Trends in International Mathematics and Science study at the fourth and eighth grades.* Chestnut Hill, MA: TIMSS & PIRLS International Study Center, Boston College.

Murdock, G. P. (1981). *Atlas of world cultures.* Pittsburgh, PA: University of Pittsburgh Press.

Nei, M., & Hughes, A. L. (1991). Polymorphism and evolution of the major histocompatibility complex loci in mammals. In R. K. Selander, A. G., Clark, & T. S. Whittam (Eds.), *Evolution at the molecular level* (pp. 222-247). Sunderland, MA: Sinauer Associates.

Neisser, U. (Ed.). (1998). *The rising curve: Long-term gains in IQ and related measures.* Washington, DC: American Psychological Association.

Neu, H. C. (1992, August 21). The crisis of antibiotic resistance. *Science, 257*, 1064-1073.

Nieder, A., Diester, I., & Tudusciuc, O. (2006, September 8). Temporal and spatial enumeration processes in the primate parietal cortex. *Science, 313*, 1431-1435.

Nowak, M. A., Komarova, N. L., & Niyogi, P. (2001, January 5). Evolution of universal grammar. *Science, 291*, 114-118.

Pepperberg, I. M. (1987). Evidence for conceptual quantitative abilities in the African grey parrot: Labeling of cardinal sets. *Ethology, 75*, 37-61.

Pica, P., Lemer, C., Izard, V., & Dehaene, S. (2004, October 15). Exact and approximate arithmetic in an Amazonian indigene group. *Science, 306*, 499-503.

Pinker, S., & Jackendoff, R. (2005). The faculty of language: What's special about it? *Cognition, 95*, 201-236.

Plomin, R., DeFries, J. C., McClearn, G. E., & McGuffin, P. (2001). *Behavioral genetics* (4th ed.). New York: Worth.

Raven, J. C., Court, J. H., & Raven, J. (1993). *Manual for Raven's Progressive Matrices and Vocabulary Scales.* London: H. K. Lewis & Co.

Reckelhoff, J. F., Fortepiani, L. A., Yanes, L. L., & Cucchiarelli, V. E. (2004). Sex differences in hypertension and renal injury. *Advances in Molecular and Cell Biology, 34,* 167-182.

Ridley, M. (1993). *The red queen: Sex and the evolution of human nature.* New York: Penguin Books.

Reid, A. (1997). Locality or class? Spatial and social differentials in infant and child mortality in England and Wales, 1895-1911. In C. A. Corsini & P. P. Viazzo (Eds.), *The decline of infant and child mortality* (pp. 129-154). Hague, Netherlands: Martinus Nijhoff.

Rivera, S. M., Reiss, A. L., Eckert, M. A., & Menon, V. (2005). Developmental changes in mental arithmetic: Evidence for increased specialization in the left inferior parietal cortex. *Cerebral Cortex, 15,* 1779-1790.

Rousseau, J. -J. (1979). *Emile: Or, on education* (A. Bloom, Trans.). New York: Basic Books. (Original work published 1762)

Saxe, G. B. (1981). Body parts as numerals: A developmental analysis of numeration among the Oksapmin of Papua New Guinea. *Child Development, 52,* 306-316.

Saxe, G. B., Guberman, S. R., & Gearhart, M. (1987). Social processes in early number development. *Monographs of the Society for Research in Child Development, 52* (No. 2, Serial No. 216).

Segerstrale, U. (2000). *Defenders of the truth: The battle for science in the sociobiology debate and beyond.* New York: Oxford University Press.

Scarr, S. (1992). Developmental theories of the 1990s: Developmental and individual differences. *Child Development, 63,* 1-19.

Siegler, R. S. (1996). *Emerging minds: The process of change in children's thinking.* New York: Oxford University Press.

Starkey, P. (1992). The early development of numerical reasoning. *Cognition, 43,* 93-126.

Starkey, P., & Cooper, R. G., Jr. (1980 November 28). Perception of numbers by human infants. *Science, 210,* 1033-1035.

Stauffer, B. L., & Leinwand, L. A. (2004). Sex differences in cardiac muscle and remodeling. *Advances in Molecular and Cell Biology, 34,* 131-145.

Stearns, S. C., & Koella, J. C. (1986). The evolution of phenotypic plasticity in life-history traits: Predictions of reaction norms for age and size at maturity. *Evolution, 40,* 893-913.

Strauss, M. S., & Curtis, L. E. (1984). Development of numerical concepts in infancy. In C. Sophian (Ed.), *Origins of cognitive skills: The eighteenth annual Carnegie symposium on cognition* (pp. 131-155). Hillsdale, NJ: Erlbaum.

Strong, E. K., Jr. (1943). *Vocational interests of men and women.* Stanford, CA: Stanford University Press.

Sweller, J., Mawer, R. F., & Ward, M. R. (1983). Development of expertise in mathematical problem solving. *Journal of Experimental Psychology: General, 112,* 639-661.

Sweller, J., & Sweller, S. (2006). Natural information processing systems. *Evolutionary Psychology, 4,* 434-458.

Tanner, J. M. (1990). *Foetus into man: Physical growth from conception to maturity.* Cambridge, MA: Harvard University Press.

Teasdale, T. W., & Owen, D. R. (1989). Continuing secular increases in intelligence and a stable prevalence of high intelligence levels. *Intelligence, 13*, 255-262.

Teasdale, T. W., & Owen, D. R. (2000). Forty-year secular trends in cognitive abilities. *Intelligence, 28*, 115-120.

Tobias, P. V. (1987). The brain of *Homo habilis*: A new level of organization in cerebral evolution. *Journal of Human Evolution, 16*, 741-761.

Turkheimer, E., Haley, A., Waldron, M., D'Onofrio, D., & Gottesman, I. I. (2003). Socioeconomic status modifies heritability of IQ in young children. *Psychological Science, 14*, 623-628.

Underhill, P. A., Passarino, G., Lin, A. A., Shen, P., Lahr, M. M., Foley, R. A., et al. (2001). The phylogeography of Y chromosome binary haplotypes and the origins of modern human populations. *Annals of Human Genetics, 65*, 43-62.

Wai, J., Lubinski, D., & Benbow, C. P. (2005). Creativity and occupational accomplishments among intellectually precocious youth: An age 13 to age 33 longitudinal study. *Journal of Educational Psychology, 97*, 484-492.

Weeden, J., & Sabini, J. (2005). Physical attractiveness and health in Western societies: A review. *Psychological Bulletin, 131*, 635-653.

Wellman, H. M., & Gelman, S. A. (1992). Cognitive development: Foundational theories of core domains. *Annual Review of Psychology, 43*, 337-375.

West-Eberhard, M. J. (2003). *Developmental plasticity and evolution*. New York: Oxford University Press.

Williams, G. C. (1957). Pleiotropy, natural selection and the evolution of senescence. *Evolution, 11*, 398-411.

Wilson, J. F., Weiss, D. A., Richards, M., Thomas, M. G., Bradman, N., & Goldstein, D. B. (2001). Genetic evidence for different male and female roles during cultural transitions in the British isles. *Proceedings of the National Academy of Sciences USA, 98*, 5078-5083.

Wilson, M., & Daly, M. (1985). Competitiveness, risk taking, and violence: The young male syndrome. *Ethology and Sociobiology, 6*, 59-73.

Wynn, K. (1992, August 27). Addition and subtraction by human infants. *Nature, 358*, 749-750.

Wynn, K., Bloom, P., & Chiang, W.-C. (2002). Enumeration of collective entities by 5-month-old infants. *Cognition, 83*, B55-B62.

Zorzi, M., Priftis, K., & Umiltá, C. (2002, May 9). Neglect disrupts the mental number line. *Nature, 417*, 138.

Printed in the United States
87441LV00002B/77/A